drinks

decaf available also

hot

coffee · house blend	1.35/1.85
or french Roast	
espresso	2.00
cappuccino	2.95
mocha	4.50
latte / chai spice latte	2.95 / 3.50
hot chocolate	2.95/3.50

* soy milk add .50¢
* flavor syrup add .50¢

tea   1.35/1.85

black
ssam breakfast
E flower earl grey
ecaf english breakfast
chai spice

green
china mao feng
japanese genmai cha
jasmine

tisanes
rimson berry
eppermint
chamomile

other
white peony
rooibos "red" latte   3.50
mate latte   3.50

do not include 7% state and local tax

cold

iced coffee and tea	2.25/
nantucket nectars	1.75
sodas	1.25/
h20 (still or bubbly)	1.50
housemade raspberry seltzer	2.25/
a tall, cold glass of milk	1.25/
kids glass of milk	.75¢
chocolate milk	2.00/3

kids corner

pb + j	4.95
grilled cheese	4.95
milk + a cookie	2.50
ham + cheese	4.95

breads made with love

flour

bakery + cafe

flour, *too*

INDISPENSABLE RECIPES *for* THE CAFÉ'S MOST LOVED SWEETS & SAVORIES

Joanne Chang

Photographs by Michael Harlan Turkell

CHRONICLE BOOKS
SAN FRANCISCO

...ndwiches   7.95 (grilled add .50¢)   ½ sandwich 4.50

1000
- ...oked Turkey, coleslaw, cheddar, island dressing
- ...ummus, spinach, tomato, carrots, sprouts
- ...pplewood-smoked Bacon, arugula, and tomato
- ...esh mozzarella, Basil Pesto, tomato
- ...rried tuna salad, apples, carrots, golden Raisins, sprouts
- ...asted Lamb, tomato chutney, goat cheese
- ...ast Chicken, mashed avocado, jicama
- ...ast Beef, horseradish mayo, crispy onions, tomato
- ...rilled Roast Chicken, brie, Roasted peppers, caramelized onions
- ...rilled Portobello melt, pesto, mozzarella, tomato
- ...reakfast Egg Sandwich, ham or Bacon, cheddar, tomato, arugula, dijonaise   6.95

...lads
- ...uinoa, tofu, spinach, veggies, portobellos, ginger-scallion dressing   8.95
- ...hite bean panzanella, fresh mozzarella, Red wine vinaigrette   8.95
- ...hopped Greek Salad, lemon-thyme Chicken, green goddess dressing   8.95
- ...mple mixed green salad   2.95/3.95   *add veggies $1.00
- ...ny Sandwich as a Salad   7.95   ...ead, on organic mesclun greens, except grilled sandwiches)

*Please note, not all ingredients are listed on the menu

...up of the day
bowl 3.50   pint 4.50

...ease inquire about delivery services.

drinks   decaf available

hot
coffee - house blend or french Roast	1.35/1.85
espresso	2.00
cappuccino	2.95
mocha	4.50
latte/chai spice latte	2.95/3
hot chocolate	2.95/3.9

* soy milk add .50¢
* flavor syrup add .50¢

tea   1.35/1.6

black
- assam breakfast
- blue flower earl grey
- decaf english breakfast
- chai spice

tisanes
- crimson berry
- peppermint
- chamomile

green
- china mao fe...
- japanese genm...
- jasmine

other
- white pe o...
- rooibos "red" l...
- mate latte

Prices do not include 7% state and...

breads

To my mom and my dad:
with infinite gratitude for always believing in me
and instilling in me an obsessive love of food.

Text copyright © 2013 by Joanne Chang.
Photographs copyright © 2013 by Michael Harlan Turkell.

Library of Congress Cataloging-in-Publication Data available.
ISBN 978-1-4521-0614-4

Manufactured in China

Designed by Alice Chau
Typesetting by Helen Lee
This book is typeset in Archer and Gotham.

10 9 8 7 6 5 4 3 2

Chronicle Books LLC
680 Second Street
San Francisco, California 94107
www.chroniclebooks.com

MAY 2014

CONTENTS

breakfast

Lunch

dinnER

Party time

drinks

Basics

INTRODUCTION

Not a day goes by that someone doesn't ask me, "How can I open a place like Flour?" I am fairly certain that they are not actually looking for step-by-step instruction on how to get into this crazy business. My guess is that instead they are just dreaming of how they can gain unlimited access to a never-ending supply of our egg sandwiches, sticky buns, gazpacho, and BLTs. When customers fall in love with our food, they fall for it hard. Each time, I smile and offer a few starting points but the truth is I often ask myself that same question. How did Flour, my little bakery-that-could, evolve into a beloved bakeshop and café that feeds literally thousands every day with made-to-order sandwiches, homemade soups, pizzas, dinners, breakfast pastries, desserts, and specialty drinks? My original business plan, while ambitious, bears just a passing resemblance to what happens at Flour every single day.

As you might imagine, the day starts early at Flour. At 4:00 a.m. the opening baker comes in and fires up the ovens. And while it's a ridiculously early hour, it's also one of the most magical at the bakery. You're alone in the kitchen about to bake off hundreds and hundreds of hand-shaped pastries and breads that within a few hours will be out on the counter and quickly consumed by delighted customers. The walk-in refrigerators are filled with towering racks of doughs that have been slowly proofing (i.e., developing flavor and texture) overnight. The first order of business is to get all of the trays of scones, brioches, and other breads out of the refrigerators and into the ovens so that they're ready to display by 7:00 a.m., when we open. It's like a dance: sliding tray upon tray of pastries into the hot ovens, poking at a scone, pulling a corner brioche that's ready before the others, giving a tray a turn, moving a pan of glorious sticky buns out of the oven and onto a cooling rack. At any one time there are sixteen trays in the ovens in various stages of baking, with another sixteen or more waiting their turn to go in.

How did it get to be 6:00 a.m.? Way too soon, the next baker arrives ready to tackle the cake orders and set up the pastry case with triple-chocolate mousse cakes and Boston cream pies. This baker spends the next eight hours writing Happy Birthday, Congratulations, and even intricate math formulas (for our MIT customers) on cakes; cooking creamy steel-cut oatmeal; slicing kiwis for fruit tarts; and making sure that every cake and tart order for the day is complete, well packaged, and passes the "mom test." In other words, would your mom (who maybe originally had dreams of your going to med school) be impressed and proud of the dessert you are making? If not, it doesn't leave the bakery.

Following on the case baker's heels is a bevy of front-of-the-house staff. The meditative quiet of the bakery is now a clanging hum as these staffers set up the pastry counter and get the sandwich station and coffee stations ready to go. Then the next baker arrives—our cookie baker. All of those perfectly baked double-chocolate cookies, macaroons, peanut butter cookies, homemade Oreos, and dozens more are his or her responsibility. We sell around a thousand cookies a day, which means that if you're the cookie baker, what you bake that day sees its way into more customers' hands than any other product. Talk about pressure! But it's a good kind of pressure when you see someone's face light up after taking a bite out of a still-warm oatmeal raisin cookie.

At this point it's hard to believe it is only 8:00 a.m. While most of the world is just getting ready for the day, our staff is already in full swing. Its time for the savory side of Flour with the arrival of Chef, along

with his prep staff. The steady buzz of the bakery evolves into a mild roar with a bit more chaos and chatter: "Good morning, Chef! Here are your quiche shells. I'll be out of the bottom deck oven in about ten minutes. How long do you need the stove for? Can you use up these overripe pears for anything?" and on and on. The prep staff confers with Chef to get the production list for the day, and "on" go the blenders for soups and the slicer for roast beef and the stove for chutneys.

Chef focuses on the daily specials—soups, pizzas, and quiche—creating a new menu each morning. The first hour of his day is often spent in the walk-in refrigerator, which, just a few hours before, was jam-packed with pastries and doughs. Typically by now the produce and meat deliveries have arrived, and he negotiates for storage space on the crowded shelves, deciding what cheeses will top his pizzas, which vegetables will go into his soups, what scrap produce and trimmings should end up in a stock today. He carefully coordinates his time and prep with the production baking team, whose members have now arrived to tackle the daily pastry production list. The stoves, ovens, countertops, walk-in refrigerator, and freezer all need to be shared among anywhere from a dozen to two dozen bakers and cooks, and trying to make it all work is a massive game of Tetris each day. The production bakers knead focaccia dough, cream butter for brown sugar–oat muffins, roll out currant scones and croissants, bake off tart shells, and assemble lemon-raspberry layer cakes while Chef works on his dinner specials and oversees his prep team. The savory cooks roast the meats, slice the cheeses, mix up the spreads, cook down the sauces, and prepare garnishes for the sandwich menu under Chef's watchful eye.

Every member of the front staff has been trained in making sandwiches, and as you poke your head out of the kitchen and peer out front, you see that that's what they do all day long. Every sandwich is made to order on bread that was baked off and sliced that morning. Large catering orders stream in; large catering platters are rolled out. Customers call all day and night to place orders for one sandwich to be picked up in ten minutes or one hundred sandwiches to be picked up the next day (or sometimes one hundred sandwiches to be picked up in ten minutes—believe me, it happens!).

But it's not just our sandwiches that draw crowds. Meg waits patiently for a carefully steamed dry cappuccino every single morning, and Jonathan and his kids are addicted to our rich hot chocolate. We know who in our neighborhood is short on time for dinner and grabs our dinner specials to take home five nights a week. Christine stops in regularly to chat with Chef and ask her for recipes for her favorite meals. We've made young David's birthday cake every year since he was born, and we've helped the South End Community Health Center celebrate the winning of a much-needed grant with humongous trays of pizzas. Whatever comes in, the staff rallies together to make it all happen with a smile. By the end of the day we've seen hundreds of happy customers who can all watch us at work in our open kitchens. The breads get shaped and ready for their overnight rest in the fridge, tomorrow's pastries are trayed up for the rack, the stocks are put on the stove for their overnight simmer. Rita, Osmin, Alonso, and Daniel scrub the kitchens and dining rooms until they are spotless from top to bottom. The lights go out for a short rest . . . and then at 4:00 a.m. it starts all over.

I know how lucky I am to be able to eat this food every day. In this book, I'm delighted to share with you our best recipes from a whole day's menu at Flour, starting with early morning breakfast sweets and savories, moving on to soups and sandwiches for lunch, and finally showcasing our most popular salads and main courses for dinner. We are the go-to place for our customers for special occasions, and here I will show you our party-ready recipes from finger foods to elaborate cakes. The house-made drinks at Flour, such as our raspberry seltzer and mulled apple cider, are just as popular as the food, and you'll learn these recipes as well.

I grew up in a food-centric Taiwanese household in which at breakfast we were thinking about lunch, at lunch we were making arrangements for dinner, and at dinner, you guessed it, we were planning the next day's breakfast. In Chinese culture, rather than greet people with "How are you?" you ask them, "Have you eaten?" My entire life has revolved around food, what I've eaten, what I'm going to eat, and when am I going to eat it.

But I never dreamed I'd end up in the food business. Like many young teens, I had no idea what I wanted to do when I grew up. When the local paper interviewed me for an award I won in high school and asked me what I thought my future might hold, I confidently replied, "I love writing and I love math, so I either want to win a Pulitzer Prize for writing or a Nobel Prize for math." (Never mind that in my youthful enthusiasm I didn't realize there is no actual Nobel math prize!) Why did I stop there? I should have told them I was going to run for president of the United States after that.

I attended Harvard College and decided on applied math and economics as my major. My plans for that future victory trip to Stockholm to claim my Nobel were quickly shot down when I met my fellow classmates. While I was a decent math student, I was nowhere near the level of my brilliant friends. I joined a terrific study group and had to learn to

add value to our regular meetings, and quickly. So I baked a batch of Toll House chocolate chip cookies—the only thing I ever baked at home growing up. I fed the group, and in turn they helped me grasp the finer points of the Riemann hypothesis.

Baking cookies on a regular basis for the study group was a fun diversion from class, and I baked leftover dough into cookies for our dormitory's student-run grill. Pretty soon I was known as the chocolate chip cookie girl. I had to double, triple, and then quadruple my batch sizes to feed both my hungry study group and the grill customers.

Although perhaps that should have been a tip-off that I was meant for the kitchen, after graduation I got a "respectable" job as a management consultant. But I didn't stop cooking and baking—quite the opposite, in fact. The more demanding my job became in terms of spreadsheets and presentations, the more I spent my free time in the kitchen, indulging my growing passion to cook and bake. I started a small side business called Joanne's Kitchen, making cookies and cakes for friends. I hosted biweekly dinner parties, cooking multicourse meals from favorite cookbooks that invariably ended with the group of us lying on the couch clutching our bellies from overindulgence. I spent my annual bonuses on cookbooks, kitchen appliances, fancy-restaurant meals, even a cooking school in Italy one summer. After two years of wearing a suit and heels to work during the day and a kitchen apron on the weekends, I decided to make the jump and get a job in a professional kitchen. With uncharacteristic bravado, I baked a batch of chocolate chip cookies; attached a cookie to each departure memo, which included the subject line, "One day these cookies will be famous!" and stuffed the memos into the mailboxes of my coworkers (this was way before email, so we all had physical mailboxes).

I spent my first year cooking at Biba, one of the top restaurants in Boston at that time, whose chef, Lydia Shire, was (and still is) rightfully famous for her immense creativity and her unparalleled passion for making extraordinary food. I threw myself into my new environment and learned how to whisk vinaigrettes properly, dice raw steak for tartare, shuck oysters. It was incredibly eye-opening to see how a love for making great food, which I shared with Lydia and her team, translated to a restaurant setting. I marveled at the attention paid to making even the simplest chicken stock. I learned the finer points of dressing salads: when to add the salt, how to pile the lettuces on the plate. I watched the care the cooks took with picking through their herbs each day before service started to ensure that only the freshest specimens were served to our guests. I ate an outrageous amount of fois gras terrine trimmings.

While I loved being in a professional kitchen setting, I slowly started to realize that I much preferred baking. The energy and bustle of restaurant service appealed to my adrenaline-addicted line-cook coworkers, but I felt sorely out of place. I longed to be elbow-deep in sugar and butter and flour, not onions and bone marrow and olive oil. I rushed through my prep so I could help the pastry cooks next to me pipe out cream puffs and slice strawberries. Sometimes we even switched outright, Francisco the pastry cook would prepare my soup stock while I baked his crème brûlées.

After a year of cooking, I got Chef Lydia's blessing to move on and get a baking job. She directed me to Rick Katz, her opening pastry chef at Biba who had gone on to open his own bakery and café. At Bentonwood Bakery in Newton Center, a suburb of Boston, I felt at home. I learned how to make everything I had been baking on my own but the right way. I fell in love with the oversized mixer, which was big enough for me to sit in (yes, I tried it out!) and helped me make dough for hundreds of pies and batter for dozens of cakes. Peeling case upon case of apples might sound tedious to you, but I got an inordinate amount of pleasure in trying to peel each apple faster and cleaner and better. Plus my insatiable sweet tooth was much happier being surrounded by fig tarts and chocolate pudding. Rick was just as fanatical about the quality of the food he served in

the café as he was about the pastries we put out in the bakery case. Every single day I worked for him, I watched as he tasted the daily soup and sampled a spoonful of each sauce and sandwich spread, giving feedback on how to improve each item. He loved nothing more than to walk by my station and poke a tasting spoon into whatever I was making and offer suggestions on how to improve the texture, the taste, the final product. Nothing left that kitchen without being thoroughly tested, whether on the savory end or the sweet end. The rigor with which he approached everything we did in the kitchen left a lasting impression on me and taught me that taking shortcuts was not an option.

My next job was working as the pastry chef at Rialto, the four-star restaurant in Cambridge owned by Jody Adams and Christopher Myers. (Christopher is now my husband. Yes. I married my boss. But that was many, many years after he was my boss. I swear.) Restaurant work was very different from bakery work. I don't think I baked a single cookie for two years. Instead I stretched my wings and created fanciful plated desserts like crêpes with caramelized bananas and tangerine custard–filled popovers and bittersweet chocolate and cherry cassata for our revolving pastry menu. Chef Jody and I collaborated on my desserts to ensure that they complemented her Mediterranean menu both in flavor and in spirit. Jody cooked from her heart, creating simple and simply delicious food for her customers and her staff, and she taught me to do the same. I absorbed the deep respect for food that she shared with everyone in her kitchen and learned the valuable lesson that, above all, cooking for others is meant to give pleasure, nothing more and nothing less. While that might sound painfully obvious, the truth is that working in a professional kitchen is just like any other job—there's stress and politics and egos—and as Jody liked to remind me when I was pulling out my hair, "Joanne, it's just dinner!" She showed me that cooking for others should be just as satisfying to us as to our guests, and if it isn't, we are approaching it the wrong way.

I eventually missed the bakery setting and moved to New York City to live in a shoebox and work for François Payard of Le Bernadin and Restaurant Daniel fame in his eponymous pâtisserie. Pastry is like a religion to the French, and I was happy to get baptized in that world. François had created a slice of Paris and plopped it in the middle of Manhattan, complete with an old-school French bistro attached to the pâtisserie and an old-school French chef. I was at home, working in the basement pastry kitchen making *macarons* and *pain aux raisins* and running upstairs to barter an armful of pastries for a taste of the daily bistro dishes. However, for all the fancy *crèmes bavaroises* and Paris-Brest the pâtisserie turned out, they couldn't make a decent chocolate chip cookie to save their lives (sorry, François!). I knew that I wanted to come back to Boston to open my own bakery, where I would make the best chocolate chip cookies, banana bread, and blueberry muffins along with fancy French pastries like *brioches au chocolat* and almond croissants. I spent my days learning classic French pastry and my nights writing a business plan for my own bakery-café that would meld my American training with my French.

I returned to Boston to scout out a location for the bakery I hoped to open, and in the meantime I worked for two years as the pastry chef at the ever-popular Mistral restaurant under Chef Jamie Mamano. I thought Mistral would be a placeholder for me—a restaurant that I could work at with relative ease and that would leave me enough free time to plan for the bakery. My time with Jamie ended up being extremely influential. He has a laser-focused approach to creating enticing menus that showcase classic dishes, each prepared with the best possible product and minimal artifice. I learned the importance of keeping it simple and flawless. Jamie led by example and his team of cooks were as loyal to him as soldiers are to a sergeant, willing to follow him to the bitter end (of dinner service) to ensure that every dish was spot on. As Jamie likes to say, "Perfect will be just fine, thank you."

At first I assumed that my bakery, which I named Flour to emphasize the simple, straightforward approach I planned to take, would make and sell only sweet treats. Morning, noon, and night I crave dessert. My ideal eating day would start with a *pain aux raisins* for breakfast (buttery brioche filled with pastry cream and golden raisins and finished with sugar glaze), sticky bun bread pudding and homemade granola bars for lunch, triple-chocolate mousse cake trimmings for afternoon snack, and a big vanilla and coffee ice cream sundae for dinner. Make Life Sweeter, Eat Dessert First! was the motto I created for Flour, and I enthusiastically promoted it by example.

But when I started thinking seriously about my bakery menu, I recognized that one cannot live on sweets alone. Most people (okay all people, including me) need more than just sugar to survive. If my goal was to create a warm, inviting neighborhood bakery that people would flock to again and again, I knew that Flour would have to be more than just a dessert Mecca. We needed to offer savory options to appeal to people throughout the day: made-to-order lunches, creative dinners, daily changing soups, fresh salads, and pizzas. And the quality and care that went into making these foods had to be just as keen and solid as they were for making pastries.

So my ideas about what Flour would look like morphed to include a commitment to making not only the best sweet foods but also the best savory ones. It wasn't far from my training—every place I'd worked had offered both. I reached out to my good friend, Chef Chris Parsons, with whom I'd worked at Rialto, and asked him if he would be interested in helping me get Flour off the ground. Chris had just left his position as sous chef at New York City's Cena, which had been awarded three stars by the *New York Times*. He fully understood that although we weren't in the fancy-restaurant business, that didn't mean we couldn't offer fresh, unpretentious, inventive, wonderful food. And that's just what we did. We developed a menu of about a dozen sandwiches that were based on classics, and then we figured out how to make them stand out, either with a house-made condiment or a different dressing or a top-quality ingredient. We knew we wanted to offer hot dishes as well, so we added daily homemade soups, individual pizzas, quiche with salads, and stuffed breads (a cousin to calzones) to the menu.

Chris planned on staying for only a few months to help me get started. He ended up staying almost three years, during which he worked relentlessly to help me educate both our customers and our staff on what we were doing. You couldn't walk by Chris's station without him grabbing a spoon and putting something delightful in your mouth as he raved about the freshness of the morels that season or the perfect tomato. It would have been easy to write an accessible popular menu and then just leave it. But Chris insisted on pushing the envelope with every-thing we did, working on our core recipes for the daily changing specials and creating soups from scratch that led our customers to wait every day in very long lines.

Our customers helped us shape our menu, too. They often stopped by Flour as we were closing and ordered sandwiches and soups to take home for a light dinner. Our suggestion bin was overflowing with requests to offer more than just sandwiches. People were too tired or too busy to cook at home, so we stretched our wings and created a changing menu of take-out dinner specials ready to be heated up at home. We responded to the many customers who wanted small snacks and party items from us with our special-occasion and catering menu and stuck with our philosophy to start with great ingredients and prepare them simply and imaginatively to highlight their flavors. It's a humble approach, and it works.

Flour now has four locations in the Boston area, which we call Flour1 (South End), Flour2 (Fort Point), Flour3 (Central Square), and Flour4 (Back Bay), and each one has its own chef who makes daily and weekly specials that I am always eager to get into the kitchens to try. In the past twelve years that Flour has been open, we've become just as well-known, if not more so, for our wide variety of savory options as for our award-winning pastries. In these pages, you'll find our very best and favorite recipes. You'll learn how to make the sandwiches that draw crowds every day—roasted lamb with tomato chutney and goat cheese, lemony hummus with cucumbers and radish sprouts, curried tuna with apples and raisins, to name a few. I'll show you how our chefs prepare the soups that our customers crave and request, ranging from chilled cucumber and yogurt in the summer to the best-ever beef stew in the winter. Dinners such as short ribs with Parmesan polenta and homemade chicken potpie fly out of our case, and now you'll be able to make these classics yourself at home. Hosting a party? Greet your guests with addictive party nibbles and tasty drinks and dazzle them with spectacular desserts for the finale.

Nothing we do is tricky or exceptionally complicated—no foams or molecular gastronomy here. But just because something is simple doesn't mean that it can't and won't knock your socks off. I've collected our staffs' and our customers' most requested dishes and meticulously tested and retested the recipes so that you can replicate them all in your own kitchen. I followed our chefs around with a notebook and a scale, driving them all batty (thank you, chefs!) as I carefully measured each spoonful of pepper and timed every minute on the stove.

Opening Flour was a way for me to share with as many people as I could what I know to be true in my own life: delicious food makes you incredibly happy. In this book, you'll see this philosophy at work. Once you learn how we cook, these recipes will become yours, and you will add your own personality to them to delight your family and friends any time of day and for any occasion.

in our
VOCABULARY

When you travel to a foreign country, at minimum you learn how to say "please" and "thank you" and "where's the bathroom?" in the local language to make sure you can get around. It's no different in cooking and baking. Be sure to familiarize yourself with the lingo before you get started so you understand exactly what you're doing before you do it. Learning basic kitchen vocabulary will help you cook and bake with ease and pleasure.

Baste To prevent meat from drying out when it is cooking in the oven, you can brush or spoon marinade, fat, or its own juices over it, a technique known as basting. It helps add color and flavor to meat, as well. Basting is also commonly used to add moisture or flavor to vegetables, fruits, and other foods, in the oven or on the grill or stove top.

Blanch Blanching is an easy technique in which you briefly immerse food (usually vegetables) in boiling water and then typically "shock" it (see facing page). It's a popular way of preparing vegetables for salads, setting their color and texture; and of loosening the skins of tomatoes and peaches.

Blind bake When you bake a pie or quiche, you want the crust to be crisp and flaky. If you fill your crust while it is raw, however, the filling will shield it from the heat of the oven and the crust will end up underbaked and soggy. Blind baking to the rescue! To blind bake is to prebake your crust before you fill it. First, line your crust with a piece of parchment and fill it with pie weights, uncooked beans or rice, or even cleaned small rocks. Then bake the crust until it is partially or almost fully baked through, depending on the recipe. When you remove the pie weights and parchment and fill the crust with filling, the crust will continue baking, and your final product will boast a fully baked, flaky shell.

Braise This classic technique usually begins with searing the ingredient (see facing page) on the stove top over high heat to get a nice caramelized flavor. Then a modest amount of liquid is added, the pot is covered, and the food cooks gently over low heat on the stove top or in a moderate oven. Braising is especially good for tough cuts of meat that break down and tenderize when cooked slowly.

Brine Brining is similar to marinating but the liquid (usually water) has a particularly high salt content. Meat is submerged in the liquid for at least a few hours or up to overnight. During the soaking period, the cells of the meat absorb the flavored liquid through osmosis. When the meat is cooked, it retains this added moisture and is tender and more flavorful.

Chop To chop is to cut food into small pieces that are not necessarily all the same size or uniform. It is arguably the simplest and most basic cooking technique since exact size and shape are of little importance.

Cream Creaming is a basic baking technique in which one or more ingredients are beaten until soft, light, and smooth. Creaming together butter and sugar is the starting point for many cake and cookie recipes, aiding in the even distribution of the sugar throughout the butter and aerating the butter with the sugar crystals.

Dice To dice is to cut food into small, same-size squares. Diced pieces tend to be smaller than chopped.

Fold When you mix ingredients, you can stir them together if you're not concerned about how they combine, or you can fold them together, which is a form of gentle mixing that preserves texture and airiness. Use a rubber spatula and cut directly down through the center of the bowl to the bottom, carefully sweep along the bottom and then up the side of the bowl, flip the spatula over, rotate the bowl a quarter turn, and repeat. Continue until the ingredients are evenly combined.

Julienne When you cut a food into long, thin, narrow strips, you are julienning. The final product should resemble matchsticks in size.

Mince To mince is to cut something into very tiny pieces. It is much finer than a dice or chop, finer still than a fine chop, but not so fine that it becomes a purée.

Purée To purée is to blend something until it has a smooth consistency and it has turned into a paste or a thick liquid.

Roast Roasting is basically cooking something uncovered in the oven, usually at relatively high heat so that it stays juicy and the exterior caramelizes a bit. Roasting in low heat is called slow roasting.

Scald To scald is to heat a liquid to just under its boiling point. You will see little bubbles forming along the sides of the pan, indicating that the liquid is about to boil.

Sear When you want a caramelized brown crust on a protein (such as meat or fish) or a vegetable or even a grain, you sear it by cooking it over really high heat in a little bit of fat for a short period until a crust forms.

Shock Typically performed after blanching (see facing page), shocking calls for plunging food into ice water to stop the cooking immediately and to preserve color and crispness.

Sweat To sweat an ingredient, such as onions, is to cook it slowly in a little fat over low heat until it starts to give off some of its natural liquid—in other words, *sweat* a bit. Stir the ingredient occasionally so it doesn't burn or caramelize. This is typically a first step used to soften ingredients before further cooking.

Temper A valuable technique, tempering allows you to combine easily two or more ingredients of different temperatures or different textures. Let's say you start with something like milk or cream that you heat in a saucepan almost to a boil. In a separate bowl, you mix eggs and sugar. Now you want to combine the hot liquid with the egg-sugar mixture. Take a little bit of the hot mixture and whisk it slowly into the cold mixture. Keep adding a bit of the hot to the cold until the cold is no longer cold. Once about half of the hot mixture is combined with the cold, you can easily mix in the rest of the hot mixture without fear of making sweetened scrambled eggs. You can use this slow-and-steady process when combining stiff ingredients with soft, hot with cold, chunky with smooth.

in our
PANTRY

Our pantry at Flour is fully stocked with a broad range of ingredients that we're fortunate to have at our disposal at all times. You don't need as extensive a selection as we have (unless you plan on making every recipe in this book), but you do need the basics. Here are the indispensable pantry items you'll want to have on hand, along with explanations of the more esoteric ingredients you'll encounter in the following pages.

NUTS

Almonds Once opened, packaged whole natural and blanched almonds and sliced blanched almonds can be stored in a cool, dark place for about three months or in the fridge for up to a year. Nuts contain oils that can go rancid, so bite into a nut before using the batch to make sure they are still fresh.

Walnuts and pecans These nuts have a high fat content, so it is best to purchase them in small quantities as you need them. Store them in the fridge for freshness.

SPICES

Bay leaves Typically sold dried, bay leaves, with a flavor reminiscent of thyme and oregano, are a common addition to stocks and soups. They are tough to chew and hard to digest, so once they have imparted their warm, pungent aroma, pluck them out of whatever you have added them to.

Black pepper Not all black pepper is the same. Tellicherry peppercorns are extra large and have a rich, deep flavor. We buy them in bulk and grind them fresh each morning with a spice grinder.

Cayenne pepper The hot cayenne chile is commonly dried and ground, yielding a gorgeous deep red pepper. It is used most often to flavor hot sauces and chili.

Chile de árbol We use beautiful dried red *chile de árbol* pods when we want to give dishes warmth and heat without burning our tongues off. They should be stored in a cool, dark, dry place. Crush them with your fingers before using.

Cinnamon Not just for baking, ground cinnamon is often used in Mexican and Middle Eastern savory dishes.

Coriander seeds The seeds of the cilantro plant, coriander imparts a warm, spicy, lemony flavor to soups and stocks.

Cumin You can purchase cumin, which has a strong, warm flavor, as whole seeds or ground. For the best flavor, we toast whole cumin seeds in a small, dry skillet over medium heat until they start to release their aroma and get toasty, about five to six minutes, and then we grind them fresh for each recipe in a spice grinder.

Curry powder There are innumerable kinds of curry powder, which is a blend of different amounts of such spices as coriander, cumin, fenugreek, garlic, mustard, turmeric, and a dozen or so others. Our curry powder is a mustardy yellow and relatively mild. Grocery stores usually offer two kinds: mild (simply labeled "curry powder") and Madras. The latter is richer and spicier than what we use, so if you prefer more spice, feel free to use the Madras instead.

Fennel seeds Although typically referred to as seeds, these small, curved pellets are actually the fruit of the fennel plant. They have an aniselike taste and add a subtle licorice flavor to marinades and stocks.

Hot red pepper flakes Not just for sprinkling on pizza, hot red pepper flakes (or HRPF in kitchen-speak) add a wonderful gentle heat to certain soups where you want some spice but it's not the star of the show.

Kosher salt Using kosher salt is so intuitive to me at this point that I am always surprised when I see iodized salt in the supermarket or at a restaurant. Kosher salt is clean and tastes of pure salt, whereas iodized salt is chemical and harshly salty. The larger granules of kosher salt are also easier to grasp between fingertips for seasoning dishes. Once you make the switch you won't go back. We use Morton coarse kosher salt.

Nigella seeds Popular in Middle Eastern and Indian cuisines, these tiny black seeds, which look a lot like black sesame seeds or poppy seeds and have a bitter, oniony flavor, are used in curries and chutneys to add depth and spice.

Nutmeg We keep whole nutmegs on hand for grating as needed. A fine-rasp Microplane grater is perfect for this. Nutmeg that you purchase already ground has lost a great deal of the essential oils that give it its distinctive warm flavor.

Smoked salt and pepper There are many kinds of smoked salts and peppers. Make sure you buy products that are made by smoking salt grains and peppercorns in a smoker and not by coating the salt and pepper with a smoke-flavored oil. Look for them in specialty spice stores or online. They add the flavor of smoke without having to light a fire.

Smoked Spanish paprika Hungarian paprika is more common and what you usually find on supermarket shelves. We use sweet smoked Spanish paprika, or *pimentón*, which has a sweeter, deeper, woodsy flavor that adds smokiness without heat. It's irreplaceable and worth seeking out, either in specialty grocery stores, spice stores, or online.

Turmeric Ground turmeric, popular in Indian, Middle Eastern, and Southeast Asian cooking, is deep orange-yellow and often used in curries. It has a warmish bitter flavor with some mustardy overtones and adds a yellowish tinge to dishes.

White pepper Milder in flavor than its black counterpart, white pepper is often used when you don't want specks of black to mar the appearance of your dish. Chef Corey at Flour1 especially likes to cook with it; he uses black pepper primarily as a finishing pepper and feels that white pepper cooks better in foods, adding a nice exotic, spicy flavor.

GRAINS AND FLOURS

All-purpose flour All-purpose, or AP, flour is just that: all-purpose. It is always good to have a large bag of AP flour on hand for baking, dredging meats, making pastas, and the like. We use unbleached, unbromated flour from King Arthur. You can certainly use another brand of flour, though you should try to buy an unbleached product, as some people find that the chemical used in bleaching leaves an unpleasant aftertaste.

Almond flour A specialty baking item, almond flour is made by grinding blanched whole almonds superfine with extra-sharp blades to make a fluffy flourlike product. It is often interchanged with almond meal, although the meal is coarser and tends to be oilier. You can mill a coarse almond flour at home by processing small amounts of blanched almonds in a clean coffee grinder or food processor and then sifting the ground nuts. The fine flour that sifts through can be used for the almond flour recipes here. For French *macarons* (page 235), use store-bought superfine almond flour (not meal) for the best results.

COUSCOUS

QUINOA

BLACK QUINOA

RED LENTILS

Bread flour This flour has a high protein content, which means that it is great for making bread doughs and other recipes in which you want a chewy substantial texture in your final product.

Bulgur wheat Bulgur is kernels of whole wheat that have been parboiled and dried, then ground to make for easy preparation and eating. It is sometimes confused with cracked wheat, which has not been parboiled or otherwise processed and thus takes much longer to cook.

Cornmeal We use cornmeal mostly to cover the bottoms of our baking sheets when we are making breads and pizzas as well as for a few select recipes such as the Cheddar scallion topping for the chicken pot pie. Ours is medium coarse: not so fine that it is a powder but not so coarse that it needs to be soaked and boiled before eating.

Couscous Made from semolina flour, couscous is actually tiny pasta granules. Most of the couscous sold in grocery stores has been presteamed and then dried, which streamlines the cooking process. Steam it and fluff it with a fork; don't boil it and stir it or it will be soggy.

Oats We have rolled oats and steel-cut oats on hand. We never use instant rolled oats, because they turn to mush when cooked.

Polenta Technically polenta is just cornmeal mush or gruel, but that's like calling truffles just a fungus or foie gras just liver. When properly cooked, it is creamy, rich, and extremely versatile. Buy cornmeal labeled "polenta" for the best texture. The difference between cornmeal and polenta is often the grind: Polenta is typically coarser and the final product is grainier and more interesting.

Quinoa Although it is not a true grain (it belongs to a different botanical family), quinoa is treated like one in the kitchen. Highly nutritious, it becomes light and fluffy and slightly nutty tasting when cooked and is great in salads.

Whole-wheat flour When milling white flour, the nutritious outer bran layer of the wheat kernel is removed; for whole-wheat flour, the bran is left intact, which makes it coarser, nuttier tasting, and heartier than white. Whole-wheat flour also goes rancid faster than white, so store it in an airtight container in your fridge.

SWEETENERS

Brown sugar We use light brown sugar, and if you're not weighing it, be sure to pack it into your measuring cup to get the right amount. You can substitute dark brown sugar if you prefer. Store brown sugar in a tightly sealed container with a piece of bread in the jar to keep it moist. If it hardens, you can soften it by putting it in the microwave for a few seconds with a small bowl of hot water alongside, or you can place a slice of apple or bread in the storage container overnight.

Confectioners' sugar Often called powdered sugar, confectioners' sugar is sugar that has been processed super fine so it is powdery in form, making it easy to dust onto pastries as a nice finishing touch. We in the kitchen call it 10X, which stands for the number of times it has been ground.

Honey You can buy honey in a few different forms and many different flavors. We use a basic pasteurized liquid clover honey. Store honey in a tightly sealed container in a cool, dark pantry for long shelf life.

Pearl sugar This type of sugar, which comes in the form of large, round balls, is typically sprinkled on pastries before baking for an attractive white sugar finish.

Sanding sugar Similar to and interchangeable with pearl sugar, sanding sugar is super-large crystals that don't melt when baked. It adds a pretty sparkly finish to pastries and desserts.

Vanilla sugar When you use the seeds from a vanilla bean in baking, save the scraped pod, wash and dry it well, and throw it into a bin of granulated sugar. After a few days the sugar will have absorbed the mellow, warm aroma of the vanilla, and you can use the sugar to add wonderful flavor to your baking recipes. (If you don't have vanilla sugar and your recipe calls for it, use 1 tsp vanilla extract per 1 cup/ 200 g of granulated sugar as a substitute.)

White sugar We use both regular granulated and superfine sugar. To make your own superfine sugar, put regular granulated in a food processor and process for fifteen to twenty seconds to reduce the granules to a finer grind. The recipes in this book will work well with either regular granulated or superfine sugar.

VINEGARS

Balsamic There are various grades of balsamic vinegar. Long-aged, expensive, sweet balsamics are served with chunks of Parmigiano-Reggiano or drizzled on fruit or even ice cream. We don't have this kind at Flour. Instead we have a large jug of a workhorse balsamic that is stronger, tarter, more acidic, and terrific for vinaigrettes and sauces.

Champagne Crisp and delicate, Champagne vinegars are best for dressing lighter salads. We have a small bottle of this specialty vinegar that we use when we're seeking a subtler, mellower vinegar flavor.

Cider Strong flavored, tangy, and at times bitingly harsh, cider vinegar is not used often in our kitchen. In fact, its claim to fame is as a folk cure for everything from acne to weight gain to diabetes. For cooking purposes, however, a small bottle is a good addition to your pantry because of how well it adds flavor in certain cooked dishes where a milder vinegar might get lost.

Distilled white Economical and versatile, this vinegar is most often used for its powerful cleaning properties but it comes in handy in cooking and baking as well for certain recipes. It's the easiest to find vinegar, available in all grocery stores.

Red wine This vinegar ranges in quality, depending on the wine from which it was made and the aging process. Red wine vinegars are particularly popular in Mediterranean and European cooking, and we use them mostly for our salad dressings and sandwich spreads. A large bottle is a good idea for a basic pantry.

Rice More popular in Asian cooking, rice vinegar (not to be confused with seasoned rice vinegar, which is sweetened and sometimes flavored) is sweet and mild and lovely for light dressings and marinades. I use this vinegar mostly at home, where I love tossing salads and vegetables with it, along with a little sugar and a little soy sauce.

Sherry This specialty Spanish vinegar made from sherry has a smooth, deep flavor that is fantastic in vinaigrettes and sauces. It can be a little hard to find; large supermarkets and gourmet stores usually carry it, and as with most things these days, it is readily available online. We have a small bottle in house that we use judiciously in certain dishes.

OILS

Extra-virgin olive We call this evoo (*EE-voo*), and we use it in salad dressings and anywhere we want to highlight the fruity flavor of the oil as a finishing touch.

Hazelnut or walnut Nut oils are specialty oils that can be bought in gourmet shops and online. They can go rancid quickly, so buy small bottles and store them in the fridge.

Sesame Made from toasted sesame seeds, dark, nutty-tasting sesame oil is a common ingredient in some Asian kitchens, where it is used more for finishing and flavoring than for cooking. We like Kadoya brand. (Another kind of sesame oil is also made from raw sesame seeds, which is mild, pale, and has a high smoke point, making it good for cooking.)

Vegetable For cooking, baking, and frying, we use a mild, flavorless oil.

CANNED, JARRED, AND BOTTLED ITEMS

Achiote paste A popular Mexican spice mix made from annatto seeds (from which it gets its red color) and flavored with oregano, cumin, black pepper, and garlic, among other pungent flavorings, achiote paste is typically sold in firm, crumbly bricks. We mix the paste with vegetable oil and slather it all over chicken breasts for awesomely flavored roasted chicken.

Beans Canned beans are okay, but dried beans that you cook at home will give you the most flavor and body. We regularly use cannellini beans, black beans, chickpeas, split peas, and lentils. Always soak the beans, though not the split peas and lentils, overnight in ample water before cooking, and save the liquid in which you cook any legumes for flavoring your soups. The liquid from canned beans is always too salty and flavorless and should not be used—ever. If you opt for canned beans, drain them and then rinse them well under running cold water before using.

Chipotle chiles We use chipotles (spicy smoke-dried jalapeños) canned in a tangy adobo sauce (tomatoes, vinegar, garlic, and spices). The chiles add smoky heat, or you can use just the adobo sauce for a milder flavor.

Coconut milk Typically sold in 13- to 14-oz/390- to 420-ml cans, coconut milk is the milky liquid that is extracted from pressing fresh coconut meat. Sometimes the fat in the coconut milk accumulates at the top of the can; just mix it into the milk and use as directed. Once a can has been opened, store any unused coconut milk in an airtight container in the fridge for up to four days or in the freezer for up to a month.

Harissa This Tunisian chile paste is a popular ingredient and table condiment in North African cooking, adding heat, spice, and warm flavor to braises, stews, and other dishes. It is made from chiles, garlic, red peppers, oil, and spices. Once you taste it, you will want to put it on everything. You can find it in the international section of larger grocery stores and online. The *harissa* we use is imported from the Fresh Olive Company in London and includes the addition of rose petals to tamp down the heat.

Horseradish Prepared horseradish is a mix of finely shredded spicy-hot horseradish root and a bit of vinegar and salt. Different brands have varying levels of heat, so taste until you find one that suits you. Look for prepared horseradish in the condiment section of your grocery store, near the vinegars, ketchups, mustards, and mayonnaises. If you see fresh horseradish root in your market, you can make your own by adding distilled white vinegar and kosher salt to taste.

Mayonnaise At my very first cooking job, the chef often proclaimed the excellence of Hellmann's and the futility of making a homemade mayo that would taste better. Who was I to argue? Sometimes we like to make our own mayo because it's easy and delicious, but for the most part we stick to Hellmann's. The same mayo carries the Best Foods label west of the Rocky Mountains.

Mustard Both mild, smooth Dijon mustard and tangy, spicy whole-grain mustard make frequent appearances in our recipes. Dijon mustard is made with a little vinegar, which keeps it from being too sharp and rounds out its flavor. Whole-grain mustard is visibly grainy from the whole mustard seeds mixed into it.

Red curry paste Red curry paste is made with lemongrass, garlic, ginger, chiles, and a host of other aromatics. A key ingredient in Thai cooking, it is often blended with coconut milk to make a sauce for curries or to season other dishes.

Soy sauce Always Kikkoman, all the time. This brand of soy sauce is naturally brewed and mild and contains no MSG. It is made with wheat (some other brands use other grains, such as rice), which gives it a pure, sweet flavor.

Sriracha This Thai hot sauce, named for a seaside town in Thailand and made with chiles, vinegar, garlic, and salt, is addictive, and we tend to put it on just about everything. The most popular brand sold in the United States comes in a clear plastic bottle with a green top and a rooster picture on the label, thus its nickname, rooster sauce.

Tahini paste A popular Middle Eastern ingredient, tahini is made by grinding sesame seeds to a paste. It can be found in specialty food stores, the health food or international section of standard grocery stores, and online.

Tomatoes Crushed, diced, or puréed, canned tomatoes are used in our kitchens all day long in soups and sauces because they are more consistent in flavor and texture than fresh tomatoes. Look for brands labeled "no salt added."

Tomato paste A small can or tube of tomato paste is invaluable for flavoring and for adding body and color to soups and stocks. Many recipes call for just a few spoonfuls; if you open a can for a recipe and use only a small amount, you can portion out the unused paste in batches of 2 tbsp and freeze them in little containers or in plastic wrap, so you always have tomato paste ready to use.

Vanilla When purchasing vanilla extract, make sure you get pure, rather than artificially flavored, vanilla extract. Store it in a tightly closed bottle at room temperature and it will last for months. Vanilla beans are often sold singly in a clear tube; they can be a bit pricey but they are worth every penny for their sweet mellow essence. Store them in a cool dark place or in the fridge and they will last for up to a year.

in our REFRIGERATOR

We call the refrigerator we have at the bakery the "walk-in," because it's big enough to walk around in. Here are some of the items we stock in it, how we use them, and how we store them.

DAIRY

Butter Always use unsalted butter. Salt acts as a preservative, so if you buy salted butter you're probably buying old butter. (Take a look at the tiny section of unsalted butter in the dairy case versus the large selection of various salted butters, which can sit in the fridge for months at a time.) Plus you don't know how much salt each dairy company puts in its salted butter, so it is best to buy the unadulterated stuff and add your own salt as needed. Fine European-style butters with a higher fat content make for great eating butter. You can certainly use them for cooking and baking, too, or you can simply use a good-quality regular unsalted butter.

Buttermilk We use nonfat buttermilk in our recipes. Be sure to shake it thoroughly before using because it does settle.

Cheddar cheese Buy sharp Cheddar for its intense flavor. The sharper and more aged it is, the more crumbly it gets, which makes for messier sandwiches. We use one that is aged six to nine months, which is enough to give it its characteristic earthy flavor but not so much that it falls apart when you use it.

Crème fraîche The wonder drug in creamy, luscious form, crème fraîche is sour cream's richer, sexier, more sophisticated cousin. You can find crème fraîche in the dairy section, or you can easily and inexpensively make your own. In a large stainless-steel, ceramic, or plastic bowl, mix together about 4 cups/ 960 ml heavy cream with about ¼ cup/60 ml buttermilk. Cover and place in a warm area overnight. The next day, stir the mixture well with a wooden spoon, and it should be thick and creamy. If it's still liquidy, re-cover and let sit in a warm area for a few more hours; sometimes it needs a little more time to thicken after it is stirred. Store crème fraîche in an airtight container in the fridge for up to a week. To make more crème fraîche, save a few dollops of what you've made and use it in place of the buttermilk for the next batch, following the same directions.

Eggs All of the eggs used in these recipes are large eggs. If you are measuring by volume, 1 large egg is equal to about 3¼ tbsp; the egg white measures about 2 tbsp and the egg yolk about 4 tsp. If you are weighing the eggs, 1 large egg weighs about 2 oz/55 g; the egg white weighs about 1 oz/30 g and the egg yolk weighs about ¾ oz/20 g.

Feta cheese Our feta comes in compact, crumbly blocks immersed in brine in large buckets. Rinse it off before you use it to rid it of excessive saltiness.

Goat cheese There are dozens of different types of goat cheeses to choose from. We use a soft, spreadable mild fresh goat cheese that is sold in the cheese section of the grocery store in 4-oz/115-g and 8-oz/ 225-g cylinders.

Half-and-half The name says it all: half whole milk and half heavy cream. If you can't find it in your local stores, you can make your own in the above ratio. Or, if you can find it, light cream is an acceptable substitute.

Heavy cream Not to be confused with whipping cream, heavy cream has at least 36 percent butterfat and whips up to a thick, voluptuous creaminess. You can't eat it every day, but you can love every moment that you do.

Milk Fat Carries Flavor! is a rallying cry at Flour. So use whole milk when cooking and baking for the best flavor. You can substitute low-fat or even nonfat milk if you must for health reasons, but know that the flavor will be compromised at least a little bit.

Mozzarella cheese We have shredded part-skim mozzarella for our pizzas and buckets of fresh mozzarella for our sandwiches. We're fortunate to have an amazing cheese purveyor, Casa Foods, that brings us tubs of superfresh and wonderfully creamy fresh mozzarella daily for our mozzarella sandwich.

Parmesan cheese True Parmesan, or Parmigiano-Reggiano, is nothing like what you find in little green containers on supermarket shelves. It's a hard cheese, milky and salty and nutty, that adds incredible flavor to dishes. For the recipes here, buy a chunk of Parmesan and grate it on the large-hole shredding disk of your food processor or on the large-hole side of a box grater. If you use a fine-rasp Microplane grater to grate your cheese, note that the volume will be different because it is so finely shredded. Not a bad thing, but be sure to adjust the amount in the recipe.

Tofu Not technically a dairy product, tofu is often found in the dairy case (unless you are lucky enough to live near an Asian grocery store, where it's in the tofu case). Made by soaking and grinding soybeans to extract the milk, then adding coagulants to the soy milk and pressing the resulting curds into blocks, tofu is growing in popularity in cooking because it is high in protein, low in calories, contains no cholesterol, and absorbs the flavors of whatever it is cooked with. It usually comes in 1-lb/455-g blocks in plastic tubs in four different types: silken, soft, firm, and extra firm.

Yogurt Plain full-fat yogurt is about as hard to find nowadays as that proverbial needle in a haystack. The shelves of the dairy case overflow with nonfat, flavored, low fat, custard, light, and more. Lucky for all of us, Greek yogurt has become popular and can be easily found. As a bonus, the full-fat plain variety is irresistible. Buy it often and in bulk, eat it with a little honey, and use it as you would sour cream.

PRODUCE

Alfalfa sprouts Often sold in plastic boxes in the produce department, alfalfa sprouts are a crisp, healthful, fresh topping for many of our sandwiches and salads. They will last three to five days in the fridge.

Avocado We use plump, dark green, bumpy-skinned Hass avocados for Luiz's avocado spread (page 141). Make sure they are soft and yield to gentle pressure before using. If they are hard, you can ripen them by leaving them out at room temperature for a few days until they soften. Once ripe, they can be stored in the fridge for up to five days.

Baby arugula Harvested when young for its more delicate flavor and smaller leaves, baby arugula is a popular ingredient in our sandwiches and salads. You can substitute regular arugula if you can't find baby leaves, but keep in mind that the flavor will be sharper and more peppery. Although not necessarily a bad thing, it does change the taste of whatever you are making.

Blood orange These flavorful oranges have a short season, depending on where you live, and are usually available in the colder winter months. They are a gorgeous deep red inside and have a somewhat tart orangey taste. If you can't find blood oranges, regular oranges are a fine, if less dramatic, substitute.

Butternut squash Probably the most popular winter squash we use at Flour, butternuts are sweet and nutty and should be stored in a cool place or in the fridge.

Celery root Also known as celeriac, celery root is a knobby, ugly root vegetable with a flavor reminiscent of celery and parsley. It has a rough, tough exterior that you trim away by slicing off a pretty thick layer with a sharp knife. Select firm celery roots with no soft spots and store them in the fridge for up to three weeks.

Cranberries Usually available in most grocery stores from around October through the end of the year, cranberries will last about a month refrigerated or up to a year in the freezer. Stock up on a few bags when you find them so you can make tart-sweet cranberry treats year-round. Fresh berries should be firm and crisp; discard any soft or discolored berries.

English cucumber We typically use long, thin, extra-crispy English cucumbers. They are often wrapped in plastic wrap at the grocery and are worth their slightly higher price tag. Their seeds are smaller and less bitter than those of regular cukes, and their skin is thinner and unwaxed. An added bonus is that they are bred to be more readily digestible than regular cucumbers, which is why they are sometimes called burpless cucumbers.

Fennel We use all of the parts: the white bulbous base and the green celery-like stalks topped with feathery fronds. The base goes into soups, the stalks are used in place of celery, and the fronds are added to the stockpot. Fennel has a mild, slightly licorice flavor that mellows into a nutty, sweet taste when cooked.

Ginger Fresh ginger keeps well in the fridge, where it will last for several weeks. The easiest way to peel it is with a spoon: scrape the bowl of the spoon firmly down the root and the peel comes right off. For baking, we like to store some fresh ginger in the freezer; once it is frozen, it grates beautifully and is less fibrous, as well.

Herbs Using fresh herbs regularly in your cooking is an instantaneous way to make your dishes shine. We always have fresh thyme, rosemary, flat-leaf parsley, sage, cilantro, Italian basil, tarragon, dill, chives, and oregano in-house. When a recipe calls for a certain amount of an herb, we trim off the stems before we measure it—except for chives, which don't have stems.

Jicama A crunchy, bulbous root vegetable, jicama (HEE-cah-mah) resembles a big, round brown turnip. Eaten raw, it has the texture of a pear or apple and is a touch sweet and very refreshing. We use it for awesome crunch on our chicken sandwich. It will keep in the fridge for up to two weeks.

Lemons and limes I know you can buy lemon and lime juice at the store because I've seen the little bottles on the shelves. That doesn't mean you should. Fresh juice that you squeeze yourself is essential to good cooking. Keep a few lemons and limes on hand in your produce drawer, so you'll always have them at your disposal. One lemon usually yields about 2 tbsp juice and 1 lime yields about 1 tbsp.

Mesclun In French, *mesclun* means "mixed," and it refers to any number of soft, young freshly picked lettuces tossed together and sold as salad greens. It is most commonly available in plastic bags in the produce section of the supermarket. We use either mesclun or baby arugula in all of our sandwiches. Feel free to substitute other salad greens or lettuce that you prefer.

Onion family We regularly use yellow onions, red onions, garlic, and shallots. Shallots, which taste like a mild onion, are shaped like an overgrown garlic bulb and, like garlic, have multiple cloves. They should have papery skins, feel firm, and be free of soft spots. Store yellow and red onions, garlic, and shallots in a cool, dark place. Despite the fact that I've listed these here in the Refrigerator section, don't store these items in the fridge or in the plastic bags that you get at the grocery, which can lead to their molding. Scallions, or green onions, are sold in clusters; these should be stored in the fridge. Both the green and the white parts are delicious. Sometimes I see home cooks throwing away the

white bit and I want to lunge into the garbage to rescue that equally flavorful section of the scallion. Leeks look like scallions on steroids. They are sold in bunches and have flat green tops that are tough and sometimes bitter. Use only the white and very light green parts of the leek. Because of the way they grow, they are often full of dirt. Take extra care to wash and soak them in cold water to clean them of stubborn grit. Like scallions, they should be stored in the fridge.

Portobello mushrooms These are large, meaty, brown cremini mushrooms in disguise. Once little cremini grow to a certain size, they are marketed as portobello or portobella mushrooms. Scrape off the dark underside gills with a spoon before using, and wipe clean with a paper towel or kitchen towel. Don't wash them, as they'll soak up the water and become soggy.

Tomatoes We use fragrant, lush vine-ripened tomatoes during their short growing season in New England. These are the ones that have been left on the vine to ripen and then picked for sale. Select tomatoes that smell sweet and warm and are just soft to the touch. Don't store them in the fridge, which will rob them of their flavor and make them mushy. Keep them on a countertop and use them within a day or two of purchase. The rest of the year, when tomatoes are not in season, we roast plum tomatoes by the case to use in our sandwiches. Plums are easy to find year-round and store well in the fridge for about a week. Roasting concentrates their flavor, making them a delicious substitute for fresh tomatoes. In fact, during the height of summer, some customers turn up their noses at the aromatic vine-ripes and beg for us to bring back the roasted plums.

MEATS

Bacon We are famous for our BLT sandwiches, and it is because of our bacon. We buy thick-cut applewood-smoked bacon from New Hampshire's North Country Smokehouse (www.ncsmokehouse.com) that is out of this world.

Black Forest ham There are a lot of different kinds of ham out there. Ours is an American-made Black Forest ham, dry cured and then smoked, with a deep, rich flavor.

Chicken Boneless, skinless chicken breast is a mainstay in our kitchen for our sandwiches and soups. Be sure to trim the breasts of the sinewy pieces that are sometimes attached to one side and of any visible fat.

Lamb Lamb top rounds can be found in most butcher shops. This is the tender, thick portion of the upper leg. If you can't find this cut, you can use boneless leg of lamb and tie it up in a bundle so it cooks evenly.

Roast beef We use the top round, which comes from the rump. You can also use the bottom round. Since this is where the cow uses the most muscle, meat from the rump can be tough. Both slow roasting it until pink and slicing it thinly against the grain make it tender.

Turkey As with ham, smoked turkey comes in many forms from many brands. Ours is smoked with applewood and it comes from North Country Smokehouse, the same place we get our bacon (see above).

in our CABINETS

We have all of the basics—wooden spoons, whisks, spatulas, and pots and pans galore. Here are the items that I recommend for a well-stocked cabinet.

Baking pan A shallow 9-by-13-in/23-by-33-cm glass or metal pan will serve you well. It is a standard size often used for baking brownies and cakes and is also great for a baked pasta or a savory strata. You can fill it with water and it becomes a water bath or put a wire cooling rack on it and use it as a roasting pan.

Baking sheet The baking sheets we use are called half-sheet pans and measure 13 by 18 in/33 by 46 cm, with about a 1-in/2.5-cm rim. They are made of heavy-duty aluminum and are handy for baking and roasting. If you place a wire cooling rack on the sheet, it serves as a great roasting pan for meats.

Blender or food processor Although they are not exactly interchangeable, if you have one of these you don't necessarily need the other. If you are trying to decide which one to buy, a food processor is a bit more versatile. Both will help you purée soups, blend drinks, and make spreads.

Bowls You need at minimum one small (big enough to whisk together a few eggs and some liquid), one medium (for whisking vinaigrettes and marinades), and one large (for folding together cake batters). I prefer bowls made of stainless steel because it is the most versatile material. Plastic can sometimes leave a film behind, even after washing, and glass breaks a lot (at least when I'm around).

Cake pans The most basic cake pan we use over and over is an 8-in/20-cm round pan. Many people have 9-in/23-cm pans—these are a fine substitute but the increased size will mean that whatever you are baking will likely take less time since it will be thinner.

Cardboard We have stacks and stacks of cardboard circles and half sheet–size rectangles for our cakes. It's handy to have a few clean pieces of sturdy cardboard for when you're making a fancy dessert that needs support on the bottom.

Colander A large bowl perforated with small holes, a colander is handy for draining pasta and washing vegetables.

Containers These can be old storage or take-out containers, little bowls, or anything else that will hold 2 to 3 cups/480 to 720 ml. You want a stack of containers around before you begin making any recipe so you can prepare and measure out your ingredients before you start to cook. They make working efficiently much easier, and having everything at your fingertips ready to go makes your time in the kitchen more enjoyable.

Dutch oven Usually made out of cast iron, or sometimes enamel, a Dutch oven is a heavy, lidded, ovenproof pot that holds 5 to 8 qt/4.7 to 7.5 L. It is especially terrific for braises and stews that start out on the stove top and finish cooking in the oven.

Immersion blender These long, wandlike blenders are super for puréeing soups and blending drink syrups and tend to be more convenient than pulling out a blender. You don't have to have one of these in your cabinet, but if you do, it saves on cleanup and time.

Knives Invest in at least one good paring knife, serrated knife, and 8- to 10-in/20- to 25-cm chef's knife. Sharpen them regularly, or in the case of the serrated knife, which can't be sharpened, replace it regularly.

Mandoline A mandoline is handy for slicing and julienning fruits and vegetables into thin, uniform pieces. It's small, rests on the countertop, and allows you to slice more precisely and quickly than you can by hand.

Measuring cups and spoons Dry measuring cups, usually of hard plastic or metal, have a straight rim and are meant to be filled to the top and then leveled with a knife or other straight edge. Wet measuring cups, usually of clear glass or plastic, look like little pitchers and are marked vertically on the side with measurements. When measuring a liquid, place your eye level with the cup to get an accurate reading. In baking, I avoid both kinds of measuring cups, preferring to use a scale for the most accurate measurements. For cooking, however, dry and wet cups are more than adequate, given the less fussy nature of the task as opposed to baking. You will also need a set of measuring spoons.

Microplane grater I remember the days before the Microplane when zesting lemons was an annoying chore and grating fresh nutmeg was pretty much unheard of in the kitchens I worked in. Now we all rush to be the lucky person who gets to swipe lemons or spices over the metal plane that makes quick work of these prep tasks. Invest in a long, skinny Microplane grater, and you'll use it all of the time for citrus, fresh ginger, spices, cheese, and more.

Muffin tin We use a home-size muffin tin for all of these recipes. It's easiest to line them with muffin papers for ease of pastry removal but you can also butter and flour the tins liberally with great success.

Parchment paper Use sheets of parchment to line baking sheets for easy cleanup and removal of food. Parchment is also good for making piping cones for decorating cakes and pastries.

Pastry brush A pastry brush is handy for applying an egg wash to pastries and for brushing soaking syrups onto cakes. One 2- to 3-in/5- to 7.5-cm brush is all you need. You can even substitute a clean paintbrush.

Pie weights You can certainly purchase pie weights for blind baking your pie crusts, or you can do what we do, which is use uncooked beans or rice. You need something small that you can pack down into the pie crust to keep it from puffing up in the oven, and the beans or rice can be saved and used again and again.

Piping bags and tips You can choose either a disposable plastic bag (which can be washed and used many times over despite its name) or a cloth bag, but whichever you choose make sure it is at least 14 to 16 in/ 35.5 to 40.5 cm long. Too often home cooks buy small dinky pastry bags that hold hardly anything, making piping a frustrating and messy endeavor. The most basic round tip is extremely versatile; it should be about ½ to ¾ in/12 mm to 2 cm in diameter.

Rolling pin My favorite rolling pin for delicate pastry tasks is a tapered wooden rod. But for laminated doughs, such as puff pastry, a standard rolling pin with two small handles connected by an internal metal rod that swivels on ball bearings is really helpful. It allows you to use your weight and power to push the dough forward while the rollers do the work of moving the pin along.

Saucepan A 3- to 4-qt/2.8- to 3.8-L saucepan is essential; if you have a smaller 2-qt/2-L saucepan, you'll use it, but there's no need to get one because you can just use the large one for the same tasks.

Scale Serious bakers consider a basic scale invaluable for accurately measuring the correct amount of flour, sugar, and the like for baking recipes that require precision. Although it is less necessary when making soups and salads, sandwiches and stews, there are enough times that it helps out with baking that I strongly suggest one for every kitchen.

Sieve For straining stocks and sauces, you will want a basic bowl-shaped metal-mesh sieve with a handle. Get one that is at least 8 to 10 in/20 to 25 cm in diameter; if your sieve is too small, it will be unwieldy and messy.

Skillets You really need only one large 12-in/30.5-cm stainless-steel ovenproof skillet and one large 10- to 12-in/25- to 30.5-cm nonstick skillet. A cast-iron skillet is a great addition for certain recipes, such as the oven-baked pancake on page 78. A smaller skillet for cooking small amounts of ingredients is useful but not necessary, as you can always use your large skillet.

Stand mixer While not imperative, a stand mixer does make certain baking projects easier. Almost anything that is done in a stand mixer can be done with a sturdy handheld mixer or by hand, so don't let the lack of a stand mixer keep you from baking.

Stockpot One 8-qt/7.5-L stainless-steel stockpot is all you need to make a multitude of soups and stocks.

Thermometer A meat thermometer is crucial for cooking basic roasts and poultry so you know how far to take them. A candy thermometer registers higher heats and is useful when caramelizing sugar or making candies. Both come in digital, instant-read, probe, dial, and other types. We use simple dial thermometers, and we test them before using them each time by sticking them in a cup of ice water to make sure they register 32°F/0°C.

Wire cooling rack A basic strong wire grid will allow you to cool pastries and bake meats when you place the rack on top of a baking sheet. Be sure to get one that is either larger than your baking sheet so it sits on the rim of the sheet or that has little feet on it, allowing it to rest on the sheet with some room underneath for air to circulate.

in our
HEADS

People who work in professional kitchens think in certain ways and follow certain basics that will help you become a better chef at home. After years of toiling in different restaurants and bakeries under various professional chefs who live and breathe these principles, I have found that they are ingrained in me as well. Let these rules guide you in making great food.

1. **Gather your** *mise en place* **before you start.** The French term *mise en place*, or "everything in its place," refers to how you prepare before starting a recipe. Recently I was teaching a reporter how to make our Roasted Pear and Cranberry Crostata at home. All of the ingredients for my *crostata* shell, almond cream filling, and ginger-roasted pears were meticulously premeasured in separate containers, allowing me to flow effortlessly through the recipe. The reporter wondered if it was somewhat contrived to have everything prepped so conveniently for us. The truth is that's how I always cook and bake, and so should you. Take the time to gather all of your ingredients and measure them out in advance and you'll avoid stumbling around trying to melt and cool your butter in time to fold it into your whipped egg–sugar mixture. Those TV chefs who have everything laid out in front of them so they can talk and chat while they make a beef bourguignonne? They've got the right idea for those of us cooking at home.

2. **Make sure your cutting board is flat and firmly anchored to the work surface.** A warped cutting board makes chopping and slicing a frustrating and risky challenge. And if it's sliding around while you're dicing, you'll want to throw it across the room. So make sure it's level, and before you use it, place a few dampened paper towels or thin dish towel on your work surface and put the cutting board on top.

The dampened towels will help to anchor the board firmly to your work surface and prevent it from moving around as you use it. It's the very first thing I do every time I start to cook.

3. **Sharpen your knives.** It's a common misconception that sharper knives are more dangerous. It's actually the opposite. If your knife is dull, it is much harder to slice and dice and chop. You're more likely to be pushing and pressing so hard that your knife will slip and you'll cut yourself. Every knife cut I have on my hands and arms is due to my being lazy and not sharpening my knife. With a super-sharp blade, your knife glides through your ingredients and makes quick, easy work of your prep tasks.

4. **Don't skimp on ingredients.** I don't mean buy fois gras or truffles for every meal. I mean make sure the produce you get is ripe, the meats you buy are good quality, the herbs you select are fresh. As often as you can, make stocks, cook beans, grind spices, juice citrus, and grate cheese rather than buy their lesser canned and jarred counterparts. Bake bread—yes bread!—from scratch and freeze what you don't eat so you always have homemade bread for sandwiches. If you make it a priority to minimize relying on prepared products and buy the best fresh stuff you can, you'll see the difference in your cooking immediately, and you'll enjoy your meals more.

5. **Clean as you go.** I polled my chefs and pastry chefs at Flour and Myers+Chang about the most important tip to pass along to home cooks and every last one told me, "Work clean." If there's one thing working in a professional kitchen has taught me, it is that working neatly and cleaning meticulously as you go is a sure way to set yourself up for success.

I remember my first week at Payard Pâtisserie. Chef François asked me to make a small wedding cake for a friend. It was a chance for me to show off my stuff to my new boss and coworkers. I came in hours before anyone arrived to work and made a glorious towering wedding cake . . . and proceeded to dirty every single worktable, sink, and mixer in the process. When my French-trained coworkers arrived, the only thing that they noticed was the pigpen-like mess that surrounded me. It made me instantly aware of how working in a kitchen isn't just about what you made but, just as important, how you made it. Once you are completely done with an item (maybe a jar of olives or a bottle of olive oil), immediately put it back in the fridge or on the counter so it is not cluttering up your workspace. Have a clean rag nearby so you can constantly clean your work surface and wipe down your cutting board. Throw away scraps right away or save them to use for stocks. The best chefs I know are all fanatical about immaculate work areas. If you keep your cooking area and tools clean and organized, your thoughts will be more focused on your task, you'll cook better, and you will enjoy the process much more.

6. Salt your food. I was invited to an impromptu casual dinner with a dear friend a few years back. She was making spaghetti and meatballs for us and her young kids. "Help me make this taste better, Joanne!" she implored me when I arrived. One taste and I knew all it needed was a hefty sprinkle of salt. Sure enough, after it was mixed in, the pasta went from blah to flavorful.

If when you go out to eat you think, "Wow, how does the chef make the food taste so good?" one "magic" ingredient is salt. For these recipes, I measured the amount of salt that we use at Flour to make them taste good to us. My testers often asked me, "Are you sure it's supposed to be X tsp salt? That seems like a lot." I know there are health implications if you are using a lot of salt, but if we're talking about simply making the food taste the way it should, there is probably a little more salt in the dish than you're

used to seeing. Try upping the salt you use in your own cooking and see the difference it makes. Along the same lines, when blanching vegetables or cooking pasta, generously salt the water until it tastes like the ocean. (Thank you, Chef Thomas Keller, for that great analogy.) The vegetables and pasta will then be flavored and ready to go into whatever you're using them in.

7. Trust your palate and taste as you go. Especially in cooking—where onions are all different sizes, lemons have varying amounts of acidity, spices sit on shelves for a few days or a few years, medium heat on one stove is low heat on another stove—you want to remember that the recipe you are following is ultimately a well-thought-out guide and not a hard-and-fast manifesto. In other words, taste continually as you are cooking and make adjustments based on the particular ingredients and equipment you are using and your own personal taste. Unlike in baking, in which every single step has been measured and accounted for and straying from the directions is frowned on, in cooking you can be a little looser, understanding that everyone's palate is different. As a trained pastry chef, I definitely had to learn to relax a bit when making these recipes. A chef would grab the salt container and start throwing pinches into his soup as I frantically chased after him with measuring spoons to document every last grain. We ultimately compromised on many dishes, recording the measured amounts of every spice and herb, and adding the phrase *season* wherever we could to account for taste differences. Remember that when seasoning, it's to *your* taste, so trust your palate and make these dishes yours.

8. Remember every bite. We regularly go out and get sandwiches from area cafés to see how we stack up. I'm amazed at how often a sandwich, made with wonderful fresh bread, well-made spread, crisp lettuce, and a flavorful filling, will be a dud because all of the filling is packed in the middle of the sandwich or the spread is only on one slice of bread, leaving the other bare and dry. When cooking, think constantly

of the people who will be eating what you are making. That means imagining your lovingly prepared dish going bite by bite into the recipient's mouth. In a sandwich, you want the bread to be spread evenly with whatever chutney or dressing is called for. You want the meat spread out and the tomatoes covering all of the meat and the lettuce arranged so that you get a few leaves with every mouthful. You want each and every bite to bring your guests as much pleasure as you got from making your marvelous creation.

9. Consolidate, label, rotate. Get into the habit—make that obsession—of always storing your ingredients in the smallest containers possible, labeling and dating them clearly, and rotating them constantly so that foods are used in the order in which they came into your kitchen (in kitchen-speak, we call this FIFO, or "first in, first out"). It's so in my blood now that I find myself FIFO-ing my makeup collection, my ever-growing stack of magazines, my sock drawer . . . you name it and I'm organizing and winnowing it down into the tightest space possible. You might not think this would help you become a better cook, but if your ingredients are kept fresh and clearly marked and easy to find, your cooking becomes less of a chaotic struggle and more of a pleasurable endeavor.

10. Think about uses for foodstuffs you would normally throw away. Parmigiano rinds, vegetable scraps, bread scraps, roasted chicken carcasses—all can be frozen and later turned into stocks, added to soups, or used in other dishes. We always have trimmings of this and that in our kitchens, and we are able to add so much more flavor to our stocks and sauces by taking advantage of these scraps. In baking, cake trimmings get ground into cake crumbs and used to decorate the sides of cakes, soft overripe fruit gets turned into jam, vanilla beans get tossed into the vanilla-sugar bin. Be creative and think of ways you can layer in and deepen flavors with scraps that others might consider throwing away.

11. Cook often for your friends and family and ask for honest feedback. It will give you a chance to improve with the next dish, so you're always growing and learning more about what works and what doesn't. Believe me, I know from (lots and lots of) personal experience that it isn't always easy to hear constructive criticism after you have spent hours in the kitchen using up every pot and pan to make a fabulous new creation. But only by pushing for real feedback will you be able to make adjustments for next time. You'll be a better cook, and you'll grow to love cooking and baking even more.

12. Eat out and read constantly. Isn't it fantastic that a highly valuable tip to becoming a better chef is something that you probably already like to do? If you love food, then the way to get better at making it is to try new dishes, cuisines, and restaurants. Expand your horizons and experiment with spices you've never heard of or a vegetable you've never seen before. Order something that you've only read about and think about how it is prepared and how you might enjoy it differently. Research how other cultures and other kitchens prepare foods that you have in common. Recipes in a book are meant to instruct you, but an even better guide is your own curiosity, which can lead you to try an unusual ingredient or to fiddle around with something that you are familiar with in a new way. Use this book and every cookbook you read as a jumping-off point to create wonderful foods that make you proud and happy.

breakfast

If I could eat breakfast for every meal of the day I would. Morning food is the most marvelous food, and the recipes here all reflect the very best and most popular of the breakfast offerings that we have at Flour and that I enjoy myself at home. Because the last thing you want to do in the morning is slave over a stove or oven for hours before you sit down to eat, all of these dishes require only minimal preparation immediately before eating. Much of the work—if not practically all of it—can be done the night before, so all you have to do is wake up and finish off your impressive breakfast or brunch feast.

sweets

CLASSIC APPLE TURNOVERS

At Flour we call these by their grown-up French name, *chausson aux pommes* (*chausson* means "slipper" and the pastries resemble bedroom slippers . . . sort of), but their genesis, I have to be honest, is the Pepperidge Farm apple turnovers that I ate as a child for special weekend breakfasts when Mom was feeling indulgent. I remember begging for them constantly and winning the battle occasionally. I would pop the frozen dough in the toaster oven and watch them transform from pale, gummy-looking triangles to flaky, shiny delights. You're supposed to wait till the filling cools to bite into them. Of course, I never did and invariably nursed a burnt tongue.

The beauty of this pastry is that you can make it over the course of many days so that when you want turnovers all you have to do is open up your freezer, like I did in my youth, and pop them in the oven. You'll be rewarded with golden brown, caramelized apple–filled treasures. Each component can be made in advance, and the final turnovers can be frozen for up to a month.

MAKES 10 TURNOVERS

CHUNKY APPLE FILLING

| 8 firm, tart apples, such as Granny Smith, peeled, halved, cored, and coarsely chopped |
| 4 tbsp/55 g unsalted butter |
| ½ tsp ground cinnamon |
| 1 cup/200 g vanilla sugar or granulated sugar |
| 1 tsp vanilla extract if using vanilla sugar, or 2 tsp vanilla extract if using granulated sugar |

| ½ batch Puff Pastry (page 286), 12 oz/340 g |
| 2 large eggs |
| 3 tbsp sanding, pearl, or granulated sugar |

SPECIAL EQUIPMENT: rimmed baking sheet, parchment paper, rolling pin, pastry brush

1. **TO MAKE THE FILLING:** In a heavy medium saucepan, combine the apples, butter, cinnamon, and sugar over low heat and cook, stirring occasionally, for 1 to 1½ hours, or until the apples break down and the mixture thickens and turns golden brown. The mixture will release a lot of water at first and bubble a lot, and then it will slowly start to caramelize and darken. There may still be some pieces of whole apple in the mixture, which is fine. Remove from the heat, stir in the vanilla extract, and let cool. You should have about 3 cups/720 ml. The filling can be stored in an airtight container in the refrigerator for up to 4 days, or it can be frozen for up to 2 weeks, then thawed overnight in the refrigerator before using. It can be used straight from the fridge or at room temperature for filling the turnovers.

2. Preheat the oven to 350°F/180°C, and place a rack in the center of the oven. Line the baking sheet with parchment paper.

3. On a well-floured work surface, roll the puff pastry into a rectangle about 28 in/70 cm wide and 12 in/30.5 cm top to bottom. The dough may seem pretty tough and difficult to roll out at first. Don't be afraid to be firm with the dough: flip it upside down, turn it side to side, pound it with the rolling pin to flatten it as you roll it into a long rectangle. Use a sharp knife to trim the edges of the rectangle to rid it of any uneven edges. Using a ruler and the knife, cut the rectangle into ten 5½-in/14-cm squares by first dividing it in half horizontally and then dividing it vertically into strips 5½ in/14 cm wide.

4. Put about ¼ cup/60 ml of the filling onto one side of each pastry square and spread the filling a little so it fills half of the square diagonally. Use a knife or the back of a spoon to spread it evenly, leaving a little bit of a border around the filling to allow for the sealing of the dough triangle. Break 1 egg into a small bowl and whisk it with a fork. Using the pastry brush, brush the exposed pastry dough with the egg wash. Carefully fold the egg-washed dough over the filling, then use your fingers to pinch the turnover triangle together. Use the tines of the fork to press the edges of the turnover firmly together, making sure the turn-over is well sealed. Continue with the remaining nine dough squares. (At this point, you can freeze the unbaked turnovers. Wrap them well with plastic wrap and store them in the freezer for up to 2 weeks. You can bake them as directed directly from the freezer.)

5. Transfer the turnovers to the prepared baking sheet. Using the top of a paring knife, cut a few small slits in the top of the turnovers to allow steam to escape while they bake. Break the second egg into a small bowl and whisk with a fork. Using the pastry brush, lightly coat the tops of the turnovers with the egg wash, and then sprinkle them evenly with the sanding sugar.

6. Bake for about 1 hour, or until the dough is entirely browned and baked through. Look at the sides of the turnovers where the pastry has puffed up to make sure this part of the turnover is golden brown, as well. Remove the turnovers from the oven and let cool on the pan on a wire rack for at least 1 hour before serving to allow the filling to cool. These turnovers are best served the same day, but you can hold them in an airtight container at room temperature for up to 2 days and refresh them in a 300°F/150°C oven for 6 to 8 minutes.

CINNAMON-CREAM BRIOCHE

We only make a few of these each morning, and as soon as they come out of the oven, they are snatched up by waiting customers. When the first *Flour* book came out, there was an outcry from these loyal cinnamon-cream devotees because the recipe was not included. It wasn't an intentional omission; in my mind, this pastry was something we kind of threw together each morning and thus it didn't really need a recipe. Clearly I was wrong.

We were inspired by a recipe for a similar pastry in Nancy Silverton's book, *Pastries from the La Brea Bakery*, called Viennese Cream Brioche, which she describes as being so sublime that it made Julia Child cry. With that description, how could we resist trying our hand at making them? The recipe uses ingredients that we always have in our fridge—brioche dough, pastry cream, crème fraîche—and puts them together in a way that makes quite an addictive treat. Be generous with the cinnamon-sugar that is showered on top; it's what makes these so crunchy and irresistible.

MAKES 8 PASTRIES

½ batch Basic Brioche dough (see page 284)

1 cup/240 ml Pastry Cream (page 290)

1½ cups/360 ml crème fraîche

1¼ cups/250 g granulated sugar

1 tsp ground cinnamon

SPECIAL EQUIPMENT: two rimmed baking sheets, parchment paper

1. Preheat the oven to 350°F/180°C, and place one rack in the center and one rack in the top third of the oven. Line the baking sheets with parchment paper.

2. Shape the brioche dough into a rectangle about 8 in/20 cm long, 4 in/10 cm wide, and 1 in/2.5 cm thick. Using a ruler and a knife, cut the rectangle into eight 2-in/5-cm squares by first dividing it in half horizontally and then dividing it vertically into strips 2 in/5 cm wide. Each square of dough should weigh about 3½ oz/100 g.

3. Stretch each dough square into a circle about 5 in/12 cm in diameter as if you are making a small pizza. Stretch the inner part of the circle so that it is quite thin and shape the edge of the circle to create a rim. The center should be almost paper-thin and the finished circle should look like you are making the crust for a mini deep-dish pizza. Place the brioche circle on one of the prepared baking sheets and repeat with the remaining dough squares, spacing them 2 to 3 in/5 to 7.5 cm apart and using both baking sheets.

4. Using the back of a spoon, spread 2 tbsp of the pastry cream over the base of each brioche circle, spreading it evenly and leaving the rim bare. Place about 3 tbsp of the crème fraîche in the center of each brioche circle and gently spread it, again covering the base of the circle and leaving the rim untouched. In a small bowl, mix together the sugar and cinnamon, then sprinkle the mixture evenly over both the crème fraîche center and the rim of each circle.

CONTINUED

5. Bake the pastries, switching the baking sheets between the racks and rotating them back to front about halfway during baking, for 25 to 30 minutes, or until they are medium golden brown along the edge. (Sometimes the crème fraîche spills out over the edge of the circle. Don't fret; when the pastries come out of the oven and cool a bit, you can scoop spillover back into the center.) Let the crème fraîche set and the brioche cool on the baking sheets for 10 to 15 minutes before serving. Cinnamon-creams should be served the day they are made; they don't hold very well overnight because of their creamy centers.

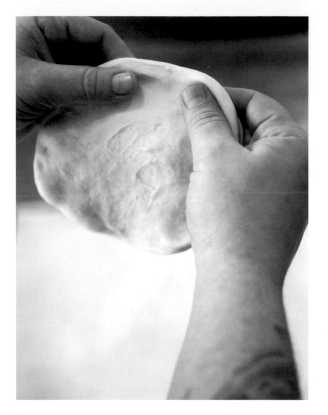

TWICE-BAKED BRIOCHE

The French are geniuses when it comes to pastry. And I don't mean that they're technically, traditionally pastry wizards (which they are); I mean that they are wonderfully inventive when it comes to creating spectacular pastries out of foods that less imaginative cooks might deem unusable. Did you know that the French translation of bread pudding, *gateau plubelle*, is actually "garbage cake"? And that French toast, *pain perdu*, translates to "lost bread"? And these are both among our most popular offerings at Flour.

Twice-baked brioche, or *bostock* as it is called in some bakeries, is a pastry that uses up day-old brioche loaves. Slices of rich, eggy brioche are dipped in almond-scented syrup, slathered with almond cream, showered with sliced almonds, and baked till golden. The buttery, crunchy, sweet result is finished off with a flourish of confectioners' sugar. As with other items on our menu that we've created to use up excess bread or pastry, we've found this treat so popular that we often end up baking extra loaves of our popular brioche to ensure that we have enough unsold day-old loaves to make these mouthwatering pastries.

MAKES 6 SLICES

¾ cup/150 g vanilla sugar

¼ tsp almond extract

One 9-in/23-cm Basic Brioche (page 284), preferably a day or two old

1¾ cups/390 g Frangipane (page 292), at spreadable room temperature

2 cups/220 g sliced blanched almonds

¼ cup/35 g confectioners' sugar for garnish

SPECIAL EQUIPMENT: rimmed baking sheet, parchment paper, offset spatula (optional), sieve or sifter

1. Preheat the oven to 350°F/180°C, and place a rack in the center of the oven. Line the baking sheet with parchment paper.

2. In a small saucepan, combine the vanilla sugar and ¾ cup/180 ml water and bring to a boil over high heat. Remove from the heat and add the almond extract. Pour the mixture into a shallow heatproof container and let cool at room temperature for 15 to 20 minutes, or until it is no longer piping hot.

3. Trim off the ends of the brioche loaf, then cut the loaf into six slices, each about 1¼ in/3 cm thick. Quickly dip both sides of one slice in the sugar syrup, giving it a slight squeeze as you remove it from the syrup to keep it from getting too soggy. Place on the prepared baking sheet. Repeat with the remaining slices. Using the offset spatula or the back of a spoon, spread about ¼ cup/55 g of the frangipane evenly over each slice and place the slices back on the baking sheet, spacing them evenly apart on the sheet. Sprinkle each slice with an equal amount of the sliced almonds, pressing them slightly into the frangipane so they don't fall off. (At this point, the brioche can be covered with plastic wrap and stored overnight in the fridge, then baked directly from the fridge.)

4. Bake for 25 to 30 minutes, or until the almonds and frangipane are golden brown on the edges and pale golden brown in the center. Remove from the oven and let cool on the baking sheet for about 15 minutes, or until cool enough to remove. Using the sieve, sprinkle with the confectioners' sugar and serve.

VEGAN VANILLA-MIXED BERRY MUFFINS

We have a rule at Flour that if something is labeled "gluten free" or "low fat," it has to be just as delicious to those who are not concerned about the label as to those who are. The same goes for our vegan items. We created this muffin to satisfy our growing number of customers who have converted to veganism, and it has as many nonvegan fans as vegan ones. In fact, most people don't believe us when we tell them that it's vegan. To the nonbelievers the proof is in the tin. In developing this muffin recipe, we realized that many vegan pastries make up for their lack of dairy and eggs by being super sweet and extra oily. We held back on the sugar and oil to create a scrumptious fluffy muffin that people of all dietary preferences will enjoy.

MAKES 12 MUFFINS

2⅔ cups/370 g all-purpose flour

2 tsp baking soda

1 tsp kosher salt

1 cup/200 g granulated sugar

¾ cup plus 2 tbsp/210 ml vegetable oil

1⅓ cups/315 ml plain soy milk

2 tbsp distilled white or cider vinegar

1 tbsp vanilla extract

1 cup/130 g fresh or frozen raspberries

1 cup/150 g fresh or frozen blueberries

SPECIAL EQUIPMENT: 12-cup standard muffin tin

1. Preheat the oven to 350°F/180°C, and place a rack in the center of the oven. Line the cups of the muffin tin with paper liners or generously oil and flour them.

2. In a medium bowl, combine the flour, baking soda, salt, and ¾ cup plus 2 tbsp/175 g of the sugar and stir until well mixed. In a separate bowl, whisk together the vegetable oil, soy milk, vinegar, and vanilla. Make a well in the dry ingredients and pour the wet ingredients into the middle of the well. Stir with a rubber spatula until well mixed. Add the raspberries and blueberries and mix until the fruit is evenly distributed.

3. Spoon an equal amount of batter into each prepared muffin cup. Sprinkle the tops with the remaining 2 tbsp sugar.

4. Bake for 25 to 30 minutes, or until the muffins are pale gold and the tops spring back when pressed gently in the middle. Let cool in the tin on a wire rack before popping them out. The muffins taste best on the day they are baked, but any uneaten muffins can be stored in a covered container at room temperature for 2 or 3 days. For the best results, refresh them in a 300°F/150°C oven for 4 to 5 minutes.

VEGAN APPLE-CINNAMON MUFFINS VARIATION: Omit the vanilla extract, raspberries, and blueberries. Mix ½ tsp ground cinnamon with the flour, baking soda, salt, and sugar. Peel, core, and chop 2 Granny Smith apples and fold them into the finished muffin batter. Proceed as directed.

BROWN SUGAR–OAT CHERRY MUFFINS

At Flour, we offer a range of muffins that vary with the season. In the spring you might see raspberry-rhubarb; during the cool fall months we feature roasted pear with ginger. These seasonal muffins are made with a simple standard muffin batter that we've used for years and that I share in my first book, *Flour*. A while back we wanted to introduce a new muffin to the mix—something that was a bit heartier and maybe even healthier, with an emphasis on whole grains. Brian, one of our pastry chefs, offered up this recipe, which we've tweaked over the years to make it ours. I didn't realize how beloved it had become until *Flour* was published. In between raving about their success with baking cupcakes and home-made Oreos, readers bemoaned the absence of this recipe and made many a desperate request for it. I'm happy to oblige here.

MAKES 12 MUFFINS

3½ cups/350 g rolled (not instant) oats

1¼ cups/300 ml crème fraîche

1 cup/240 ml whole milk, at room temperature

½ cup/115 g unsalted butter, melted and cooled to room temperature

2 large eggs

⅔ cup/135 g granulated sugar

¾ cup/165 g packed brown sugar

1½ cups/210 g frozen or fresh sweet or sour cherries, pitted and chopped

1¼ cups/210 g whole-wheat flour

2 tsp baking powder

½ tsp baking soda

1 tsp kosher salt

BROWN SUGAR–OAT TOPPING

¼ cup/25 g rolled (not instant) oats

3 tbsp packed brown sugar

Pinch of ground cinnamon

SPECIAL EQUIPMENT: 12-cup standard muffin tin, rimmed baking sheet

1. In a medium bowl, stir together the rolled oats, crème fraîche, milk, and butter with a wooden spoon until combined. In a small bowl, whisk the eggs together and stir into the oat mixture. Add the granulated sugar, brown sugar, and cherries and continue to stir until well combined.

2. In a separate small bowl, combine the whole-wheat flour, baking powder, baking soda, and salt and stir until well mixed. Gently fold the dry ingredients into the wet oat mixture. The batter will be gloppy. Transfer the batter to an airtight container and place in the fridge. Let the batter sit for at least 8 hours or up to overnight in the refrigerator.

CONTINUED

3. When ready to bake, preheat the oven to 350°F/180°C, and place a rack in the center of the oven. Line the cups of the muffin tin with paper liners, coat liberally with nonstick spray, or butter and flour them. Spoon about 1 cup/240 ml of the batter into each muffin cup, filling it all the way to the brim and wa-a-a-y over. (It will seem like there's too much batter for the tins, but if you want the characteristic muffin top you need to overfill them. You can make smaller muffins if you prefer and reduce the baking time by about 10 minutes.) The batter will be stiff and firm.

4. **TO MAKE THE TOPPING:** In a small bowl, stir together the oats, brown sugar, and cinnamon. Sprinkle the topping evenly over the muffins and place the muffin tin on a baking sheet to catch any drips. Bake for 45 to 55 minutes, or until the muffins are golden brown on top and spring back when pressed in the middle with a fingertip. Let cool in the tin on a wire rack for 20 minutes and then remove the muffins from the pan.

5. These muffins taste best the day they are made, but you can store them in an airtight container at room temperature for up to 2 days. If you keep them for longer than a day, refresh them in a 300°F/150°C oven for 5 to 6 minutes. Or, you can freeze them, well wrapped in plastic wrap, for up to 1 week. Reheat directly from the freezer in a 300°F/150°C oven for about 10 minutes.

CRANBERRY VARIATION: For a winter version of this addictive muffin, substitute 1½ cups/150 g chopped fresh or frozen cranberries for the cherries. Proceed as directed.

FABULOUS FRENCH TOAST

The most important thing about making great French toast is starting with great bread. It doesn't have to be fresh (in fact—the older, the better, because the bread will soak up more custard when it's dried out and stale), but it should be a hearty country-style loaf. The bread spends the night in the fridge in a simple custard bath: vanilla sugar, eggs, half-and-half. By the time you cook it it's so filled with custard that it almost seems to soufflé. You start it in a skillet to give it a lovely caramelized crust on the outside and then you finish it in the oven. It's so deliciously airy and eggy that I usually eat it as is, sans butter and syrup, but for a special breakfast treat do it up right with all of the trimmings.

MAKES 6 SLICES

6 large eggs

⅔ cup/135 g vanilla sugar

½ tsp kosher salt

2 cups/480 ml half-and-half

6 slices country-style sourdough bread, 1 in/2.5 cm thick, preferably 1 day old

3 to 4 tbsp unsalted butter, plus extra for serving

2 tbsp confectioners' sugar for garnish

Maple syrup for serving

SPECIAL EQUIPMENT: large, flat nonstick skillet, rimmed baking sheet, sieve or sifter

1. Into a small bowl, crack the eggs and slowly whisk in the sugar and salt. Whisk in the half-and-half. Place the bread in a single layer in a shallow container and pour the egg mixture over the bread. Turn the bread over to coat both sides and cover with plastic wrap. Refrigerate overnight.

2. The next morning, turn the bread over again. Preheat the oven to 350°F/180°C, and place a rack in the center of the oven.

3. In the skillet, heat about 1 tbsp of the butter over medium-high heat. Sprinkle a few drops of water into the pan; if the water sizzles on contact, the pan is ready. Place two slices of French toast in the pan and cook on one side for 2 to 3 minutes, or until golden brown. Flip them over and cook for 2 to 3 minutes longer, or until the second side is golden brown. Remove from the heat and place on the baking sheet. Repeat with the remaining French toast in two batches, adding 1 tbsp or so of the butter to the skillet each time.

4. When all the slices have been fried, place the baking sheet in the oven for 8 to 10 minutes to finish the cooking. When the French toast is done, the insides will be custardy and soft but no longer soggy and wet. Using the sieve, dust the tops with the confectioners' sugar. Serve immediately with butter and maple syrup.

DECADENT SUNDAY WAFFLES

One of the benefits of working in a bakery is having a wonderful selection of tempting break-fast items to enjoy each morning. Shall I have an apple turnover today or an egg sandwich with special secret sauce? On my weekends, however, I like to take the time to make things that we don't offer at Flour. My husband especially enjoys the new dishes I create from my experiments. Waffles are his weakness, and after years of experimenting with every waffle recipe under the sun, this one was declared our hands-down favorite. I shouldn't be surprised; I love crème fraîche in (or on) just about everything, and its addition to this basic waffle batter makes these super-rich and deca-dent. The soda water adds a little oomph to the batter, so your waffles are extra light and crispy.

MAKES 6 WAFFLES

1½ cups/210 g all-purpose flour

3 tbsp packed brown sugar

1½ tsp baking powder

½ tsp baking soda

½ tsp kosher salt

¾ cup/180 ml nonfat buttermilk, at room temperature

½ cup/120 ml crème fraîche

¼ cup/60 ml soda water, at room temperature

4 tbsp/55 g unsalted butter, melted and cooled, plus more at room temperature for serving

2 large eggs

1 tsp vanilla extract

Maple syrup for serving

SPECIAL EQUIPMENT: waffle maker

1. Preheat the waffle maker. The higher heat settings are better, because the outside of the waffle will turn crisper faster.

2. In a medium bowl, whisk together the flour, brown sugar, baking powder, baking soda, and salt. If necessary, break up the brown sugar lumps with your fingers to make sure the sugar is evenly mixed. In a separate bowl, whisk together the buttermilk, crème fraîche, soda water, melted butter, eggs, and vanilla until well combined. Make a well in the middle of the dry ingredients and pour the wet ingredients into the well. Using a whisk and a fold-ing motion, gently fold the wet and dry ingredients together until combined.

3. Brush the preheated waffle grids with melted butter or vegetable oil or coat with nonstick spray. Ladle the batter onto the bottom grid according to the manufacturer's directions and close the lid. Be sure to bake the waffles until they are golden brown; if underbaked, they will be floppy and more like bumpy pancakes than crisp, light waffles. Serve the waffles hot with softened butter and copious amounts of maple syrup.

CJ'S SPICED BANANA PANCAKES

Chef Jeff at Flour2 made these pancakes for his son, Julian, one weekend and raved about them so much I asked him to make some for us to try at work. Before I knew it, I had eaten four at one sitting. That's how I know when something is up to Flour standards: I can't stop eating it. There's so much banana in here that the pancakes are incredibly moist and naturally sweet. A touch of freshly ground pepper and allspice elevates this homey breakfast treat to something truly special. I'll bet that like me you can't eat just one.

MAKES 7 OR 8 PANCAKES

1 cup/140 g all-purpose flour

2 tsp baking powder

½ tsp kosher salt

1½ tsp ground allspice

¾ tsp freshly ground black pepper

2 tbsp packed brown sugar

1 large egg

1 cup/240 ml whole milk

2 tbsp vegetable oil

4 medium ripe bananas, cut into ½-in/12-mm pieces

2 to 3 tbsp unsalted butter for cooking pancakes, plus more for serving

Maple syrup for serving

SPECIAL EQUIPMENT: rimmed baking sheet, large flat nonstick skillet

1. Preheat the oven to 200°F/95°C, and place a rack in the center of the oven. Put a wire rack on the baking sheet and place it in the oven.

2. In a medium bowl, whisk together the flour, baking powder, salt, allspice, pepper, and brown sugar. In another medium bowl, whisk together the egg, milk, and vegetable oil until blended; add about 3 of the bananas (reserving the rest for serving). Make a well in the dry ingredients and pour in the wet ingredients. With a rubber spatula or wooden spoon, fold the wet ingredients into the dry ingredients just until combined. Don't overmix. It will be a thick, gloppy, lumpy batter. (Sounds delicious so far, doesn't it?)

CONTINUED

3. In the skillet, melt about 1 tsp of the butter over medium heat. Sprinkle a few drops of water into the pan; if the water sizzles on contact, the pan is ready. Pour a scant 1/2 cup/120 ml of batter into the skillet and cook for about 3 minutes, or until the edges of the pancake start to brown and small bubbles begin forming along the edges and in the middle of the cake. With a flat metal or plastic spatula, carefully flip the pancake over; the first side should be golden brown. Cook slowly for another 2 to 3 minutes. Gently press the pancake in the middle with the spatula to flatten it out a bit and make sure the center is cooked through. Adjust the heat as needed so the pancake browns nicely but doesn't burn on the second side. Remove the finished pancake from the skillet and place it on the wire rack in the oven to keep warm while you cook the remaining pancakes.

4. Cook the remaining pancakes the same way, adding another 1 tsp or so of butter before adding the batter each time. For these pancakes, a slower and lower heat is better; once the pan has been seasoned by the first pancake, you should be able to cook the remaining pancakes on medium-low heat. Serve immediately with butter, maple syrup, and the remaining banana.

DENISE'S DUTCH BABY

When you are a professional baker, most people shy away from baking for you, because they think that there's no way they can impress you. The truth is I love to be presented with a home-made dessert or pastry. That's why I got into this business in the first place: I love spreading (and receiving) the joy that sweets bring to people. Denise Drower Swidey, a dear friend, former coworker, and amazing cook, is always baking and sharing, and I'm the lucky recipient of many a scrumptious treat. She had Christopher and me over for brunch one Sunday and served us a decadent apple pancake. I pleaded for the recipe, and she generously agreed. It's essentially a Dutch baby, which is a pouffy baked pancake that rises dramatically in the oven and then gently deflates as you take it out and serve it to your guests. The sugar and butter caramelize around the edge of the pancake, making a delicious counterpart to the soft, custardy middle.

**MAKES 1 LARGE PANCAKE
(SERVES 3 OR 4)**

1 large Granny Smith apple, peeled, halved, cored, and thinly sliced

4 tbsp/50 g granulated sugar

¼ cup/55 g packed brown sugar

½ tsp ground cinnamon

½ cup/120 ml whole milk

2 large eggs

½ cup/70 g all-purpose flour

½ tsp kosher salt

2 tbsp unsalted butter

¼ lemon, wedge-cut

2 tbsp confectioners' sugar

SPECIAL EQUIPMENT: blender or food processor, 10-in/25-cm seasoned cast-iron skillet, rimmed baking sheet, sieve or sifter

1. Preheat the oven to 425°F/220°C, and place a rack in the center of the oven.

2. In a medium bowl, toss the apple slices with 2 tbsp of the granulated sugar, all of the brown sugar, and the cinnamon. Set aside.

3. Pour the milk and eggs into the blender or food processor and pulse a few times to combine. Add the flour, the remaining 2 tbsp granulated sugar, and the salt and blend for 6 to 8 seconds to combine if using a blender, or pulse 8 to 10 times until well blended and frothy if using a processor.

4. Heat the cast-iron skillet over medium-high heat. When the pan is hot, add the butter. When the butter has melted, add the apple-sugar mixture and cook, stirring often, for about 2 minutes, or until the sugar melts and bubbles. The apples will finish cooking in the oven, so don't worry about cooking them through. Cook them just until the sugar starts to bubble. Remove the skillet from the heat, arrange the apples so that they cover the bottom of the pan evenly, and pour the batter evenly over the apples. The batter will fill the skillet and go under and over the apples.

5. Place the skillet on the baking sheet to avoid spills on your oven floor and bake for 20 to 30 minutes, or until the pancake is puffed and golden brown. Remove from the oven, squeeze the lemon wedge over the pancake, then, using the sieve, dust the top with the confectioners' sugar. Serve immediately. The pancake will stick to the pan if you don't remove it while it is still hot, so be sure to get it out within 15 minutes of pulling the pan from the oven (or be prepared to scrape the pan).

STEEL-CUT OATS
with Pear Compote and Crunchy Pecans

I always thought oatmeal came in little packets that you add hot water to, stir, and eat. It wasn't until the staff at Flour clamored to offer a hot cereal option to our customers that I discovered steel-cut oats, which are made by cutting oat kernels into little pieces with steel blades, rather than rolling them flat into flakes with rollers. What results is a world away from the mushy porridge I dutifully ate when I was growing up. Steel-cut oats are chewy, nutty, and far more flavorful and interesting to eat. This recipe will change your outlook on oatmeal. The easy-to-make, barely sweetened pecans are a great crunchy topping for more than just oatmeal. Try them on ice cream, pancakes, or waffles, or just eat them out of hand.

SERVES 3 OR 4

PEAR COMPOTE

3 medium Bosc pears, peeled, halved, cored, and roughly chopped

¼ cup/55 g packed brown sugar

¼ tsp vanilla extract

Pinch of kosher salt

CRUNCHY PECANS

2 tbsp granulated sugar

¾ cup/75 g pecans, lightly toasted and chopped

OATMEAL

2 cups/480 ml whole milk

¼ tsp kosher salt

1 cup/180 g steel-cut oats

¼ tsp freshly grated nutmeg

¼ tsp ground cinnamon

SPECIAL EQUIPMENT: Microplane or other fine-rasp grater

1. **TO MAKE THE COMPOTE:** In a small saucepan, combine the pears, brown sugar, vanilla, and salt and cook over medium-high heat, stirring, until the sugar melts and starts to simmer. Continue cooking, stirring occasionally, for about 5 minutes, or until the pears have softened. Remove from the heat. The compote can be made up to 3 days in advance and stored in an airtight container in the refrigerator.

2. **TO MAKE THE PECANS:** In a small saucepan, mix together the sugar and 2 tbsp water and bring to a boil over high heat. Watch the pan carefully as the sugar syrup starts to color. As soon as the syrup begins to turn brown, add the pecans, reduce the heat to low, and quickly stir the pecans into the syrup. The nuts will clump and it won't look like there is enough syrup to cover them. Stir over low heat for about 1 minute, or until the syrup is well mixed with the nuts (you may start to see some sugar-syrup threads clinging to the nuts). Remove from the heat, scrape the nuts onto a heatproof plate or a clean work surface, and let cool. When cool, break into small bite-size pieces.

3. **TO MAKE THE OATMEAL:** In a medium saucepan, combine the milk, 2 cups/480 ml water, the salt, and oats and bring to a boil over high heat. Stir, reduce the heat to medium-low, and simmer, stirring occasionally, for about 30 minutes. (To speed up the cooking, combine the milk, water, salt, and oats in an airtight container and let soak overnight in the fridge. In the morning, transfer the mixture to a medium saucepan and proceed as directed. Cooking time will be reduced by about half.) Add the nutmeg and cinnamon to the oatmeal and stir to combine.

4. When ready to serve, divide the oatmeal equally among four bowls and top with the pear compote and the nuts.

BLUEBERRY COMPOTE VARIATION: Omit the pears. Mix 3 cups/450 g frozen or fresh blueberries with the brown sugar, vanilla, and salt. In a medium saucepan over medium heat, cook just until the sugar melts and starts to simmer, about 1 minute. Remove from the heat. The compote can be made up to 3 days in advance and stored in an airtight container in the refrigerator.

SAVORIES

GARLIC AND ROSEMARY HOME FRIES

Truffle pigs are renowned for their ability to sniff out aromatic truffles, highly sought-after and difficult-to-find delicacies that grow deep in the forest; I am notorious for being able to sense when Chef Jeff is making these home fries all the way from the other side of the kitchen. Regardless of the buttery cookies coming out of the oven or the luscious cakes being draped in chocolate ganache, it's these home fries that lure me out of the office or away from the mixer, and I end up hovering at Jeff's station, where trays of these crispy, garlicky, piping-hot potatoes await. I try to limit myself to just one or two ("Testing Chef! Making sure they're okay!"), but it's usually about half a tray later before I pull myself away.

SERVES 4

2 lb/910 g Yukon gold potatoes, scrubbed clean and unpeeled

⅓ cup/80 ml vegetable oil

1 tbsp chopped fresh thyme

1 tbsp chopped fresh rosemary

4 garlic cloves, smashed and cut in half

1¼ tsp kosher salt

½ tsp freshly ground black pepper

SPECIAL EQUIPMENT: rimmed baking sheet

1. Preheat the oven to 375°F/190°C, and place a rack in the center of the oven.

2. Cut the potatoes into 1- to 1½-in/2.5- to 3-cm pieces and place in a large bowl. Set aside.

3. In a small saucepan, combine the vegetable oil, thyme, rosemary, and garlic. Warm over medium-low heat for 3 to 4 minutes, or until the oil is hot. Turn off the heat and let the seasonings sit for 2 minutes. Pluck out the garlic halves and discard.

4. Pour the hot oil over the potatoes, add the salt and pepper, and toss well. Spread the potatoes on the baking sheet. Bake, turning the baking sheet from back to front and stirring the potatoes once halfway through baking, for 40 to 45 minutes, or until the potatoes are cooked through and golden brown. Serve immediately.

FLOUR'S FAMOUS EGG SANDWICH

We never meant for our egg sandwiches to become famous. In fact, for the first seven or so years we were open, we only offered them on Sundays in a limited amount and on a first-come, first-served basis. The original Flour is just a short walk from one of Boston's classic diners, Mike's City Diner, which serves a killer egg sandwich along with its characteristic sassy attitude. We figured our customers would come to us for pastries and head to Mike's if they wanted a more substantial eggy breakfast.

Since our kitchen isn't really set up for a diner-style egg sandwich, with eggs cracked into a skillet and fried to order, we had to come up with a way to precook the eggs so they could simply be reheated and assembled quickly to order by the counter staff. We tried to bake the eggs ahead of time, but they turned rubbery as soon as they were chilled. So we brought in our pastry knowledge that fat—in this case, half-and-half—keeps eggs tender and soft. Thus our egg soufflé was born. We bake the eggs in advance and then reheat them with cheese, meat, and tomato to order. Our homemade focaccia roll is slathered with dijonnaise, a mix of Dijon mustard and mayonnaise that we dub our (not any longer) "secret sauce." These egg sandwiches have become so beloved that now we offer them seven days a week all day long, and some customers only know us as the Egg Sandwich Place.

MAKES 4 SANDWICHES

Small handful of cornmeal for sprinkling on the baking sheet

½ batch Flour Focaccia dough (see page 282), or 1 lb/455 g store-bought pizza dough

Small handful of all-purpose flour for sprinkling on the rolls

9 large eggs

¾ cup/180 ml half-and-half

¾ tsp kosher salt

Pinch of freshly ground black pepper

½ tsp chopped fresh thyme

4 slices sharp Cheddar cheese

4 slices good-quality ham, or 8 slices thick-cut applewood-smoked bacon, cooked in the oven until barely crisp (see page 150)

¼ cup/60 ml good-quality mayonnaise

¼ cup/60 ml Dijon mustard

2 cups/40 g mesclun greens or other mild lettuce

1 ripe tomato, cut into 4 thick slices

SPECIAL EQUIPMENT: rimmed baking sheet, 8-in/20-cm square or round cake pan, roasting pan, or other large, shallow pan

1. Sprinkle the baking sheet liberally with the cornmeal. Set aside.

2. Shape the dough into a 4-in/10-cm square, then divide the square into four equal pieces. Shape each piece of dough into a ball by stretching it flat on a work surface and then bringing the edges inward to meet in the center. Turn the dough piece over and keep tucking the edges of the dough underneath until you have a small ball with a taut surface. Place the dough ball on the prepared baking sheet and repeat with the remaining three dough pieces. Sprinkle the dough balls with some of the flour, lightly cover them with plastic wrap or a lint-free cloth, and place them in a warm area (78° to 82°F/25° to 27°C is ideal) for about 2 hours, or until the dough has doubled in size and is soft and wobbly.

CONTINUED

3. About 30 minutes before you are ready to bake the rolls, preheat the oven to 400°F/200°C, and place a rack in the center of the oven. Coat the bottom and sides of the cake pan with nonstick spray or liberally coat the bottom and sides with vegetable oil.

4. Uncover the dough balls. Sprinkle them with the remaining flour, and then slap each ball flat with the palm of your hand to deflate it. Bake the rolls for 15 to 20 minutes, or until golden brown. Transfer the rolls to a wire rack to cool. Reduce the oven temperature to 300°F/150°C.

5. In a large bowl, whisk the eggs together until blended. Whisk in the half-and-half and salt until combined. Pour the egg mixture into the prepared cake pan.

6. Place the cake pan in the roasting pan, and place the roasting pan on the center oven rack. Pour hot water into the roasting pan to reach halfway up the sides of the cake pan. This water bath will ensure that the egg soufflé will cook slowly and evenly. Drape a piece of aluminum foil over the cake pan or place a baking sheet directly on top of it, then carefully slide in the oven rack and close the oven door. Bake for 15 to 20 minutes, then remove the foil or baking sheet and sprinkle the pepper and thyme evenly over the top. Cover again and continue baking for about 20 minutes longer, or until the center of the egg mixture is just barely set and no longer wiggles when you jiggle the pan.

7. Remove both pans from the oven, and carefully remove the cake pan holding the eggs from the water bath. Leave the oven on. Let the eggs cool and set in the pan for about 10 minutes, or until cool enough to handle. Cut the eggs into four equal portions. Using a spatula, carefully remove the egg patties from the cake pan. (Egg patties may be made in advance and stored in an airtight container in the refrigerator.) Place the egg patties on the baking sheet and top each patty with 1 slice of the Cheddar and 1 slice of the ham or 2 strips of bacon. Put the baking sheet in the oven for 4 to 5 minutes, or until the cheese starts to melt.

8. Meanwhile, in a small bowl, combine the mayonnaise and mustard and stir until blended. Split each cooled roll in half horizontally, and spread the mayo-mustard mixture evenly on both cut sides of each roll. Divide the mesclun equally among the roll bottoms. Remove the egg patties from the oven, place a patty on top of the greens, then top each with 1 tomato slice. Close each sandwich with a roll top and press down to smush everything together. Serve immediately.

SMOKED SALMON SANDWICHES

with Herbed Cream Cheese, Arugula, and Red Onion

I remember the first time I went to a fancy hotel brunch buffet: I was in college, and I was wowed by the endless rows of eggs, breakfast meats, pastries, fruit, and more. I hadn't really grown up with typical breakfast or brunch foods, so I was fascinated by the array. Omelet stations, Belgian waffle stations, Canadian bacon, sausage links—it was like a culinary Disney World to a food fanatic like me. What caught my eye especially was a large platter of smoked salmon with mounds of cream cheese, capers, chives, minced red onion, lemon wedges and a pile of bagels waiting to be toasted. I knew about toasted bagels with cream cheese, but what was all of this other paraphernalia? I watched and learned and soon became hooked on this traditional brunch treat.

Years later when I opened Flour, I wanted to offer something like that smoked salmon spread offering on our Sunday brunch menu. We don't do bagels, but we do have awesome focaccia toast, which makes spectacular sandwiches. We added the lemon and capers and chives to the cream cheese, and today we serve dozens of these sandwiches each weekend, slathered with cream cheese, piled high with salmon, and accompanied with arugula and red onion.

MAKES 4 SANDWICHES

HERBED CREAM CHEESE

8 oz/225 g cream cheese, at room temperature

1 tsp grated lemon zest

1 tsp freshly squeezed lemon juice

¼ cup/15 g minced fresh chives

1 tsp chopped capers

8 slices Flour Focaccia (page 282) or other good-quality white or wheat bread

2 cups/50 g loosely packed baby arugula

¼ red onion, cut into very thin slices

12 oz/340 g sliced smoked salmon

SPECIAL EQUIPMENT: Microplane or other fine-rasp grater

1. **TO MAKE THE HERBED CREAM CHEESE:** In a small bowl, beat the cream cheese with a wooden spoon until softened. Add the lemon zest, lemon juice, chives, and capers and mix until well combined.

2. Toast the bread and lay the slices out on a clean, dry work surface. Spread each slice evenly with about 2 tbsp of the cream cheese. Divide the arugula equally among four slices and top each tangle with an equal amount of the red onion. Add the smoked salmon, again dividing evenly, and top each sandwich, cream cheese–side down, with a remaining bread slice.

HAM AND VERMONT CHEDDAR HOT POCKETS

As someone who always likes something sweet to eat in the morning, I've struggled over the years at Flour to create appealing offerings for our customers who don't want sugar for breakfast. After all, we have a plethora of savory breakfast ingredients at our fingertips, so all I needed was some inspiration to develop something that was Flour yummy. Enter these hot pockets. We take our fantastic focaccia bread dough and roll it out into a long oval. Thinly sliced smoked country ham and sharp Vermont Cheddar go on top, then we fold the dough over in half to make a pocket. When these golden beauties come out of the oven, the cheese sometimes oozes out a bit on the side and bakes into a crunchy cheese snack that we all fight over in the kitchen.

MAKES 5 POCKETS

Small handful of cornmeal or all-purpose flour for sprinkling on the baking sheet

½ batch Flour Focaccia dough (see page 282), or 1 lb/455 g store-bought pizza dough

8 oz/225 g Black Forest ham, thinly sliced

8 oz/225 g sharp Cheddar cheese, thinly sliced

Dijon mustard for serving (optional)

SPECIAL EQUIPMENT: rimmed baking sheet, rolling pin

1. Preheat the oven to 400°F/200°C, and place a rack in the center of the oven. Sprinkle the baking sheet with the cornmeal.

2. Shape the dough into a rough square, then divide it into five equal pieces. Liberally flour both your work surface and the dough. Using the rolling pin, roll each piece into a thin oval about 4 by 8 in/10 by 20 cm.

3. Place one-fifth of the ham and Cheddar slices over half of one oval, covering about 2 by 4 in/5 by 10 cm and leaving a ½-in/12-cm border uncovered along the edge. Fold the oval in half lengthwise to cover the ham and cheese, then seal the edges by pressing them together and then pinching them shut. Do not fold over the edges or you'll end up with a thick, crusty layer with no ham or cheese in it. Repeat with the remaining ovals, ham, and cheese.

4. Place the pockets on the baking sheet about 2 in/5 cm apart. Bake for 25 to 30 minutes, or until the pockets are golden brown. Remove from the oven and let the pockets cool on the pan on a wire rack for about 10 minutes before serving. Some customers like their pockets with a side of Dijon mustard.

BREAKFAST PIZZAS

We offer so many mouthwatering buttery, sugary, fruity, chocolaty sweet breakfast treats in the morning that it can be almost impossible to choose just one ("I'll have one of each" is a common humorous request from new customers). That is, unless you're one of those people who need to start off the day with eggs or bacon or anything not sweet. For those customers, we've created the ultimate quick grab-'n'-go breakfast using items we already have in-house: brioche dough, cheese, breakfast meats, and eggs. The dough, after an overnight rest in the refrigerator during which it develops flavor, is stretched and pulled like you would a pizza dough to make a flat round.

I've suggested a few of our best topping combinations here, but feel free to use whatever mixture of meats, cheeses, and vegetables you prefer. The egg on top is what makes the pizza shine. After creating a border of meats and vegetables around the edge of each brioche circle, you bake the pizzas about halfway through. Then you crack a whole egg in the middle of each one, blanket them with cheese, and bake until the eggs are just barely set. It's a bit of a messy breakfast, but you won't care once you taste how good it is.

MAKES 8 PIZZAS

½ batch Basic Brioche dough (see page 284)

½ cup/120 ml crème fraîche

12 slices thick-cut applewood-smoked bacon, cooked in the oven until barely crisp (see page 150)

1 cup/90 g Caramelized Onions (page 278)

8 large eggs

2 cups/225 g shredded part-skim mozzarella cheese

SPECIAL EQUIPMENT: two rimmed baking sheets, parchment paper

1. Preheat the oven to 350°F/180°C, and place one rack in the center and one rack in the top third of the oven. Line the baking sheets with parchment paper.

2. Shape the brioche dough into a rectangle about 8 in/20 cm long, 4 in/10 cm wide, and 1 in/2.5 cm thick. Using a ruler and a knife, cut the rectangle into eight 2-in/5-cm squares by first dividing it in half horizontally and then dividing it vertically into strips 2 in/5 cm wide. Each square of dough should weigh about 3½ oz/100 g. Stretch each square into a circle about 5 in/12 cm in diameter as if you are making a small pizza. Stretch the inner part of the circle so that it is quite thin and shape the edge of the circle to create a rim. The center should be almost paper-thin, and the finished circle should look like you are making the crust for a mini deep-dish pizza. Place the brioche circle on one of the prepared baking sheets and repeat with the remaining dough squares, spacing them 2 to 3 in/5 to 7.5 cm apart and using both baking sheets.

3. Using the back of a spoon, spread 1 tbsp of the crème fraîche over the base of each brioche circle, spreading it evenly over the base but leaving the rim bare. Cut the bacon slices in half. For each pizza, press three half slices of bacon against the brioche rim to create a bacon wall. Divide the caramelized onions evenly among the pizzas, spooning and spreading the onions next to the bacon and leaving the center of the circle bare except for the crème fraîche.

CONTINUED

4. Bake the pizzas, switching the baking sheets between the racks and rotating them back to front about halfway during baking, for about 15 minutes, or until the edges of the pizza start to turn light brown. Remove the baking sheets from the oven and carefully crack an egg into the center of each pizza. Sprinkle about 1/4 cup/30 g of the mozzarella on top of each pizza, covering both the egg and the exposed rim of brioche. Bake for another 8 to 10 minutes, again switching the baking sheets between the racks and rotating them back to front about halfway during baking, or until the cheese has melted, the edges of the egg are cooked but the yolk is still wiggly, and the edges of the pizza are golden brown. Remove from the oven. Let the pizzas cool for 8 to 10 minutes to allow the eggs to set up a bit before serving.

HAM, RICOTTA, AND PARMESAN VARIATION: Omit the bacon, onions, and mozzarella. Substitute 4 oz/115 g sliced ham, 1 cup/250 g fresh whole-milk ricotta cheese, and 1 cup/100 g freshly grated Parmesan cheese. Using about 1/2 oz/15 g ham per pizza, tear the ham into small pieces and press the pieces against the brioche rim to create a ham wall. Spread 2 tbsp of the ricotta along the edges of each pizza next to the ham, leaving the center of the brioche circle bare except for the crème fraîche. Bake as directed, substituting 2 tbsp of the grated Parmesan in place of the mozzarella sprinkled over the egg on each pizza. Let cool for 8 to 10 minutes before serving.

TOMATO AND CHEDDAR: Omit the bacon, onions, and mozzarella. Substitute 2 ripe tomatoes, thinly sliced, and 8 oz/225 g Cheddar cheese, thinly sliced. Using 2 to 3 tomato slices per pizza, tear the slices into pieces and press the pieces against the edge of the brioche rim to create a tomato wall, leaving the center of the brioche circle bare except for the crème fraîche. Bake as directed, substituting 1 oz/30 g of the sliced Cheddar in place of the mozzarella sprinkled over the egg on each pizza. Let cool for 8 to 10 minutes before serving.

CHRISTOPHER'S OVEN-BAKED POTATO AND RED PEPPER TORTILLA

Spanish tortillas are a popular snack found in bars and tapas restaurants around Spain. Layers of fried potato baked with onion and egg are served warm or at room temperature for breakfast, lunch, dinner, and every hour in-between. Our opening chef, Chris, made this dish occasionally on weekends, and we offered it as a special during those first few slow opening months. Then we got really busy, and Chris had less and less time to make it. And when he left, the dish just slipped our minds.

I recently found the recipe in an old file—basically a scrap of paper with a list of ingredients and a few lines of direction. My husband, Christopher, remembered it from our early days and eagerly made it for brunch. Clearly something was missing in the scribbled notes. So he made it again . . . and again . . . and again . . . (we hosted quite a few brunches during this time) until he came up with his own version, which is even better than what we fondly remembered from a decade earlier. To spice it up, serve Sriracha or Tabasco sauce on the side.

SERVES 6 TO 8

2 large or 3 medium Yukon gold potatoes

6 large eggs

¾ cup/180 ml whole milk

1 cup/100 g freshly grated Parmesan cheese

4 scallions, white and green parts, minced

3 tbsp chopped fresh flat-leaf parsley

¾ tsp kosher salt

½ tsp freshly ground black pepper

5 tbsp/75 ml extra-virgin olive oil

1 medium yellow onion, cut into ½-in/12-mm pieces

1 medium red bell pepper, cut into 1-in/2.5-cm pieces

3 garlic cloves, smashed and minced

½ teaspoon smoked Spanish paprika (*pimentón*)

SPECIAL EQUIPMENT: ovenproof 12-inch skillet

1. In a medium saucepan, combine the potatoes with water to cover and bring to a boil over high heat. Reduce the heat to medium-low and simmer until the potatoes are cooked through and can be easily pierced with a fork; the timing will depend on the size of the potatoes. Drain and transfer the potatoes to a bowl. Set aside until cool enough to handle, then peel (the skins should come off quite easily) and cut crosswise into slices ½ in/12 mm thick.

2. Preheat the oven to 450°F/230°C, and place a rack in the center of the oven.

3. In a medium bowl, whisk together the eggs, milk, Parmesan, scallions, and parsley. Season with ¼ tsp each of the salt and pepper. Set aside.

4. In the skillet, heat 1 tbsp of the olive oil over medium-high heat. Add the yellow onion, bell pepper, and garlic and sweat for several minutes, or until the vegetables soften. Season with ¼ tsp salt and ⅛ tsp pepper. Transfer the vegetables to a bowl and set aside.

CONTINUED

5. In the same skillet, heat 3 tbsp of the oil over high heat. Carefully add the potatoes and reduce the heat to medium. Sprinkle evenly with the paprika, the remaining $\frac{1}{4}$ tsp salt, and the remaining $\frac{1}{8}$ tsp pepper. Do not turn the potatoes for 3 to 4 minutes. Once the potatoes are nicely browned on the first side, flip them over and drizzle the remaining 1 tbsp oil into the skillet. Let the second side brown for a few more minutes. Don't worry if not all of the potatoes get browned; the point is to get a nice crust on some of the potatoes. Remove the skillet from the heat.

6. Spread the vegetable mixture evenly over the potatoes, then carefully pour the egg mixture evenly over the potatoes and vegetables. Bake for 16 to 20 minutes, or until the egg puffs and browns and the middle is just barely set when tested with a knife tip. Remove from the oven and let cool in the skillet for 5 to 10 minutes. Serve warm or at room temperature. The tortilla can be made up to 2 days in advance and stored in an airtight container in the fridge. Bring to room temperature or warm in a 300°F/150°C oven for 15 minutes before serving.

WINTER GREENS, MUSHROOM, AND PARMESAN STRATA

Baking a strata is perfect for a late-morning brunch when you want something special but aren't quite up to making a full-blown quiche, flaky crust and all. Most of the prep can be done the night before, so all you have to do when you wake up is quickly cook the vegetables, add them to the soaked bread, and pop the dish into the oven. Less than an hour later, you will be sitting down to a cheesy, eggy breakfast. Feel free to improvise with ingredients. I've included a few of our most popular options, but this dish is really meant to be created with the bits and ends of meats and vegetables and cheeses in your fridge. You won't believe the delicious result from such humble beginnings.

SERVES 8 TO 10

6 cups/360 g day-old bread, cubed

2 large eggs

6 egg yolks

¼ cup/35 g all-purpose flour

4 cups/960 ml half-and-half

2 tsp kosher salt

1 tsp freshly ground pepper

1 tsp chopped fresh thyme

¼ tsp freshly grated nutmeg

4 tbsp/60 ml vegetable oil

1 garlic clove, smashed and minced

2 cups/85 g lightly packed chopped winter greens, such as escarole or kale

2 shallots, sliced

1½ cups/140 g sliced mushrooms, such as oyster, shiitake, hen-of-the-woods (maitake), or portobello mushrooms

1 cup/100 g freshly grated Parmesan cheese

SPECIAL EQUIPMENT: 9-by-13-in/23-by-33-cm baking pan, Microplane or other fine-rasp grater, large skillet

1. Place the bread in the baking pan. In a medium bowl, whisk together the eggs, egg yolks, and flour until well combined. Whisk in the half-and-half, 1 tsp of the salt, ½ tsp of the pepper, the thyme, and nutmeg. Pour the mixture evenly over the bread, cover the dish with plastic wrap, and refrigerate overnight.

2. The next day, preheat the oven to 350°F/180°C, and place a rack in the center of the oven.

3. In the skillet, heat 2 tbsp of the vegetable oil over high heat. Add the garlic and greens and cook, stirring, for 2 to 3 minutes, or until the greens have wilted. Season with 1/2 tsp salt and 1/4 tsp pepper. Using a slotted spoon, transfer the greens to a bowl and set aside. Add the remaining 2 tbsp oil to the skillet and heat over high heat. Add the shallots and mushrooms and cook, stirring, for 4 to 5 minutes, or until the mushrooms are browned. Season with the remaining 1/2 tsp salt and 1/4 tsp pepper. Transfer the mushroom mixture to the bowl with the greens.

4. Unwrap the pan of soaking bread. Add the cooked vegetables and 3/4 cup/75 g of the Parmesan and stir until mixed. Sprinkle the top evenly with the remaining 1/4 cup/25 g Parmesan.

5. Bake for 35 to 40 minutes, or until the top is browned and set. You can test the doneness by inserting a knife in the middle of the pan and bending the blade backward a little bit to see if the custard mixture has set up. If liquid fills the hole that you have made with your knife, the strata needs more time.

6. When the strata is ready, remove from the oven and let rest for 15 minutes before serving. Cut into squares and serve warm. Any leftover strata can be tightly covered and stored in the fridge for up to 3 days; reheat in a 300°F/150°C oven for 10 to 15 minutes, or until heated through.

BROCCOLI AND CHEDDAR VARIATION: Even broccoli haters love this savory strata—maybe it's all the melty, yummy Cheddar cheese. For terrific hors d'oeuvres, cut it into small squares. Omit the vegetable oil, garlic, winter greens, shallots, mushrooms, and Parmesan cheese. Substitute 1 lb/455 g broccoli florets and 1½ cups/170 g shredded sharp Cheddar cheese. Prepare the bread and egg mixture and soak overnight as directed. The next day, chop the broccoli florets into small pieces and toss them with the remaining 1 tsp salt and remaining ½ tsp pepper. Mix the broccoli and ¾ cup/85 g of the Cheddar into the soaked bread, then sprinkle the top with the remaining ¾ cup/85 g Cheddar. Bake and serve as directed.

ASPARAGUS, GOAT CHEESE, AND LEMON VARIATION: This springtime version also makes a great lunch or light dinner with a side salad. Omit the vegetable oil, garlic, winter greens, shallots, mushrooms, and Parmesan cheese. Substitute 2 lb/910 g asparagus; 8 oz/255 g soft fresh goat cheese, crumbled; and 1 tbsp grated lemon zest. Prepare the bread and egg mixture and soak overnight as directed. The next day, snap off the woody bottoms and peel the base of the asparagus spears, then cut crosswise into 1-in/2.5-cm pieces. In a medium bowl, toss the asparagus with the remaining 1 tsp salt and remaining ½ tsp pepper. Gently mix the asparagus, tablespoon-size dollops of the goat cheese, and the lemon zest into the soaked bread. Bake and serve as directed.

Lunch

Dinner might be America's main meal of the day, but you'd never guess that if you walked into Flour at lunchtime and witnessed the mob scene of patrons waiting patiently for their orders. Our daily-changing homemade soups and our inventive, crave-worthy sandwiches all draw crowds and for good reason. We are fanatical about making sure we use the freshest, most seasonal ingredients we can get our hands on. Chefs Chris, Aniceto, Corey, and Jeff have tested and retested these recipes until they are fan-worthy; now you can skip the line and replicate what we make at Flour for your family and friends.

Soups

CHILLED SPANISH WHITE GAZPACHO

We sell enough of our traditional tomato-based gazpacho in the hot summer months to fill a swimming pool. Most of our customers prefer chilled soups when it's steamy outside, and with the bounty of vine-ripened tomatoes and fresh cucumbers and peppers, gazpacho is a no-brainer. One morning a few summers back, I noticed a huge flat of green grapes among the crates of fresh produce that had been delivered to our South End location. Perhaps we were making a large number of fresh fruit cups or maybe a big fruit platter had been ordered? Then Chef Corey told me he was making Spanish gazpacho, a variation of the more common tomatoey kind. It is made with grapes, almonds, cucumbers, and lots of garlic that are all puréed to a beautiful pale celery-green. We've had customers from all over, even from Spain, proclaim this gazpacho the best. People have begged for the recipe, promising to sign contracts never ever to divulge it if they can just make it for themselves at home. It's fantastic and unique, and I share it here without making you sign your life away.

MAKES ABOUT 2 QT/2 L
(SERVES 4 TO 6)

2 lb/910 g seedless green grapes, stemmed

½ cup/70 g whole blanched almonds

2 garlic cloves

6 tbsp/25 g minced fresh cilantro

3 tbsp good-quality sherry vinegar

2 tbsp freshly squeezed lime juice

1¼ tsp kosher salt

2 English cucumbers, cut crosswise into 1- to 2-in/2.5- to 5-cm pieces

3 tbsp extra-virgin olive oil, plus 1½ to 2 tbsp for finishing

SPECIAL EQUIPMENT: blender or food processor

1. Working in batches, combine the grapes, almonds, garlic, cilantro, vinegar, lime juice, and salt in the blender and pulse until the almonds and garlic are chopped but not too finely. Add the cucumbers and pulse again until the cucumbers are blended. Do not overblend; you want the soup to have some texture. Using a spatula or wooden spoon, stir in the olive oil.

2. Refrigerate for at least 1 hour to chill the soup and to allow the flavors blend. (Taste and add more salt as needed.) Ladle into bowls and drizzle each with about 1 tsp olive oil before serving. The soup will keep in an airtight container in the fridge for up to 3 days.

CHILLED CUCUMBER, YOGURT, AND FRESH HERBS

A chilled soup is a lovely choice for a quick lunch when you want something light and refreshing. We offer this soup throughout the sweltering summer months, and both the staff and the customers can be seen sipping it throughout the day. Thick, tangy Greek yogurt lends a richness and creaminess that's hard to replicate with regular yogurt, so be sure to seek it out.

MAKES ABOUT 2 QT/2 L (SERVES 4 TO 6)

4 English cucumbers

2 cups/500 g plain full-fat Greek yogurt

2 tbsp freshly squeezed lemon juice

1 tbsp Dijon mustard

4 tbsp/15 g minced fresh chives

2 tbsp chopped fresh flat-leaf parsley

1 tsp chopped fresh thyme

1 tsp kosher salt

½ tsp freshly ground black pepper

SPECIAL EQUIPMENT: blender or food processor

1. Peel, halve lengthwise, and seed the cucumbers. Chop finely and place in a large bowl; stir in the yogurt. Transfer about 2 cups/280 g of the chopped cucumber mix to a blender or food processor and blend on low speed for 8 to 10 seconds, or until puréed. (Blending a small amount of the cucumber mixture first helps to achieve a smoother soup when you add the remainder of the mixture.) Add the remaining cucumber mixture in several batches, blending well after each addition until smooth. The soup should be thin enough to pour but still have some body. Add the lemon juice, mustard, 3 tbsp of the chives, the parsley, thyme, salt, and pepper and blend again for several seconds until combined.

2. Refrigerate for at least 1 hour to chill the soup and to allow the flavors to blend. (Don't skip this step! The soup will thicken a bit and taste much better after a rest in the fridge.) Taste and adjust the seasoning if needed. Ladle into bowls and garnish each with a sprinkle of the remaining 1 tbsp chives before serving. The soup will keep in an airtight container in the fridge for up to 2 days. Stir well before serving.

VEGAN CARROT AND GINGER

We call Chef Jeff the vegan-soup whisperer. He has an uncanny ability to coax incredible flavor out of vegetables and fruits to make soups that make even the most ardent meat lovers swoon. This carrot-ginger soup is one of our customers' favorites. It starts with slow-roasted carrots and fennel, lots of grated fresh ginger, a little bit of apple for sweetness, and a touch of nutmeg at the end for depth. I strongly suggest finding a whole nutmeg and grating it fresh for this soup; the aromatic deep flavor of freshly grated really makes a difference. I showed Chef Jeff a tip for grating fresh ginger that we use often in pastry: freezing it before grating removes much of the fibrous texture. In turn, he taught me his tip for peeling ginger: peel it with a spoon, and the rounded edge of the spoon easily separates the papery skin from the ginger flesh.

**MAKES ABOUT 2 QT/2 L
(SERVES 4 TO 6)**

2 lb/910 g carrots, peeled and cut crosswise into about 1-in/2.5-cm chunks

3 tbsp extra-virgin olive oil

2 tsp chopped fresh thyme

3 tsp kosher salt

½ tsp freshly ground black pepper

1 medium onion, cut into ½-in/12-mm pieces

1 celery stalk, cut into ½-in/12-mm pieces

1 medium fennel bulb, leafy tops trimmed and bulb thinly sliced

3 garlic cloves, smashed and minced

2-in/5-cm piece fresh ginger, peeled and grated

6 cups/1.4 L Vegetable Stock (page 279)

1 small Granny Smith or other tart apple, peeled, halved, cored, and diced

½ tsp freshly grated nutmeg

SPECIAL EQUIPMENT: Microplane or other fine-rasp grater, rimmed baking sheet, large stockpot, blender or food processor

1. Preheat the oven to 400°F/200°C, and place a rack in the center of the oven.

2. Spread the carrots on the baking sheet. Drizzle them with 2 tbsp of the olive oil and sprinkle them with the thyme, 1 tsp of the salt, and ¼ tsp of the pepper. Roast the carrots for 35 to 45 minutes, or until tender; roasting brings out the natural sweetness of the carrots. Set aside.

3. In the stockpot, heat the remaining 1 tbsp olive oil over medium-high heat. Add the onion, celery, fennel, and garlic; reduce the heat to medium; and sweat the vegetables, stirring often with a wooden spoon, for 6 to 8 minutes, or until they soften and the onion is translucent. Stir in the ginger, add the roasted carrots and stock, and bring to a boil. Launch in (Chef Jeff's lingo) the apple and simmer for about 1 minute. Remove from the heat.

4. Working in batches, blend the soup in the blender until smooth. Return the soup to the pot, add the remaining 2 tsp salt, the remaining ¼ tsp pepper, and the nutmeg and stir well. Bring back to a simmer. If the soup seems too thick, add a little water or stock to thin it. Taste and adjust the seasoning if needed.

5. Ladle into bowls and serve. The soup may be stored in an airtight container in the fridge for up to 3 days or in the freezer for up to 1 month.

SPICY PEANUT-SQUASH
with Chickpeas

When Chef Corey at Flour1 first made this soup, I honestly thought he'd gone a bit off the deep end. Peanuts? Squash? Chickpeas? All together? The slew of emails and phone calls we received after we offered it proved that he was once again tuned into what our customers love. It turns out that peanut soups are traditional in many African cuisines, where peanuts are a plentiful, inexpensive source of protein. The cream added at the end rounds out the flavor and makes the soup a bit richer. But if you're a vegan or you don't want a richer soup (or you don't have cream in your fridge), you can skip this step, and you'll still have a satisfying, earthy, simple soup that makes a terrific meal in a bowl.

MAKES 3 QT/2.8 L
(SERVES 6 TO 8)

⅔ cup/120 g dried chickpeas, or one 15-oz/430-g can chickpeas

One 2- to 3-lb/910-g to 1.4-kg butternut squash

1 tbsp vegetable oil

1 medium onion, cut into ½-in/12-mm pieces

6 garlic cloves, smashed and minced

2 tsp kosher salt

½ tsp ground cumin

2 tbsp crushed *chile de árbol*

2 tsp Sriracha sauce

¼ tsp freshly ground black pepper

4 cups/960 ml Vegetable Stock (page 279)

1 cup/260 g smooth peanut butter

½ cup/120 ml heavy cream (optional)

¼ cup/60 ml freshly squeezed lime juice

¼ cup/15 g chopped fresh cilantro

2 scallions, white and green parts, minced for garnish

½ cup/65 g chopped, salted, roasted peanuts for garnish

SPECIAL EQUIPMENT: large stockpot

1. If using dried chickpeas, place in a bowl or other container, add 5 to 6 cups/1.2 to 1.4 L water, cover, and refrigerate overnight. The next day, drain and rinse the chickpeas. In a medium saucepan, bring the chickpeas and about 6 cups/1.4 L fresh water to a boil over high heat. Reduce the heat to medium-low and simmer for 1 to 1½ hours, or until the chickpeas are tender. Remove from the heat, drain, and set aside. If using canned chickpeas, drain, rinse under cold running water, and set aside.

2. Peel, seed, and dice the squash. In the stockpot, heat the vegetable oil over medium-high heat. Add the onion and garlic and cook, stirring occasionally, for about 1 minute. Add the squash, salt, cumin, chile, Sriracha sauce, and pepper and stir to combine. Cook over medium heat, stirring occasionally, for about 10 minutes. Add the stock and drained chickpeas and bring to a boil. Reduce the heat to medium–low, add the peanut butter, and simmer, stirring occasionally, for about 15 minutes. Add the cream (if using) and bring the soup back to a simmer. (If the soup seems too thick, add a little water or stock to thin it.) Turn off the heat and stir in the lime juice and cilantro. Taste and adjust the seasoning if needed.

3. Ladle the soup into bowls and top each with the scallions and peanuts before serving. The soup can be stored in an airtight container in the fridge for up to 3 days or in the freezer for up to 1 month.

SWEET POTATO
with Thai Curry and Coconut

Chef Jeff loves to make squash soups during the fall. He flavors them with apples and sage, or with fresh ginger and orange, or sometimes with just a little cream and black pepper. When you make soup every day (for five years and counting), the challenge is to keep things interesting for both yourself and your customer. To branch out, he started playing around with sweet potatoes, using the same basic flavor variations as he uses for squash. The starchy potato made for a much thicker soup, which our customers loved for its heartiness. Looking around the kitchen for inspiration one day, he noticed the coconut milk that we use in pastry for coconut pastry cream, and he threw it into the soup. A can of Thai curry paste caught his eye and it went in as well. The creamy sweetness of the potato is the perfect foil for the rich coconut milk and spicy curry paste, and now this is one of our most requested soups at Fort Point.

MAKES ABOUT 3 QT/2.8 L (SERVES 6 TO 8)

5 large or 6 or 7 medium sweet potatoes, scrubbed clean

3 tbsp vegetable oil

1 medium onion, cut into ½-in/12-mm pieces

3 garlic cloves, smashed and minced

1 large carrot, peeled and cut into ½-in/12-mm pieces

1 celery stalk, cut into ½-in/12-mm pieces

½ medium fennel bulb, leafy tops trimmed and bulb cut crosswise into pieces 1 in/2.5 cm wide

6 cups/1.4 L Vegetable Stock (page 279)

One 13- to 14-oz/390- to 420-ml can coconut milk

2 tbsp Thai red curry paste

2¼ tsp kosher salt

1 tsp freshly ground black pepper

¼ cup/10 g fresh cilantro leaves for garnish

½ lime for garnish

SPECIAL EQUIPMENT: rimmed baking sheet, large stockpot, blender or food processor

1. Preheat the oven to 400°F/200°C, and place a rack in the center of the oven.

2. Place the sweet potatoes on the baking sheet and pierce each one several times with a knife tip or fork. Roast for 1 to 1½ hours, or until they can be easily pierced in the center with a fork. Set aside to cool.

3. In the stockpot, heat the vegetable oil over medium-high heat. Add the onion, garlic, carrot, celery, and fennel; reduce the heat to medium-low; and sweat the vegetables, stirring often with a wooden spoon, for 6 to 8 minutes, or until they soften and the onion is translucent.

4. Peel the cooled sweet potatoes, cut them into large chunks, and add them to the vegetables in the stockpot. Add the stock, raise the heat to medium-high, and bring to a simmer. Reduce the heat to medium-low and simmer gently for 20 to 25 minutes to blend the flavors.

5. Turn off the heat and add the coconut milk, curry paste, salt, and pepper. Working in batches, blend the soup in the blender until very smooth. Return the soup to the pot and bring back to a simmer. Taste and adjust the seasoning if needed.

6. Ladle the soup into bowls and garnish each with the cilantro and a squeeze of lime before serving. The soup can be stored in an airtight container in the fridge for up to 3 days or in the freezer for up to 1 month.

EGGPLANT PARMESAN

A customer came in recently, asked for a taste of the soup of the day without reading the daily specials board, and exclaimed, "This soup tastes exactly like eggplant parm!" The staff chuckled as they pointed to the "Eggplant Parmesan Soup" written on the chalkboard.

I asked Corey what made him think of making a soup version of this popular Italian classic, and it turns out he has a list of dishes he has either already made or is determined to make into soup. He rattled off macaroni and cheese, cheeseburger, BLT (on rye with mayo)—the list goes on and on. I haven't yet tried any of his other attempts, but this one works: tomatoes, cheese, garlic, bread, fresh basil—delicious!

MAKES ABOUT 3 QT/2.8 L
(SERVES 6 TO 8)

3 tbsp vegetable oil

2 medium onions, cut into ½-in/12-mm pieces

3 garlic cloves, smashed and minced

2 large eggplants, chopped into 1- to 2-in/2.5- to 5-cm pieces

One 28-oz/680 g can "no salt added" diced tomatoes, with juice

2 cups/120 g bread, cubed

1 cup/55 g chopped fresh basil

1½ cups/150 g freshly grated Parmesan cheese

2 tbsp red wine vinegar

2½ tsp kosher salt

¼ tsp freshly ground black pepper

SPECIAL EQUIPMENT: large stockpot, blender or food processor

1. In the stockpot, heat the vegetable oil over high heat. Add the onions and garlic and stir for 1 to 2 minutes, or until the onions just start to soften. Add the eggplants and reduce the heat to medium. Cook, stirring occasionally, for 8 to 10 minutes, or until the eggplants break down a bit and become slightly mushy.

2. Add the tomatoes and the same amount of water to the pot (just use the empty tomato can as a measure). Bring to a simmer over medium heat and simmer for about 5 minutes. Add the bread cubes and stir for 1 minute, or until the bread breaks down in the soup. Stir in the basil and Parmesan, turn off the heat, and let cool slightly.

3. In the blender, purée the soup in batches until very smooth. Return the soup to the pot and bring back to a simmer. Season with the vinegar, salt, and pepper. If the soup seems too thick, thin with a little water. Taste and adjust the seasoning.

4. Ladle the soup into bowls and serve immediately. The soup can be stored in an airtight container in the fridge for up to 3 days or in the freezer for up to 1 month.

SMOKY TOMATO AND POTATO

Tomato soup might sound boring if you are used to the stuff from the can. Tomato soup made from scratch, however, is a very different product. All of our chefs make stellar tomato soups, which are especially popular with our customers during the frigid winter months. I particularly like this version because of the many layers of flavor that are developed throughout the soup-making process.

Chef Aniceto taught me to start off with a cold pan and cold oil so that the garlic will toast slowly in the oil. That tip adds a lot of flavor and makes it less likely that the garlic will burn, which would add a bitter taste. The carrot lends a sweetness to the soup that helps balance the acidity of the tomatoes. A couple spoonfuls of tomato paste heighten the tomato flavor. The addition of smoked salt and smoked pepper is the final step in distancing this soup from the humdrum stuff of your childhood. Search out these two seasonings for a quick and easy way to add smoky flavor to your food without breaking out wood chips, unearthing a smoking vessel, and setting off your smoke alarm. If you prefer a nonsmoky soup, the variation that follows calls for a generous amount of freshly grated Parmesan and a touch of half-and-half for an excellent tomato and Parmesan version.

MAKES ABOUT 2 QT/2 L
(SERVES 4 TO 6)

3 tbsp extra-virgin olive oil

2 garlic cloves, smashed

1 medium onion, cut into ½-in/12-mm pieces

1 large carrot, peeled and cut into ½-in/12-mm pieces

1 small russet potato, peeled and cut into ½-in/12-mm pieces

2 tbsp tomato paste

Two 28-oz/680-g cans whole tomatoes, with juice

3 cups/720 ml Vegetable Stock (page 279) or water

¼ tsp hot red pepper flakes

½ tsp smoked salt

¼ tsp smoked black pepper

SPECIAL EQUIPMENT: large stockpot, blender or food processor

1. In the stockpot, add the olive oil and garlic. Turn on the heat to medium and toast the garlic, stirring constantly, for 3 to 4 minutes, or until golden brown. Remove the garlic and set aside.

2. Add the onion, carrot, potato, and tomato paste to the pot and stir over medium heat for 5 to 6 minutes, or until the vegetables are coated and the onion has started to soften. Return the garlic to the pot and stir. Add the tomatoes and crush them into pieces with a wooden spoon. Add the stock, red pepper flakes, smoked salt, and smoked pepper; raise the heat to high; and bring the soup to a boil. Reduce the heat to medium and simmer for about 15 minutes.

3. Remove from the heat. In the blender, purée the soup in batches until very smooth, roughly 2 to 3 minutes for each batch. Return the soup to the pot and bring back to a simmer. Taste and adjust the seasoning if needed.

4. Ladle the soup into bowls and serve immediately. The soup can be stored in an airtight container in the fridge for up to 3 days or in the freezer for up to 1 month.

CREAMY TOMATO-PARMESAN VARIATION: If you want to try a cheese-rich variation of this soup, omit the smoked salt and the smoked pepper. Add ½ tsp kosher salt, ¼ tsp freshly ground black pepper, 1 cup/100 g freshly grated Parmesan cheese, and ¼ cup/60 ml half-and-half with the stock. Proceed as directed. Serve with more grated Parmesan sprinkled on top.

CREAMY SUNCHOKE

The sunchoke is one of those vegetables that you look at and wonder, who was the first person who decided that this might be something worth eating? Knobby and wizened and flecked with brown, sunchokes resemble overgrown fresh ginger tubers and are closest in flavor and texture to a water chestnut crossed with a potato crossed with an artichoke heart. Until recently they were known as Jerusalem artichokes, even though they are not related to Jerusalem or artichokes. They are actually a relative of the sunflower. One theory suggests that Italian settlers in the United States called them *girasole*, the Italian word for "sunflower," and the pronunciation morphed into "Jerusalem." Their taste is similar to that of artichokes, so they became known as Jerusalem artichokes. To avoid confusion, they were renamed sunchokes in the 1960s.

This creamy soup showcases their delicate, sweet, nutty flavor. Don't peel them, because the peel is where most of the flavor is. Just scrub them with a stiff vegetable brush to get rid of any debris.

MAKES ABOUT 1¾ QT/1.75 L
(SERVES 4 TO 6)

2 lb/910 g sunchokes

2 tbsp unsalted butter

2 cloves garlic, thinly sliced

8 shallots, thinly sliced

4 cups/960 ml Chicken Stock (page 280)

1 cup/240 ml half-and-half

1¾ tsp kosher salt

¼ tsp freshly ground white pepper

2 tbsp minced fresh flat-leaf parsley for garnish

SPECIAL EQUIPMENT: large stockpot, blender or food processor

1. Scrub the sunchokes but do not peel. Cut into 2-in/5-cm pieces and set aside.

2. In the stockpot, melt the butter over medium-high heat for 1 to 2 minutes, or until it foams. When the foam begins to subside, add the garlic and shallots and cook, stirring frequently, for 2 to 3 minutes, or until soft and translucent. Add the sunchokes and cook, stirring, for 5 minutes. Add the stock and bring to a boil. Reduce the heat to medium and simmer for 10 minutes.

3. Remove the pot from the heat and let cool slightly. In the blender, purée the soup in batches until smooth. Return the soup to the pot and place over medium-low heat. Stir in the half-and-half and add the salt and white pepper. Simmer for 5 minutes more and then remove from the heat.

4. Ladle the soup into deep bowls, garnish with the parsley, and serve. The soup can be stored in an airtight container in the fridge for up to 3 days.

SPICY THREE-BEAN AND CORN CHILI

One of our most popular soups is this meatless chili. It has an extraordinary amount of flavor and is relatively quick to put together. Even our heartiest meat-loving customers are sold on this chili, and more than one has counseled us to omit the word *vegan* from the name to make it more appealing to nonvegans. So now we just call it Spicy Three-Bean and Corn Chili and it sells out every time. If you like, you can garnish each serving with sliced scallions. Or, for a nonvegan option, garnish with sour cream or grated cheese.

I strongly recommend that you use dried beans for the best flavor. But if you're stuck for time and have only canned beans in your pantry, this soup is still fantastic. Just be sure to rinse the beans well before using, because the liquid they are packed in tastes stale and salty.

MAKES 3 QT/2.8 L
(SERVES 6 TO 8)

⅔ cup/120 g dried cannellini beans, or one 15-oz/430-g can cannellini beans

⅔ cup/120 g dried black beans, or one 15-oz/430-g can black beans

⅔ cup/120 g dried chickpeas, or one 15-oz/430-g can chickpeas

2 tbsp vegetable oil

1 onion, cut into ½-in/12-mm pieces

1 large carrot, peeled and cut into ½-in/12-mm pieces

1 celery stalk, cut into ½-in/12-mm pieces

1 medium sweet potato, peeled and cut into ½-in/12-mm pieces

2 garlic cloves, smashed and minced

One 15¼-oz/435-g can corn kernels, drained and rinsed

One 4-oz/115-g can minced mild green chiles

Two 14½-oz/415-g cans "no salt added" diced tomatoes, with juice

1 tbsp sherry vinegar

2 tbsp packed brown sugar

1 tbsp plus 1 tsp chili powder

1 tbsp smoked Spanish paprika

2 tsp cocoa powder

¼ tsp cayenne pepper

1 tbsp plus 1 tsp kosher salt

½ tsp freshly ground white pepper

SPECIAL EQUIPMENT: large stockpot

1. If using dried beans, place them together in a bowl or other container, add 2½ qt/2.5 L water, cover, and refrigerate overnight. The next day, drain and rinse the beans. In a large sauce-pan, bring the beans and about 2½ qt/2.5 L fresh water to a boil over high heat. Reduce the heat to medium-low and simmer for 1 to 1½ hours, or until the beans are tender. Remove from the heat and drain the beans, reserving the cooking liquid. Set the beans and liquid aside separately. If using canned beans, drain, rinse under cold running water, and set aside.

CONTINUED

2. In the stockpot, heat the vegetable oil over medium heat. Add the onion, carrot, celery, sweet potato, and garlic and cook, stirring occasionally, over medium heat for 6 to 8 minutes, or until the vegetables start to soften, the onion starts to turn translucent, and you can smell the vegetables cooking. Add the drained beans, corn, green chiles, tomatoes, and 4 cups/960 ml of the bean cooking liquid, or water if you have used canned beans, and bring to a simmer over medium-high heat. Add the vinegar, brown sugar, chili powder, paprika, cocoa powder, cayenne, salt, and white pepper. Stir until well mixed and bring back to a simmer. Reduce the heat to medium-low and simmer for 20 to 30 minutes, or until the mixture thickens a bit.

3. The chili can be ladled into bowls and served immediately, or it can be cooled, covered, and refrigerated overnight to develop flavor and texture. It can also be stored in an airtight container in the fridge for up to 3 days or in the freezer for up to 1 month.

THREE-BEAN AND CORN CHILI WITH RICE VARIATION: To make this chili even heartier, add ½ cup/100 g uncooked medium-grain rice and an additional 1 cup/ 240 ml water when adding the beans and liquid to pot. Continue as directed.

CHIPOTLE CHICKEN AND BLACK BEAN

Chef Chris, Flour's opening chef, set the soup bar pretty darned high for every chef that has followed him at Flour. We opened Flour with the goal of having at least one if not two rotating, daily changing soups, and very quickly we became adored for them locally. Even back then, before I knew we would have more than one Flour and before I ever dreamed that I would write a book, I remember asking Chris for this recipe. It was so addictive that I wanted to have this in my back pocket for whenever I had a craving for it. I love how deeply flavorful it is. The distinctive scent of chopped fresh cilantro and the bright limey notes at the end really make this soup.

MAKES 3¾ QT/3.5 L
(SERVES 6 TO 8)

1⅓ cups/240 g dried black beans, or two 15-oz/430-g cans black beans

2 tbsp vegetable oil

1 medium onion, cut into ½-in/12-mm pieces

2 large carrots, peeled and cut into ½-in/12-mm pieces

3 garlic cloves, smashed and minced

2 lb/910 g bone-in, skin-on chicken breasts

1 canned chipotle chile, seeded and minced

½ tsp ground cumin

One 20-oz/570-g can "no salt added" crushed tomatoes, with juice

2½ tsp kosher salt

½ tsp freshly ground black pepper

½ cup/100 g uncooked long-grain white rice

2 medium zucchini, quartered lengthwise and cut crosswise into ½-in/12-mm pieces

2 tbsp chopped fresh oregano

½ cup/30 g minced fresh cilantro

1 lime

SPECIAL EQUIPMENT: large stockpot

1.   If using dried beans, place them in a bowl or other container, add 2 qt/2 L water, cover, and refrigerate overnight. The next day, drain and rinse the beans. In a medium saucepan, bring the beans and about 2 qt/2 L fresh water to a boil over high heat. Reduce the heat to medium-low and simmer for 1 to 1½ hours, or until the beans are tender. Remove from the heat and drain the beans, reserving the cooking liquid. Set the beans and liquid aside separately. If using canned beans, drain, rinse under cold running water, and set aside.

2.   In the stockpot, heat the vegetable oil over medium-high heat. Add the onion, carrots, and garlic; reduce the heat to medium; and sweat the vegetables for 6 to 8 minutes, stirring often with a wooden spoon, or until they start to soften and the onion is translucent. Add the chicken breasts, chipotle chile, and ground cumin and brown the chicken, turning occasionally, for 8 to 10 minutes.

2. Add the onion, garlic, carrot, and celery to the stockpot and stir over medium-high heat with a wooden spoon for a few minutes, scraping up the browned bits that have stuck to the bottom of the pan. This residue is called the fond and it will add lots of flavor to your soup. When all of the fond has been scraped from the bottom, reduce the heat to medium-low, add the tomato paste and the 1/2 tsp salt, and stir to combine. Add the bay leaves and stir for 2 to 3 minutes, or until the vegetables are thoroughly coated with the tomato paste. Reduce the heat to low. Add the paprika, thyme, turmeric, oregano, cumin, fennel seeds, curry powder, and cinnamon and stir for 3 to 4 minutes to toast the spices.

3. Add the reserved sausage and stir until evenly coated with the spice mixture. Raise the heat to medium; add the potato, parsnip, leek, mushrooms, turnip, and squash; and cook, stirring, for a few minutes. Add the stock and tomatoes and stir in the remaining 1 tbsp salt and the pepper. Raise the heat to high and bring the soup to a boil. Reduce the heat to medium and simmer for about 10 minutes.

4. Add the lentils and simmer, stirring occasionally, for 40 to 45 minutes, or until the lentils are tender. Add the winter greens and stir well. Let the soup simmer for 1 minute, or until the escarole is cooked. The soup should be thick and stewy. Fish out the bay leaves and discard. Ladle into bowls and serve immediately. The soup can be stored in an airtight container in the fridge for up to 3 days or in the freezer for up to 1 month.

VEGETARIAN VARIATION: Omit the sausage. Increase the vegetable oil to 3 tbsp, add the onion, garlic, carrot, and celery, and sauté the vegetables for a few minutes over medium heat. Then reduce the heat to medium-low, add the tomato paste, and proceed as directed.

SUMMER VARIATION: Omit the parsnip, leek, mushrooms, turnips, squash, and winter greens. Substitute about 2 cups/250 g diced zucchini, 2 cups/250 g diced summer squash, 1 cup/135 g corn kernels, and 2 cups/50 g baby spinach.

BEAN VARIATION: For a bean version, omit the lentils. Place 2/3 cup/120 g dried chickpeas, 2/3 cup/120 g dried cannellini beans, and 2/3 cup/120 g dried black beans overnight in a bowl or other container, add water to cover by about 3 in/7.5 cm, cover, and refrigerate overnight. The next day, preheat the oven to 350°F/180°C. Drain and rinse the beans. In a Dutch oven or other large oven-proof pot, combine 1/2 onion, chopped; 1/2 carrot, peeled and chopped; 1 tomato, halved; 2 bay leaves; 1/4 tsp hot red pepper flakes; 2 tbsp extra-virgin olive oil; and water to cover the beans by 2 in/5 cm. Bring to a boil over high heat. Cover with a lid or a piece of aluminum foil, transfer to the oven, and braise for 30 to 45 minutes, or until the beans are tender. Add the beans and their liquid to the soup in place of the lentils and simmer until heated through. Add the winter greens and proceed as directed to finish the soup. This version will yield 5 to 5½ qt/4.7 to 5.2 L soup (serves 10 to 12).

MAMA CHANG'S HOT AND SOUR

Here are all of the bright and peppery flavors of the hot-and-sour soup you get at a restaurant with none of the glop. Ground pork is not tradi- tional, but it makes the preparation of this soup ultraquick. Wood ear mushrooms, sometimes labeled "tree fungus" (now there's an appetizing name), are a standard addition, but they can be hard to find unless you live near an Asian grocery store. I substitute easy-to-find button mushrooms, which don't have the same crunch but add a nice earthy flavor. Egg, not flavorless cornstarch, acts as the thickener, allowing the flavors of pork, sesame, vinegar, and pepper to come shining through. My mom used to whip this up as a fast lunch for my brother and me, and I have taught it to the Flour chefs, so they now offer it as a daily soup special. It always sells out, and Mom is thrilled to be part of the Flour menu.

MAKES ABOUT 1¾ QT/1.75 L (SERVES 4)

2 tbsp vegetable oil

1 garlic clove, smashed and minced

1 tbsp peeled and minced fresh ginger

4 scallions, white and green parts, minced, plus 2 tbsp chopped for garnish

8 oz/225 g ground pork

4 cups/960 ml Chicken Stock (page 280)

1-lb/455-g block soft or firm tofu (not silken and not extra-firm), cut into ½-in/12-mm cubes

4 or 5 medium button mushrooms, wiped clean and thinly sliced

1 tsp granulated sugar

⅔ cup/160 ml rice vinegar

3 tbsp soy sauce

1 tsp freshly ground black pepper

1 tbsp sesame oil, plus 2 tsp for garnish

1 tbsp Sriracha sauce

2 large eggs

White pepper for garnish

SPECIAL EQUIPMENT: large saucepan

1. In the saucepan, heat the vegetable oil over medium-high heat until hot. Add the garlic, ginger, scallions, and ground pork and cook, stirring occa- sionally, for about 1 minute. Break up the pork into smaller pieces but don't worry about breaking it down completely. Add the stock and bring to a simmer.

2. Add the tofu, mushrooms, sugar, vinegar, soy sauce, black pepper, sesame oil, and Sriracha sauce and bring the soup back to a simmer over medium-high heat. (Taste the soup. If you want it hotter, add more Sriracha sauce; if you want it more sour, add more vinegar.)

3. In a small bowl, whisk the eggs until blended. With the soup at a steady simmer, slowly whisk in the eggs so they form strands. Bring the soup back to a simmer. Divide the soup among four bowls and garnish each with a little sesame oil, scallion, and white pepper. Serve immediately. The soup can be stored in an airtight container in the fridge for up to 3 days.

CLASSIC SPLIT GREEN PEA
with Smoked Ham

Filling and comforting, this soup is one of Chef Aniceto's favorites to both make and eat. He prepares it at home during winter and eats it out of a coffee mug as a quick meal after a long, busy workday. When he makes it for us at Flour, I do the same, enjoying it for lunch, midday snack, or early dinner. It's thick and satisfying and full of flavor.

MAKES ABOUT 2½ QT/2.5 L
(SERVES 4 TO 6)

3 tbsp vegetable oil

1 medium onion, cut into ½-in/12-mm pieces

1 large carrot, peeled and cut into ½-inch pieces

1 large leek, white and tender green parts, well rinsed and cut into 1-in/2.5-cm pieces

2 garlic cloves, smashed and minced

1 tsp finely chopped fresh thyme

1 bay leaf

1 to 1½ lb/455 to 680 g smoked ham hock or shank (shanks are meatier than hocks)

2 qt/2 L Vegetable Stock (page 279)

1½ cups/300 g green split peas, rinsed

1 small russet potato, peeled and cut into ½-in/12-mm pieces

2 tsp Dijon mustard

2 tsp whole-grain mustard

1 tsp kosher salt

½ tsp freshly ground black pepper

2 tbsp freshly squeezed lemon juice

3 tbsp chopped fresh flat-leaf parsley

SPECIAL EQUIPMENT: large stockpot, blender or food processor

1. In the stockpot, heat the vegetable oil over medium-high heat. Add the onion, carrot, leek, and garlic; reduce the heat to medium-low; and sweat the vegetables, stirring often with a wooden spoon, for 6 to 8 minutes, or until they soften and the onion turns translucent. Add the thyme, bay leaf, and ham hock; then pour in the stock, raise the heat to medium-high, and bring to a boil. Reduce the heat to low and simmer, stirring occasionally, for about 1½ hours.

2. Stir in the split peas, potato, and about 2 cups/ 480 ml water. Simmer over medium-low heat, stirring occasionally, for another 1 to 1¼ hours, or until the peas are tender.

3. When the peas have softened, fish out the bay leaf and discard. Carefully fish out the ham hock and set it aside until it is cool enough to handle. Remove the meat from the bone, chop the meat, and set it aside.

4. Add the Dijon and whole-grain mustards, salt, and pepper to the soup and stir well. In the blender or food processor, purée about half of the soup until smooth and return it to the pot. Add the reserved ham, lemon juice, and parsley and stir well. If the soup seems too thick, add up to ½ cup/120 ml water to thin as needed, then taste and adjust the seasoning if needed. Bring the soup back to a simmer and turn off the heat.

5. Ladle the soup into bowls and serve immediately. The soup can be stored in an airtight container in the fridge for up to 3 days or in the freezer for up to 1 month.

BEST-EVER BEEF STEW
with Pearl Onions, Mushrooms, and Red Wine

When I was a little kid, my mom used to make a Taiwanese beef stew redolent with star anise, ginger, and soy. In addition to large chunks of tender beef, the stew was filled with hard-boiled eggs, spinach, and chewy wheat noodles. We ate it at least once a week during the winter, sometimes more, and I was unaware of any other kind of beef stew in my early years.

Then I started to eat lunch at the school cafeteria, and I saw that there was another kind of beef stew. It looked a lot like the picture on the Dinty Moore beef stew cans that I'd seen at the grocery store. I tried it once and found it gloppy and oddly devoid of flavor. Mom's cooking was best after all.

Flour's beef stew, created by Chef Jeff, made me rethink the whole beef-stew paradigm. While Mom's beef stew is indisputably delicious, it turns out that classic American-style beef stew with carrots, potatoes, mushrooms, and onions is also sensational when done right. At Flour, we make it with a super-rich beef stock, though in a pinch we've used chicken stock with great success. Accompanied with crusty rolls and a salad, this stew makes a really terrific cold-weather dinner.

MAKES ABOUT 2¾ QT/2.7 L
(SERVES 6 TO 8)

Heaping 1 cup/150 g all-purpose flour

1 tbsp kosher salt

1 tsp freshly ground black pepper

1½ lb/680 g boneless beef chuck, cut into 1-in/2.5-cm cubes

6 tbsp/85 g unsalted butter

1 medium yellow onion, cut into ½-in/12-mm pieces

2 garlic cloves, smashed and minced

1 large carrot, peeled and cut into 1-in/2.5-cm rounds

2 celery stalks, cut into 1-in/2.5-cm pieces

½ medium fennel bulb, leafy tops trimmed and bulb chopped into 1-in/2.5-cm pieces

2 tbsp tomato paste

2 qt/2 L Beef Stock (page 281) or Chicken Stock (page 280)

2 tsp chopped fresh rosemary

2 tsp chopped fresh thyme

2 large or 3 medium Yukon gold potatoes, peeled and cut into 1-in/2.5-cm pieces

8 oz/225 g pearl onions, peeled and trimmed

4 oz/115 g button mushrooms, wiped clean and halved

¾ cup/180 ml red wine

¼ cup/15 g chopped fresh flat-leaf parsley

SPECIAL EQUIPMENT: large stockpot

1. In a medium bowl, whisk together the flour, 1 tsp of the salt, and ¼ tsp of the pepper. Add the beef and toss until the pieces are evenly coated with the flour.

2. In the stockpot, melt 2 tbsp of the butter over medium heat until it foams. When the foam begins to subside, add about half of the beef cubes, shaking them a bit to remove the excess flour before you toss them in the pot. Brown the beef cubes, turning them as needed, for 2 to 3 minutes, or until evenly browned on all sides. Using a slotted spoon, transfer the meat to a medium bowl. Add 2 tbsp butter to the pot and brown the remaining beef cubes the same way and transfer to the bowl. Set aside.

3. In the same stockpot, add the remaining 2 tbsp butter and heat over medium heat until hot. Add the yellow onion, garlic, carrot, celery, and fennel and sweat the vegetables, stirring occasionally with a wooden spoon, for 6 to 8 minutes, or until the vegetables soften and the onion is translucent. Stir in the tomato paste. Return the beef to the pot and stir over medium heat for about 1 minute. Add the stock, the remaining 2 tsp salt, and the remaining ¾ tsp pepper and bring to a simmer over medium-high heat.

4. Reduce the heat to low and simmer, stirring occasionally, for about 1½ hours to thicken the stew slowly. Add the rosemary, thyme, potatoes, pearl onions, mushrooms, and ½ cup/120 ml of the wine and simmer for another 35 to 45 minutes, or until the stew thickens to the point that it coats the vegetables. Add the remaining ¼ cup/60 ml wine and bring the stew to a boil. Turn off the heat and stir in the chopped parsley.

5. Ladle the stew into bowls and serve immediately. The stew can be stored in an airtight container in the fridge for up to 3 days or in the freezer for up to 1 month.

SandwicHes

FRESH MOZZARELLA
with Pesto and Tomatoes

Chef Chris, our opening chef, was instrumental in designing our opening menu and developing recipes that still guide us today. I told him I wanted a traditional mozzarella, tomato, and pesto sandwich—nothing fancy, just the best he could come up with. So he created a heady aromatic pesto that you can smell throughout the whole bakery and dining room when it is being prepared. Instead of traditional pine nuts, it calls for blanched almonds, which are just as rich and satisfying. He insisted on the freshest fresh mozzarella we could find (and you should too), and he taught us that if the tomatoes aren't perfectly ripe, you'll end up with a shoddy sandwich. In the winter months we go to roasted tomatoes, which aren't quite as fragrant as vine-ripened ones but are just as popular with our customers.

The pesto recipe makes more than you need for the sandwiches, but it's hard to make a smaller amount given the already small amounts of almonds and Parmesan. It keeps marvelously in the fridge and in the freezer, however, and can be stirred into pasta for a quick, easy side dish, mixed into soups for extra flavor and richness, or dolloped onto roasted meats or fish.

MAKES 4 SANDWICHES

PESTO

1 lb/455 g fresh basil

⅓ cup/40 g sliced blanched almonds

⅓ cup/35 g freshly grated Parmesan cheese

2 garlic cloves, smashed

½ cup/120 ml extra-virgin olive oil

2 tsp freshly squeezed lemon juice

1 tsp kosher salt

¼ tsp freshly ground black pepper

8 slices Flour Focaccia (page 282) or other good-quality white or wheat bread

4 cups/100 g loosely packed baby arugula

12 oz/340 g fresh mozzarella cheese, cut into slices ¼ in/6 mm thick

2 tbsp Balsamic Vinaigrette (page 275)

2 vine-ripened tomatoes, thinly sliced, or 1 batch Roasted Tomatoes (page 276)

¼ tsp kosher salt, if using fresh tomatoes

SPECIAL EQUIPMENT: large stockpot or saucepan, food processor or blender

1. **TO MAKE THE PESTO:** Fill the stockpot with water and bring to a boil over high heat. While the water is heating, fill a medium bowl about three-fourths full with ice and then add cold water just to cover the ice. Blanch the basil—that is, plunge it into the boiling water—for about 30 seconds. Scoop out the basil and immediately plunge it into the ice water to stop the cooking. Remove the basil from the ice bath and squeeze it dry. Roughly chop the basil (it might be a bit difficult to chop at this point) and set aside.

2. In the food processor or blender, combine the almonds and Parmesan and process for 30 seconds. Add the garlic and process for another 30 seconds. Scrape down the sides of bowl and the blade. Add the chopped basil and the olive oil and process until smooth, then again scrape down the sides of the bowl and the blade. Add the lemon juice, salt, and pepper and process until blended. You will have about 1³/₄ cups/420 ml. Set aside ¹/₂ cup/120 ml for the sandwiches. To store the remaining pesto, transfer it to an airtight container and press a piece of parchment or wax paper directly onto the surface of the pesto. Cover and refrigerate for up to 1 week or freeze for up to 3 months. The surface of the pesto will turn a bit brown over time; simply scrape off the discolored portion before using.

3. Lay the bread slices out on a clean, dry counter and spread each slice with 1 tbsp of the pesto. Top four of the slices with the arugula, dividing it evenly, then top each mound of greens with an equal number of mozzarella slices. Drizzle the vinaigrette evenly over the mozzarella. Top with the tomatoes; if using fresh tomato slices, sprinkle with the salt. Close each sandwich with a second focaccia slice, pesto-side down, then cut in half and serve.

GRILLED TOFU
with Olive Tapenade and Roasted Vegetables

Tofu is sadly misunderstood. As a Taiwanese American, I grew up with tofu at almost every meal and didn't realize the maligned reputation it has among many eaters. Bland and flavorless are how some people view it; for me, it's a marvelous canvas for whatever flavors you want to cook or eat with it. In this sandwich, firm tofu is roasted with salt, pepper, and olive oil so that it's lightly seasoned and has a little bit of chew to it. Then the tofu is layered on thick slices of our focaccia that have been spread with our signature Kalamata olive tapenade.

We used to make the tapenade for our tuna sandwich before we changed up the menu and introduced our Curried Tuna with Apples and Golden Raisins (page 139). The tapenade version was a customer favorite, however, and many customers were quite vocal against the substitution. The curried tuna quickly became just as popular, but we, too, missed the tapenade. In trying to come up with a vegan sandwich offering, we reintroduced the tapenade, pairing it with tofu for a perfect match. You'll have a little tapenade left over after you make the four sandwiches. It's great as a topping on meat or fish and is also good spread on toast for a simple hors d'oeuvre.

For crunch and flavor, we add roasted zucchini, onions, and bell peppers to this sandwich, which is a healthful, yummy lunch that is guaranteed to convert even tofu haters. At the bakery, we grill this sandwich on a panini press; if you have one, definitely use it here. But if you don't, this sandwich is great on toasted focaccia slices.

MAKES 4 SANDWICHES

TAPENADE

1½ cups/250 g pitted Kalamata olives

2 garlic cloves, smashed and minced

1 tbsp capers

8 or 9 large leaves fresh basil, chopped

2 tsp freshly squeezed lemon juice

2 tsp extra-virgin olive oil

¼ tsp kosher salt

⅛ tsp freshly ground black pepper

2 tbsp extra-virgin olive oil

1 tsp kosher salt

½ tsp freshly ground black pepper

1-lb/455-g block extra-firm tofu

1 large or 2 medium zucchini

2 large red bell peppers

8 slices Flour Focaccia (page 282) or other good-quality white or wheat bread

4 cups/100 g loosely packed baby arugula

1 cup/90 g Caramelized Onions (page 278)

SPECIAL EQUIPMENT: food processor or blender, two rimmed baking sheets

1. **TO MAKE THE TAPENADE:** In the food processor or blender, combine the olives, garlic, capers, basil, lemon juice, olive oil, salt, and pepper and pulse until somewhat smooth but not perfectly smooth. You don't want a purée; you want the tapenade to have some small olive pieces. It can be made up to 4 days in advance and stored in an airtight container in the fridge.

2. Preheat the oven to 400°F/200°C, and place a rack in the center of the oven.

3. Drizzle one of the baking sheets with 1 tbsp of the olive oil and sprinkle evenly with ½ tsp of the salt and ¼ tsp of the pepper. Slice the tofu into eight equal slices, each ¼ to ½ in/6 to 12 mm thick. Blot each slice with paper towels to remove any excess moisture. Place each slice on the baking sheet, then flip it to coat it evenly with the seasoned oil. Arrange the tofu slices in a single layer and roast for about 10 minutes, or until the tofu is soft and a bit pouffy. Remove from the oven.

4. Halve the zucchini crosswise, then cut each half lengthwise into slices $1/2$ in/12 mm thick. Place in a large bowl. Cut the bell peppers lengthwise into strips $1/2$ in/12 mm wide. Be sure to trim off the bitter white inner membranes. Add to the bowl with the zucchini. Drizzle the vegetables with the remaining 1 tbsp oil and sprinkle with the remaining $1/2$ tsp salt and $1/4$ tsp pepper. Toss to coat evenly. Arrange the vegetables in a single layer on the second baking sheet and bake for 20 to 25 minutes, or until the zucchini is somewhat soft to the touch and the peppers have softened. Remove from the oven.

5. If you don't have a panini press, toast the focaccia slices.

6. Lay the bread slices on a clean, dry counter and spread each slice evenly with tapenade, using about $11/2$ tbsp for each slice. Top four of the slices with the arugula, dividing it evenly, then top each mound of greens with two tofu slices. Divide the zucchini slices and pepper strips evenly among the sandwiches, arranging them on the tofu, then top with an equal amount of the onions. Close each sandwich with a second focaccia slice, tapenade-side down. If using a panini press, grill the sandwiches until the bread is golden brown. Cut in half and serve.

LEMONY HUMMUS
with Cucumber, Radish Sprouts, and Red Onion

During my time as a management consultant just out of college, I spent many a late evening at the office pouring over spreadsheets. I wasn't alone; all of the beginning consultants often pulled all-nighters, and we took advantage of the dining allowance that was granted us if we worked past a certain hour. Eating take-out from fast-food joints and restaurants gets old pretty quickly, however. One of my coworkers, Eric, routinely brought his own bagged dinner instead, which he freely shared on those regular late nights. It was through him that I was introduced to the Best Hummus in the World. It was garlicky, lemony, bright, perfect. I couldn't get enough of it. After I left consulting, I would buy hummus at the store, hoping to find something similar. I tried making it at home. Nothing came close. All I had was my taste memory.

When Aniceto wanted to add a new sandwich to the menu I asked him if he could re-create my vivid memory. I described it in detail. He worked tirelessly, coming up with one recipe that we used for a few years and then tweaking it again a few years later until he came up with this one. We fold in whole chickpeas, which add great texture, and a pinch of cumin, which makes it especially interesting and flavorful. The recipe makes about twice as much as you will need for the four sandwiches, but the leftover makes a terrific dip for crudités and crackers.

MAKES 4 SANDWICHES

LEMONY HUMMUS

1⅓ cups/240 g dried chickpeas, or two 15-oz/430-g cans chickpeas

6 tbsp/90 ml extra-virgin olive oil

¼ cup/60 ml freshly squeezed lemon juice

2 tbsp tahini paste

2 medium garlic cloves, smashed

½ tsp ground cumin

¾ tsp kosher salt

¼ tsp freshly ground black pepper

8 slices Flour Focaccia (page 282) or other good-quality white or wheat bread

4 cups/85 g loosely packed mesclun greens or other mild lettuce

1 English cucumber, thinly sliced crosswise

2 vine-ripened tomatoes, thinly sliced, or 1 batch Roasted Tomatoes (page 276)

¼ tsp kosher salt, if using fresh tomatoes

1½ cups/140 g loosely packed alfalfa sprouts

2 medium carrots, peeled and shredded

¼ red onion, thinly sliced

SPECIAL EQUIPMENT: food processor or blender

1. **TO MAKE THE HUMMUS:** If using dried chickpeas, place them in a bowl or other container, add 6 to 8 cups/1.4 to 2 L water, cover, and refrigerate overnight. The next day, drain and rinse the chickpeas. In a medium saucepan, bring the chickpeas and about 2 qt/2 L fresh water to a boil over high heat. Reduce the heat to medium-low and simmer for 1 to 1½ hours, or until the chickpeas are tender. Remove from the heat and drain the chickpeas. If using canned chickpeas, drain and rinse under cold running water.

CONTINUED

2. Set aside about ¾ cup/150 g of the chickpeas. In the food processor or blender, combine the remaining chickpeas with the olive oil, lemon juice, tahini paste, garlic, cumin, salt, and pepper and purée until smooth, stopping and scraping down the sides of the bowl as needed to make sure the hummus is well blended and smooth. Transfer the hummus to a bowl and fold in the reserved chickpeas. Use immediately, or store in an airtight container in the fridge for up to 4 days.

3. Lay the bread slices on a clean, dry counter, and spread each slice evenly with hummus, using about ¼ cup/55 g per slice. Top four of the slices with the greens, dividing them evenly. Top the greens with cucumber slices, then with the tomatoes; if using fresh tomato slices, sprinkle with the salt. Top the tomatoes with equal amounts of alfalfa sprouts, shredded carrot, and onion slices. Close each sandwich with a second focaccia slice, hummus-side down, then cut in half and serve.

CURRIED TUNA
with Apples and Golden Raisins

If there's a running theme in the food at Flour, it's that we take classic dishes and add a special twist to make them ours. Maybe it's an upgrade on a key ingredient or an additional herb or a reworked sauce. In the case of our curried tuna sandwich, we decided to turn the traditional upside down and try something completely new. Just about everyone has eaten the basic tuna sandwich: tuna, mayo, and maybe some celery or onion. It's a staple in cafeterias and lunch boxes everywhere. Chef Aniceto created a completely different style of tuna sandwich: a grown-up version spiced with curry and made bright with crunchy diced apple and sweet golden raisins. Crisp alfalfa sprouts and shredded carrot top off the tuna salad, making this sandwich recipe the most often requested at Flour. I'm thrilled to be able to share it with you.

MAKES 4 SANDWICHES

CURRIED TUNA

Two 5-oz/140-g cans water-packed albacore tuna, drained

½ cup/120 ml mayonnaise

1 small Granny Smith apple, peeled, halved, cored, and cut into ¼-in/6-mm pieces

3 tbsp golden raisins, soaked in hot water for 1 minute and drained

2 tbsp minced red onion

1 tbsp mild curry powder

2 tbsp freshly squeezed lime juice

¼ tsp kosher salt

⅛ tsp freshly ground black pepper

8 slices Flour Focaccia (page 282) or other good-quality white or wheat bread

4 cups/85 g loosely packed mesclun greens or other mild lettuce

2 medium carrots, peeled and shredded

1½ cups/140 g loosely packed alfalfa sprouts

2 vine-ripened tomatoes, thinly sliced, or 1 batch Roasted Tomatoes (page 276)

¼ tsp kosher salt, if using fresh tomatoes

1. **TO MAKE THE CURRIED TUNA:** In a medium bowl, using a large spoon, mix together the tuna, mayonnaise, apple, raisins, onion, curry powder, lime juice, salt, and pepper until well blended. The mixture will not be very stiff. In fact, it may be a little soupy and a bit gloppy. The tuna can be made up to 2 days in advance and stored in an airtight container in the refrigerator.

2. Very lightly toast the bread slices, then lay them out on a clean, dry counter. Top four slices with an equal amount of the greens. Top each mound of greens with an equal amount of the tuna, followed by equal amounts of the carrots, alfalfa sprouts, and tomatoes; if using fresh tomatoes, sprinkle evenly with the salt. Close each sandwich with a second slice of focaccia, pressing down slightly to make the whole sandwich stick together, then cut in half and serve.

CHICKEN
with Avocado and Jicama

People think that when you work in a restaurant you eat like a king all day long. The truth is you are often so busy prepping and cooking that you rarely have time to sit for a meal yourself. When I was the pastry chef at Mistral, I shared the kitchen with a skeleton crew that came in with me to help prep the food needed for dinner service. When we were hungry, we'd just grab a snack on the fly, maybe some leftover stew or a hastily prepared salad.

But every now and then, one of us would be inspired to cook for the team, and I made my fair share of quick-'n'-easy stir-fries with all of the vegetable ends and meat scraps in the fridge. To return the favor one day, Luiz, the head prep cook, made us the most amazing sandwiches I'd ever eaten. He put together a quick mash of perfectly ripe avocado with lime juice, cilantro, and some chipotles for heat. Then he julienned jicama, a crispy, crunchy root vegetable with a mild taste of a nonsweet apple. Next came sliced roasted chicken breast from the previous night's dinner service. He piled these components on that morning's fresh bread, and the first thought I had in my head was, "This sandwich is definitely going on my menu someday." Luiz's sister, Ana, is now one of our best bakers at Flour. I know she's as proud as I am that her brother is the creator of one of our most popular sandwiches and by far my personal favorite.

Much of the success of this sandwich is due to Luiz's avocado spread. Yes, you could simply call it guacamole. But it's so much more delicious than any guacamole I've ever had that I always call it Luiz's Avocado. Slathered on multigrain or wheat toast and drizzled with some extra-virgin olive oil, it is one of life's great pleasures . . . one that many Flour workers enjoy every day.

MAKES 4 SANDWICHES

1 lb/455 g boneless, skinless chicken breasts
2 tsp achiote paste
5 tsp vegetable oil
½ tsp kosher salt
¼ tsp freshly ground black pepper
1 small jicama
1 lime
1 tbsp honey

LUIZ'S AVOCADO

2 ripe avocados
1 tbsp plus 1 tsp freshly squeezed lime juice
1 tbsp finely chopped red onion
½ tsp seeded and minced canned chipotle chile
1 tbsp plus 1 tsp finely chopped fresh cilantro
½ tsp kosher salt
¼ tsp freshly ground black pepper

8 slices Flour Focaccia (page 282) or other good-quality white or wheat bread
4 cups/85 g loosely packed mesclun greens or other mild lettuce

SPECIAL EQUIPMENT: rimmed baking sheet or 9-by-13-in/23-by-33-cm baking pan, meat thermometer, Microplane or other fine-rasp grater

1. Trim the chicken of any fat, gristle, or sinew. In a small bowl, mix together the achiote paste, vegetable oil, salt, and pepper. Rub the chicken all over with the mixture, then place in a covered container in the fridge for at least 2 hours or up to overnight.

2. About 20 minutes before you are ready to cook the chicken, preheat the oven to 300°F/150°C, and place a rack in the center of the oven.

3. Remove the chicken from the fridge and place it on the baking sheet. Roast for 35 to 40 minutes, or until cooked through. Check the doneness by inserting the thermometer into the thickest part of the breast; it should register an internal temperature of 165°F/74°C. Remove the chicken from the oven and let cool. The chicken can be roasted up to 1 day in advance and stored in an airtight container in the fridge.

4. Peel the jicama and cut into julienne. First, slice the jicama into thin circles. Then stack the circles and cut the stack into thin matchsticks. The pieces should be 2 to 3 in/5 to 7.5 cm long and 1/8 in/3 mm wide and thick. If the pieces are too long, cut them in half. Put the jicama matchsticks in a medium bowl. Using the Microplane grater, grate the lime directly over the matchsticks, and then halve the lime and squeeze the juice over them. Add the honey and toss to combine. The jicama can be prepared up to a day in advance and stored in an airtight container in the fridge.

5. **TO MAKE LUIZ'S AVOCADO:** Halve and pit the avocados and scoop the flesh into a medium bowl. Add the lime juice, onion, chile, cilantro, salt, and pepper and mash together with a fork until thoroughly mixed. The avocado will still be somewhat lumpy, but the mixture should be spreadable. (Taste the mixture, and if you want a spicier spread, add up to 1/2 tsp more minced chile.) The spread can be made up to 3 days in advance. Transfer to an airtight container, press a piece of parchment or wax paper directly onto the surface of the mixture, cover, and refrigerate. The surface will turn a bit brown over time; simply scrape off the discolored portion before using.

6. Lay the bread slices out on a clean, dry counter and spread each slice evenly with the avocado mixture, using about 2 tbsp for each slice. Top four slices with equal amounts of the greens. Cut the chicken breasts into slices 1/4 in/6 mm thick. Top each mound of greens with an equal number of chicken slices and top the chicken with an equal amount of the jicama. Close each sandwich with a second focaccia slice, avocado-side down, then cut in half and serve.

SMOKED TURKEY
with Sharp Cheddar and Cranberry Chutney

As fall nears in New England, fresh cranberries begin showing up in the supermarkets and farmers' markets and everyone's thoughts start to turn to Thanksgiving. We opened Flour in late September, and I put this sandwich on the menu as a nod to the upcoming holiday. We make a sweet-tart cranberry chutney flavored with orange and ginger and use it as a spread for a sandwich that is filled with roasted turkey and thick slices of sharp Vermont Cheddar. I never expected that we'd keep it on the menu after Thanksgiving, but it gained such a following after that first winter that we've never taken it off. I love that we bring a little bit of my favorite holiday to our customers year-round. To replicate this Flour favorite at home, first make sure you can find cranberries; they're not always readily available, and you may need to search a few stores before you find them either fresh or frozen. Get good-quality smoked turkey and nice sharp Cheddar—the sandwich will be only as good as your filling ingredients.

MAKES 4 SANDWICHES

CRANBERRY CHUTNEY

2¼ cups/225 g fresh or frozen whole cranberries

1 tbsp balsamic vinegar

3 tbsp packed light or dark brown sugar

1 orange, peeled, seeded, and roughly chopped

1 tbsp peeled and chopped fresh ginger

¼ tsp kosher salt

⅛ tsp freshly ground black pepper

8 slices Flour Focaccia (page 282) or other good-quality white or wheat bread

4 cups/85 g loosely packed mesclun greens or other mild lettuce

8 oz/225 g sharp Cheddar cheese, thinly sliced

1 lb/455 g smoked turkey, thinly sliced

1. **TO MAKE THE CHUTNEY:** In a small saucepan, cook cranberries over low heat for 1 to 2 minutes, or until they begin to get very soft and start to lose their shape. Add the vinegar, brown sugar, orange, ginger, salt, and pepper and stir well. Continue to cook over low heat for 8 to 10 minutes, or until the mixture is thick and spreadable. Transfer the chutney to a heatproof container and set aside to cool. The chutney can be stored in an airtight container in the fridge for up to 1 week.

2. Lay the bread slices out on a clean, dry counter and spread each slice evenly with the chutney, using about 3 tbsp for each slice. Top four slices of the bread with the greens, dividing them evenly, then top the greens with the cheese slices followed by the turkey slices. Close each sandwich with a second focaccia slice, chutney-side down, then cut in half and serve.

ROAST BEEF
with Horseradish Mayo, Crispy Onions, and Tomato

I have a hard time with change. It makes me all prickly inside, and I resist it completely. Now, of course, this isn't entirely true, because I'm always up for improving how we do things, and I've learned that pushing myself outside my comfort zone often leads to good results. But when it comes to Flour sandwiches, I admit that I have a harder time with change than usual. Chef Aniceto teases me about how long and hard he worked to get me to even consider making changes on the sandwich menu. I think he's right in saying that I eventually did it to appease him more than anything else. This roast beef was one of the happy results of his persistence. Customers complained for a few weeks about the change (we removed another sandwich to make room for this one), but now it is a wildly popular menu staple. Like with the lamb top round in the roasted lamb sandwich (see page 146), you'll have a little roast beef left over after making four sandwiches. You can roast a smaller cut, of course, but be careful because it will roast more quickly and can easily overcook.

MAKES 4 SANDWICHES

1½- to 2-lb/680- to 910-g beef roast, top or bottom round

4 tsp kosher salt

1 tsp freshly ground black pepper

CRISPY ONIONS

Vegetable oil for deep-frying

2 large onions

About 2 cups/270 g all-purpose flour

½ tsp kosher salt

HORSERADISH MAYONNAISE

¼ cup/60 ml prepared horseradish, drained

1 tbsp crème fraîche

¼ cup/60 ml good-quality mayonnaise

1½ tsp Dijon mustard

1½ tsp whole-grain mustard

8 slices Flour Focaccia (page 282) or other good-quality white or wheat bread

4 cups/85 g loosely packed mesclun greens or other mild lettuce

2 vine-ripened tomatoes, thinly sliced, or 1 batch Roasted Tomatoes (page 276)

¼ tsp kosher salt, if using fresh tomatoes

SPECIAL EQUIPMENT: two rimmed baking sheets, roasting rack, meat thermometer, deep-fry thermometer, metal slotted spoon

1. The night before, rub the beef all over with the salt and pepper, cover with plastic wrap or place in a container with a tight-fitting lid, and let rest overnight in the fridge.

2. The next day, take the beef out of the fridge and let rest for about 1 hour at room temperature.

3. About 20 minutes before you are ready to roast the beef, preheat the oven to 300°F/150°C, and place a rack in the center of the oven.

CONTINUED

4. Put the roasting rack on one of the baking sheets and put the roast on the rack. Roast the beef for 50 to 60 minutes for a 1½-lb/680-g roast or 65 to 75 minutes for a 2-lb/910-g roast, or until the meat thermometer inserted into the thickest part of the roast registers 130°F/54°C. Start checking after 45 minutes. Once the temperature hits 100°F/38°C, the cooking goes quickly, so check every 5 minutes or so. When the temperature reaches 130°F/54°C, remove the roast from the oven and let cool. Let the roast rest in the fridge for at least 3 hours or up to overnight.

5. MEANWHILE, PREPARE THE ONIONS: Line the second baking sheet with paper towels and set aside. Pour the vegetable oil to a depth of about 2 in/5 cm into a large saucepan and heat over medium-high heat to 350°F/180°C on the deep-fry thermometer. While the oil is heating, slice the onions as thinly as possible. Scoop the flour into a large bowl. Add the onions and toss until thoroughly coated.

6. When the oil is ready, remove about half of the onions from the flour bowl, shake them to remove the excess flour, and carefully drop them into the hot oil. As soon as you immerse the onions in the oil, the temperature of the oil will drop, so turn the heat to high to bring the oil back to 350°F/180°C. Cook the onions, stirring constantly with a slotted spoon to avoid overbrowning, for 5 to 7 minutes, or until golden brown. Using the slotted spoon, transfer the onions to the prepared baking sheet and sprinkle with ¼ tsp of the salt. When the oil has returned to 350°F/180°C, cook the remaining onions the same way, then transfer them to the baking sheet and sprinkle with the remaining ¼ tsp salt. The onions can be cooked up to 2 days in advance and stored in an airtight container at room temperature.

7. TO MAKE THE HORSERADISH MAYONNAISE: In a small bowl, stir together the horseradish, crème fraîche, mayonnaise, Dijon mustard, and whole-grain mustard until well combined. The mayonnaise can be stored in an airtight container in the fridge for up to 2 weeks.

8. Remove the well-chilled roast from the refrigerator and slice it against the grain as thinly as possible. Set the slices aside.

9. Lay the bread slices out on a clean, dry counter and spread them evenly with the horseradish mayo, using about 1 tbsp for each slice. Top four of the slices with the greens, dividing them evenly. Top the greens with the tomatoes; if using fresh tomatoes, sprinkle evenly with the salt. Top each sandwich with 5 to 6 oz/140 to 170 g of the sliced beef, and top the beef with the onions, dividing them evenly. Close each sandwich with a second focaccia slice, mayonnaise-side down, cut in half, and serve.

ROAST LAMB
with Tomato Chutney and Rosemary Goat Cheese

"I have dreams about your lamb and goat cheese sandwich." "I want to marry the lamb sandwich." "The lamb sandwich is seriously the most delectable sandwich in the world . . . make that the *universe*." These are actual love letters elicited by this sandwich. We pack thin slices of rosemary-scented rare roast lamb with herbed goat cheese and a tangy tomato chutney between two slices of our soft focaccia sandwich bread. At Flour we use lamb top round, a tender boneless cut from the leg. If you can't find it in your grocery or at your butcher shop, I've included an easier-to-find alternative, boneless leg. Either way you'll probably end up with more lamb than you need for the four sandwiches. If you opt for a smaller cut, keep in mind that it will roast more quickly. Make sure the lamb roasts long and low so it turns out juicy and a nice reddish pink.

MAKES 4 SANDWICHES

1½- to 2-lb/680- to 910-g lamb top round or boneless leg of lamb

4 tsp kosher salt

1 tsp freshly ground black pepper

2 garlic cloves, smashed and minced

2 tsp finely chopped fresh rosemary

2 tbsp extra-virgin olive oil

TOMATO CHUTNEY

2 tsp vegetable oil

¼ small onion, cut into ¼-in/6-mm pieces

2 tbsp granulated sugar

2 tbsp red wine vinegar

One 14½-oz/415-g can "no salt added" diced tomatoes, with juice

2 tbsp golden raisins

2 tbsp dried currants

⅛ tsp kosher salt

⅛ tsp freshly ground black pepper

¼ cup/15 g minced fresh flat-leaf parsley

ROSEMARY GOAT CHEESE

8 oz/225 g soft fresh goat cheese, at room temperature

½ tsp finely chopped fresh rosemary

½ tsp finely chopped fresh flat-leaf parsley

½ tsp finely chopped fresh thyme

¼ tsp kosher salt

⅛ tsp ground black pepper

8 slices Flour Focaccia (page 282) or other good-quality white or wheat bread

4 cups/85 g loosely packed mesclun greens or other mild lettuce

SPECIAL EQUIPMENT: roasting rack, rimmed baking sheet, meat thermometer

1. The night before, rub the lamb all over with the salt and pepper, cover with plastic wrap or place in a container with a tight-fitting lid, and let rest overnight in the fridge.

2. The next day, take the lamb out of the fridge. If using leg of lamb, roll the lamb into a bundle and tie together tightly with kitchen twine. Rub the surface of the lamb with the garlic, rosemary, and olive oil. Let rest for about 1 hour at room temperature.

3. About 20 minutes before you are ready to roast the lamb, preheat the oven to 300°F/150°C, and place a rack in the center of the oven.

4. Place the roasting rack on the baking sheet, and put the roast on the rack. Roast for 50 to 60 minutes for a 1½-lb/680-g roast or 65 to 75 minutes for a 2-lb/910-g lamb top, or until the thermometer inserted into the center of the roast registers 130°F/54°C. Start checking the lamb after 45 minutes. Once it hits 100°F/38°C, the cooking goes quickly, so check every 5 minutes or so. When the internal temperature reaches 130°F/54°C, remove the roast from the oven and let cool. Let the roast rest in the fridge for at least 3 hours or up to overnight.

5. **MEANWHILE, MAKE THE TOMATO CHUTNEY:** In a medium skillet, heat the vegetable oil over medium-high heat. Add the onion and cook, stirring constantly, for about 2 minutes, or until softened a bit. Add the sugar and vinegar and stir for 1 minute until the sugar starts to dissolve. Add the tomatoes, raisins, and currants and bring to a simmer. Reduce the heat to low and simmer, stirring occasionally and using the back of a wooden spoon to press down on the tomato pieces to break them up. The chutney should darken and the liquid will eventually evaporate. Let reduce and thicken for 10 to 15 minutes. Stir in the salt, pepper, and parsley; remove from the heat; and let cool. The chutney can be stored in an airtight container in the fridge for up to 1 week.

6. **TO MAKE THE ROSEMARY GOAT CHEESE:** In a small bowl, combine the goat cheese, rosemary, parsley, thyme, salt, and pepper and mix with a wooden spoon until well blended. The rosemary cheese can be stored in an airtight container in the fridge for up to 1 week; bring to room temperature before using so it spreads easily.

7. Trim the well-chilled lamb of any fat and slice it against the grain as thinly as possible. Set the slices aside.

8. Lay the bread slices out on a clean, dry counter and spread four of the slices with the chutney, dividing it evenly. Spread the remaining four slices with the goat cheese, again dividing it evenly. Top each of the chutney-spread slices with an equal amount of the greens. Top each of the goat cheese–spread slices with 5 to 6 oz/140 to 170 g of the sliced lamb. Close each sandwich, then cut in half and serve.

APPLEWOOD-SMOKED BLT

To me this sandwich is like the "Emperor has no clothes." Customers go crazy for it—among many folks we're better known for this sandwich than for any of our pastries. People stop me on the street and beg me for the recipe. We make between 200 and 250 of these each day, and if you hang out at Flour for any amount of time, you're guaranteed to leave with a little eau de bacon lingering on your clothes. And all that fuss is about the simplest of recipes. The trick is to be really picky about what the B and the L and the T are: thick-cut applewood-smoked bacon; tender, peppery baby arugula; vine-ripened tomatoes (or slow-roasted plum tomatoes when it's not tomato season) on lightly mayonnaise-slathered lightly toasted bread.

MAKES 4 SANDWICHES

16 slices thick-cut applewood-smoked bacon

8 slices Flour Focaccia (page 282) or other good-quality white or wheat bread

¾ cup/180 ml good-quality mayonnaise

4 cups/100 g loosely packed baby arugula

2 vine-ripened tomatoes, thinly sliced, or 1 batch Roasted Tomatoes (page 276)

¼ tsp kosher salt, if using fresh tomatoes

2 tbsp Balsamic Vinaigrette (page 275)

SPECIAL EQUIPMENT: rimmed baking sheet, parchment paper (optional)

1. Preheat the oven to 300°F/150°C, and place a rack in the center of the oven. Line the baking sheet with parchment paper or aluminum foil. Arrange the bacon slices in a single layer on the prepared sheet and bake for 22 to 26 minutes, or until the slices are half crispy and half still a little bendy. Remove the bacon from the oven and set aside.

2. Lightly toast the bread slices and spread each slice with about 1½ tbsp of the mayonnaise. Top four of the slices with the arugula, dividing it evenly. Top the greens with the tomatoes; if using fresh tomato slices, sprinkle with the salt. Drizzle the vinaigrette over the tomatoes. Top each sandwich with four bacon slices. Close each sandwich with a second focaccia slice, mayonnaise-side down, and press down to make the sandwich stick together. Cut in half and serve.

dinnER

By our fourth year, we were fortunate enough to have a wonderful loyal group of hungry customers who were eating three meals a day with us. Although we were not offering dinner of any sort at that time, people were making hearty meals out of our soups and quiches and pizzas. Chef Aniceto was itching to stretch his wings, so we developed a take-out dinner menu with selections that he created from scratch and changed weekly. Today, each chef at each location comes up with a weekly menu of dinners that range from homey classics to more exotic offerings. What follows are our best, most requested dishes, the salads and main courses that we love the most. Make them for family and friends, sit back, and enjoy the compliments.

SaLads

HEIRLOOM TOMATO SALAD

with Feta, Pistachios, Watermelon, and Nigella Seeds

I once ate all four servings of this salad in one sitting. Each bite won me over with its interplay of sweet, crunchy, salty, spicy flavors, which kept me coming back for more. This isn't just another run-of-the-mill heirloom tomato salad. Feta and pistachios and watermelon are not uncommon ingredients, but putting them together with the tomatoes highlights Chef Aniceto's time at Sofra, a beloved Boston Middle Eastern bakery. The nigella seeds are a more unusual influence; they look like poppy seeds and have a slightly peppery, oniony taste. All together, dressed with a simple delicious red wine vinaigrette and piled on perfectly ripe (yes, you can only make this salad in the full height of summer!) heirloom tomatoes, this salad exemplifies what I love most about Aniceto's cooking. It is always perfectly balanced, perfectly seasonal, and exactly what I want to eat.

SERVES 4

RED WINE VINAIGRETTE

1 medium shallot, minced

2 tbsp red wine vinegar

2 tsp freshly squeezed lemon juice

2 tsp Dijon mustard

1 tsp honey

¾ cup/180 ml extra-virgin olive oil

½ tsp kosher salt

¼ tsp freshly ground black pepper

½ tsp chopped fresh thyme

½ cup/60 g shelled pistachios

4 to 6 medium-to-large perfectly ripe heirloom tomatoes, cut into slices ½-in/12-mm thick

¼ tsp kosher salt

1 cup/150 g crumbled feta cheese

2 cups/300 g cubed seeded watermelon (1-in/2.5-cm cubes)

4 oz/115 g watercress, tough stems removed

1 tbsp nigella seeds

SPECIAL EQUIPMENT: rimmed baking sheet

1. **TO MAKE THE VINAIGRETTE:** In a small bowl, whisk together the shallot, vinegar, lemon juice, mustard, and honey until combined. Whisking continuously, slowly drizzle in the olive oil and whisk until the oil is thoroughly blended and the dressing is well combined. Whisk in the salt, pepper, and thyme. The vinaigrette can be made up to 1 week in advance and stored in an airtight container in the refrigerator. Bring back to room temperature before using.

2. Preheat the oven to 350°F/180°C, and place a rack in the center of the oven.

3. Spread the pistachios on the baking sheet and toast in the oven, shaking the pan once or twice for even toasting, for 6 to 8 minutes, or until they are light golden brown. Set aside to cool.

4. Arrange an equal number of tomato slices on four salad plates. Sprinkle the tomato slices with the salt and drizzle about 1 tbsp of the vinaigrette over each serving. Sprinkle each plate evenly with an equal amount of the feta and top with the watermelon. Pile one-fourth of the watercress in the center of each salad, and top with 2 tbsp of the pistachios. Sprinkle each salad evenly with the nigella seeds and drizzle with the remaining vinaigrette, dividing it evenly. Serve immediately.

FARMERS' MARKET SALAD
with Buttermilk-Chive Dressing

During the summer when the local farmers' markets are in full swing, our chefs reach out to area farmers to take advantage of the natural bounty of the season. We have a brief but amazing growing season here in the Northeast, with irresistible produce making an appearance for just a few short months. Chef Corey created this delightfully fresh and simple salad from a mismatched box of produce that arrived with our regular vegetable order one day. He wanted to highlight the crispy, crunchy vegetables with a light, tangy classic dressing. This makes a terrific salad for a light lunch or brunch; it is beautiful and simple to put together. Feel free to vary the vegetables to suit what is in season near you and what appeals to your taste. To turn this salad into a heartier meal, crumble some blue cheese and/or some crispy bacon slices over the top and serve with crusty bread.

SERVES 4 AS A MAIN COURSE OR 6 TO 8 AS A FIRST COURSE

BUTTERMILK-CHIVE DRESSING

½ cup/120 ml nonfat buttermilk

¼ cup/60 ml sour cream or crème fraîche

2 tbsp good-quality mayonnaise

1 tbsp freshly squeezed lemon juice

¼ cup/15 g minced fresh chives

½ tsp kosher salt

¼ tsp freshly ground black pepper

4 large eggs

8 oz/225 g baby carrots, peeled and trimmed to leave 1 in/2.5 cm of stem

1 lb/455 g English peas, shucked

8 oz/225 g green beans, trimmed and halved crosswise

8 oz/225 g small Red Bliss potatoes, unpeeled and quartered

8 cups/170 g loosely packed mixed organic lettuces

One 6-oz/170-g bag radishes, trimmed and quartered lengthwise

1 pt/300 g cherry tomatoes

SPECIAL EQUIPMENT: rimmed baking sheet, sieve

1. **TO MAKE THE DRESSING:** In a small bowl, mix together the buttermilk, sour cream, mayonnaise, lemon juice, chives, salt, and pepper until well blended. The dressing can be made up to 3 days in advance and stored in an airtight container in the fridge.

2. Place the eggs in a small saucepan, add cold water to cover, and bring to a boil over high heat. As soon as the water begins to boil, turn off the heat, cover the pan, and let the eggs sit for 15 minutes, or until cool enough to handle. Remove the eggs from the water. Working with one egg at a time, softly and gently crack each eggshell all around and carefully peel it off while holding the egg under running cool water. Pat the eggs dry, halve lengthwise, and set aside.

CONTINUED

3. In a large saucepan, bring 3 qt/2.8 L lightly salted water to a boil over high heat. While waiting for the water to boil, fill a large bowl about half full with ice and then add cold water just to cover the ice. Line the baking sheet with paper towels.

4. Drop the carrots into the boiling water and boil for 3 to 4 minutes. Using the sieve, remove the carrots from the water and plunge them, sieve and all, into the ice bath. Remove the carrots from the ice water, drain, and dump them out onto the prepared baking sheet. This process, called "shocking," will halt the cooking so the vegetables retain their bright color and fresh crunch.

5. Bring the water back to a boil and repeat with the peas, leaving them in the boiling water for about 30 seconds, and then with the green beans, leaving them in the boiling water for 2 to 3 minutes, before shocking each of them, in turn, in the ice water and transferring them to the baking sheet. Replenish the ice bath as needed with more ice to keep it ice-cold.

6. Bring the water back to a boil and add the potatoes. Reduce the heat to medium and simmer for 10 to 12 minutes, or until you can pierce them easily with a fork. Shock the potatoes in the ice water, scoop them out, and then dump them onto the baking sheet with the other vegetables.

7. Decoratively arrange the lettuce, radishes, tomatoes, eggs, potatoes, carrots, peas, and green beans in four shallow salad bowls. Serve the dressing on the side.

SUMMER THREE-BEAN AND POTATO SALAD
with Fresh Herbs

If you are a chef at Flour, as in most kitchens, you don't really have an office. You have a station, usually near the stove or the oven, that you call yours, and when people need to talk with you they hover at your station until you have a free moment between searing off this and marinating that.

Chef Aniceto's station is in the center of our kitchen at Flour3, and I often find myself perched there as I observe the bakers, prep cooks, counter staff, and customers. It's an ideal spot to see it all. That's where I watched him come up with this gorgeous fresh summer salad that he was serving as a side for his fried chicken dinner special. The three-bean salad that I grew up with was typically a drab conglomeration of canned green beans, floppy yellow beans, and mealy red kidney beans in a sharp dressing. This one is something else altogether: crisp fresh beans, earthy black-eyed peas, radishes and carrots for color, and potato for soaking up all of the lemony, herby vinaigrette.

**SERVES 4 AS A MAIN COURSE OR
6 TO 8 AS A FIRST COURSE**

⅔ cup/120 g dried black-eyed peas, or one 15-oz/430-g can black-eyed peas

8 oz/225 g wax beans, trimmed and halved crosswise

8 oz/225 g green beans, trimmed and halved crosswise

1 medium carrot, peeled and thinly sliced

1 large russet potato, unpeeled and cut in half crosswise

5 radishes, trimmed and thinly sliced

4 scallions, white and green parts, thinly sliced

1 tbsp finely chopped fresh dill

1 tbsp finely chopped fresh flat-leaf parsley

1 tbsp finely chopped fresh tarragon

6 tbsp/90 ml extra-virgin olive oil

2 tbsp freshly squeezed lemon juice

1 tbsp red wine vinegar

1 tsp kosher salt

¼ tsp freshly ground black pepper

SPECIAL EQUIPMENT: sieve

1. If using dried black-eyed peas, place them in a medium bowl or other container, add about 6 cups/1.5 L water, cover, and refrigerate overnight. The next day, drain and rinse the peas. In a medium saucepan, bring the black-eyed peas and about 6 cups/1.5 L fresh water to a boil over high heat. Reduce the heat to medium-low and simmer for 1 to 1½ hours, or until the peas are tender. Remove from the heat, drain, and set aside. If using canned black-eyed peas, drain, rinse under cold running water, and set aside.

2. Fill a large saucepan with lightly salted water and bring to a boil. While waiting for the water to boil, fill a large bowl about half full with ice and then add cold water just to cover the ice.

CONTINUED

3. Add the wax beans and the green beans to the boiling water and boil for 1 to 2 minutes, or until the beans are barely tender and still a bit crunchy. Using the sieve, remove them from the boiling water and plunge them, sieve and all, into the ice bath. Drain them well and place in a large bowl. Bring the water back to a boil, add the carrot, and boil for about 1 minute. Scoop the carrot out of the boiling water with a sieve and plunge, sieve and all, into the ice batch. Drain well and add to beans.

4. Bring the water back to a boil, add the potato, reduce the heat to medium, and simmer for about 15 minutes, or until cooked through.

5. While the potato is cooking, add the black-eyed peas, radishes, scallions, dill, parsley, and tarragon to the beans and carrots and stir together gently with a wooden spoon. Drizzle the vegetables with the olive oil, lemon juice, vinegar, salt, and pepper and stir again with the wooden spoon until well mixed.

6. Using the sieve, remove the potato from the boiling water. While still warm, cut the potato into 1-in/2.5-cm chunks. Add the potato to the vegetables and mix well. (Taste and add more salt and pepper and red wine vinegar as needed.) Serve warm or at room temperature.

ASIAN CELERY, FENNEL, AND EDAMAME SALAD
with Candied Lemon

This wonderful salad is crunchy, fresh, lemony, and a perfect start to any meal. We serve it at Myers+Chang, and the chefs at Flour have borrowed the dressing recipe when they want something simple and light for summer salads. You can easily improvise with various vegetables: mushrooms, radishes, cucumbers, salad greens are all terrific variations. The dressing can be made a couple weeks in advance and stored in an airtight container in the refrigerator.

SERVES 6 AS A FIRST COURSE

DRESSING

½ cup/120 ml rice vinegar

6 tbsp/90 ml soy sauce

⅓ cup/70 g granulated sugar

2 tsp Sriracha sauce

2 tbsp sesame oil

1 tsp kosher salt

½ tsp freshly ground black pepper

18 oz/500 g candied lemon (recipe follows), coarsely chopped

8 celery stalks, thinly sliced

1 medium fennel bulb, leafy tops trimmed and bulb quartered, then thinly sliced on the mandoline

3 medium shallots, thinly sliced

2 cups/280 g frozen edamame beans, thawed

Leaves from 10 to 12 fresh flat-leaf parsley sprigs

1 tbsp white sesame seeds for garnish

1 tbsp black sesame seeds for garnish

SPECIAL EQUIPMENT: mandoline

1. **TO MAKE THE DRESSING:** In a medium bowl, whisk together the vinegar, soy sauce, sugar, Sriracha sauce, sesame oil, salt, pepper, and candied lemon.

2. Put the celery, fennel, shallots, edamame, and parsley in a large bowl. Pour the dressing over the vegetables and toss until well combined. Divide equally among six bowls and sprinkle evenly with the black and white sesame seeds. Serve immediately.

Candied Lemon

MAKES ABOUT ¼ CUP/75 G

1 lemon, unpeeled and sliced as thinly as possible

½ cup/100 g granulated sugar

In a medium saucepan, combine the lemon slices, sugar, and 1½ cups/360 ml water and bring to a boil over high heat. Reduce the heat and simmer uncovered, stirring occasionally, for about 1 hour, or until the lemon slices are translucent. Remove the pan from the heat and let the slices cool completely in the syrup. The candied lemon can be made up to 2 weeks in advance and stored in an airtight container in the fridge.

WINTER PAPER SALAD
with Hazelnut Vinaigrette

Even though at Flour we are surrounded by food all day long, it's not unusual to see someone at lunch unpack a container filled with leftovers from his or her previous night's dinner. As much as we all love Flour food, there are only so many days a week that you can eat soup and sandwiches before you start wanting something new and different.

Nicole, our executive pastry chef, brought this salad to work one day and shared a bit with Chef Corey. He went crazy for it and begged Nicole for the recipe. As with most recipes that get shared around Flour, it went through some tweaking before Corey offered his version as a dinner special. At that point, I tried it and went crazy for it and begged him for the recipe. This is a combination of Nicole's original and Chef Corey's variation. Nicole uses hickory nuts rather than hazelnuts, so if you can find them, use them.

SERVES 4 AS A MAIN COURSE OR
6 TO 8 AS A FIRST COURSE

HAZELNUT VINAIGRETTE

2 tbsp Dijon mustard

2 tbsp Champagne vinegar

1 tbsp freshly squeezed lemon juice

2 tbsp honey

1 garlic clove, smashed and minced

¼ cup/60 ml hazelnut oil

2 tbsp extra-virgin olive oil

½ tsp kosher salt

½ cup/75 g raw hazelnuts

¼ cup/60 ml freshly squeezed lemon juice

1 medium head fennel, leafy tops trimmed

2 medium Gala apples, cored and unpeeled

1 small celery root, peeled

2 celery stalks, thinly sliced

2 shallots, thinly sliced

¼ cup/15 g minced fresh flat-leaf parsley

½ tsp kosher salt

⅛ tsp freshly ground black pepper

2 oz/55 g pecorino or other dry, firm cheese, shaved into thin slices with the mandoline or a vegetable peeler

SPECIAL EQUIPMENT: baking sheet, mandoline

1. **TO MAKE THE VINAIGRETTE:** In a small bowl, whisk together the mustard, vinegar, lemon juice, honey, and garlic until combined. Whisking continuously, slowly drizzle in the hazelnut oil and olive oil and whisk until the oils are thoroughly blended and the dressing is well combined. Whisk in the salt. The dressing can be made up to 1 week in advance and stored in an airtight container in the fridge. Before using, bring back to room temperature and rewhisk to combine all of the ingredients.

2. Preheat the oven to 350°F/180°C, and place a rack in the center of the oven.

3. Put the hazelnuts on the baking sheet and toast in the oven, shaking the pan once or twice for even toasting, for 8 to 10 minutes, or until the nuts are light golden brown. Set aside to cool.

4. Pour the lemon juice into a large bowl. Using the mandoline, shave the fennel bulb into paper-thin slices. Add the sliced fennel to the bowl and toss to coat with the lemon juice. Repeat with the apples and celery root, add to the bowl, and toss to coat with the lemon juice. Then add the celery and shallots, toss again, and sprinkle with the parsley, salt, and pepper. Drizzle with the vinaigrette and toss to coat thoroughly. Divide the salad equally among four bowls and top with the hazelnuts and pecorino. Serve immediately.

BLOOD ORANGE AND BEET SALAD
with Toasted Walnuts, Goat Cheese, and Blood Orange Vinaigrette

In Boston in the dead of winter, when the skies are gray day in and day out and you can't remember which snowfall caused the slushy snowbanks just outside the window, this salad is a welcome reprieve. Chef Corey at Flour1 created this brightly colored appetizer for one of our holiday menus. The day before Christmas, when the bulk of our customers were picking up their orders, Corey had his worktable and the pastry table next to it lined up with container after container of gorgeous ruby red citrus and sun gold and magenta beets. He arranged a little arugula underneath the oranges and beets and scattered generous dollops of soft goat cheese on top. It was stunning. When making this at home, toss the salad with the tangy blood orange vinaigrette at the last minute so that the various colors don't run.

SERVES 6 TO 8 AS A FIRST COURSE

2 lb/910 g beets, a mix of red and gold

1 tsp kosher salt

1 cup/115 g walnut pieces

2 blood oranges
(or regular oranges if you can't find blood oranges)

BLOOD ORANGE VINAIGRETTE

1 blood orange
(or regular orange if you can't find blood oranges)

1 small shallot, finely diced

2 tsp Dijon mustard

2 tsp honey

1 tsp kosher salt

⅛ tsp freshly ground black pepper

3 tbsp sherry vinegar

¼ cup/60 ml extra-virgin olive oil

8 cups/200 g loosely packed baby arugula

8 oz/225 g soft fresh goat cheese

SPECIAL EQUIPMENT: rimmed baking sheet, Microplane or other fine-rasp grater

1. Cut the tops from the beets, leaving a little of the stem intact, and scrub them well. Put the beets in a large saucepan, sprinkle with the salt, and add water to cover by about 2 in/5 cm. Cover and bring to a boil over high heat. Reduce the heat to medium-low and simmer for about 1 hour, or until the beets are tender and can be easily pierced with a paring knife. Drain and set aside until the beets are just cool enough to be handled comfortably. Using a kitchen towel (find an old one that you won't mind staining) to hold the beets, remove the skins by rubbing the towel firmly against the beets. When the beets are completely cool, cut them into bite-size wedges.

2. Meanwhile, preheat the oven to 350°F/150°C, and place a rack in the center of the oven. Spread the walnuts in a single layer on the baking sheet and toast in the oven, shaking the pan once or twice for even toasting, for 8 to 10 minutes, or until the nuts are golden brown. Remove from the oven and let cool.

3. Cut the top and bottom off of each orange. Stand one of the oranges on a flat end. Using a sharp paring knife, carve away the rind from the orange, starting from the top and cutting downward and curving inward, until all the rind is gone and you are left with just the fruit. Repeat with the remaining orange. Cut the oranges crosswise into thin slices and set aside for the salad.

4. **TO MAKE THE VINAIGRETTE:** Working directly over a small bowl, grate the zest from the orange with the Microplane. Cut the orange in half and squeeze the juice into the grated zest. Add the shallot, Dijon mustard, honey, salt, and pepper. Whisk in the vinegar and then slowly whisk in the olive oil until well blended. Taste and adjust the seasoning if needed. The vinaigrette can be made up to 1 week in advance and stored in an airtight container in the fridge. Bring back to room temperature and rewhisk to combine the ingredients before using.

5. Arrange the arugula in a large, shallow bowl. In a medium bowl, toss the beets with 2 to 3 tbsp of the vinaigrette, coating them evenly. Top the arugula with the beets, orange slices, walnuts, and dollops of the goat cheese. Serve the remaining dressing on the side.

WARM QUINOA SALAD

with Roasted Autumn Vegetables and Ginger-Scallion Dressing

Over the last few years, quinoa (pronounced KEEN-wah) has been touted as the next great superfood. It's considered by most to be a grain, but it is actually an amino-acid–rich seed full of protein and magnesium and a host of other minerals. Crunchy and nutty in taste, it is also extremely easy to prepare.

This recipe is a winner in all respects. It's simple to make, absolutely delicious, and about the most healthful dish you could ever eat. Chef Corey created it as part of his perpetual quest to expand our repertoire of meatless options that will satisfy even the most devoted carnivore. It's my favorite dish from Flour to make at home.

SERVES 4 AS A MAIN COURSE OR 6 TO 8 AS A FIRST COURSE

6 or 7 Brussels sprouts, trimmed and quartered lengthwise

1 large parsnip, peeled and cut into ½-in/12-mm pieces

1 large carrot, peeled and cut into ½-in/12-mm pieces

1 small sweet potato, peeled and cut into ½-in/12-mm pieces

2 or 3 baby white turnips or purple-top turnips, peeled and cut into ½-in/12-mm pieces

3 tbsp olive oil

1 teaspoon kosher salt

¼ tsp freshly ground black pepper

1¼ cups/225 g quinoa

8 or 9 scallions, white and green parts, thinly sliced

3 tbsp peeled and minced fresh ginger

2 tbsp sherry vinegar

3 tbsp soy sauce

3 tbsp vegetable oil

1 tsp sesame oil

¼ cup/15 g chopped fresh cilantro for garnish (optional)

SPECIAL EQUIPMENT: rimmed baking sheet, sieve

1. Preheat the oven to 400°F/200°C, and place a rack in the center of the oven.

2. In a medium bowl, toss the Brussels sprouts, parsnip, carrot, sweet potato, and turnips with the olive oil, salt, and pepper. Transfer the vegetables to the baking sheet, arranging them in a single layer. Roast the vegetables, stirring every 5 minutes or so, for 18 to 20 minutes, or until they are tender and cooked through. Remove from the oven and set aside.

CONTINUED

3. While the vegetables are roasting, in a large saucepan, combine the quinoa and about 6 cups/ 1.4 L water and bring to a boil over high heat. Reduce the heat to medium-low, cover, and simmer for about 20 minutes, or until the quinoa grains "pop" (a white halo appears around each grain) and are cooked through. Drain the quinoa in the sieve and transfer to a medium bowl. The quinoa can be cooked up to 3 days in advance and store in an airtight container in the fridge; bring to room temperature or reheat in a medium skillet over medium heat for 6 to 8 minutes, or until warmed through, before using.

4. Add the roasted vegetables to the quinoa and toss well. In a small bowl, whisk together the scallions, ginger, vinegar, soy sauce, vegetable oil, and sesame oil until combined. Pour the dressing over the quinoa and vegetables and mix well. Divide equally among four bowls and top with the cilantro (if using). Serve warm or at room temperature.

SEARED FLANK STEAK SALAD

with Crumbled Blue Cheese, Glazed Onions, and Worcestershire Vinaigrette

Chef Corey created this salad as a tribute to Aaron, our former general manager of ten years. Corey had just started at Flour, and he and Aaron were on their way to becoming great friends. It was summertime, and Aaron talked often about grilling steaks and making summer salads at home. Aaron is known for conveying incredibly contagious passion when talking about the things he loves to eat. You always want to be a part of every meal he's describing. Corey came up with this salad to thank him for his inspiring energy and love of great food; Aaron loved it so much he told him, "This dressing is so good I could drink it."

**SERVES 4 AS A MAIN COURSE OR
6 TO 8 AS A FIRST COURSE**

WORCESTERSHIRE VINAIGRETTE

¼ cup/60 ml Worcestershire sauce

1 tsp Dijon mustard

1 tbsp sherry vinegar

½ tsp minced fresh thyme

⅛ tsp kosher salt

⅛ tsp freshly ground black pepper

5 tbsp/75 ml extra-virgin olive oil

1¼ lb/570 g flank steak

2 tsp kosher salt

1 tsp freshly ground black pepper

8 oz/225 g small Red Bliss potatoes, unpeeled and halved

3 tbsp extra-virgin olive oil

2 tbsp balsamic vinegar

1 tbsp packed brown sugar

1 medium red onion, peeled and cut into 4 thick rings

1 large or 2 small heads of romaine lettuce, trimmed and chopped into 2-in/5-cm pieces

2 large tomatoes, each cut into 8 wedges

1 large ripe avocado, halved, pitted, peeled, and sliced

1 cup/150 g crumbled blue cheese

SPECIAL EQUIPMENT: rimmed baking sheet, meat thermometer

1. **TO MAKE THE VINAIGRETTE:** In a medium bowl, whisk together the Worcestershire sauce, mustard, sherry vinegar, thyme, salt, and pepper until blended. Whisking continuously, slowly add the olive oil and whisk until well combined. The dressing can be stored in an airtight container in the fridge for up to 1 month. Bring back to room temperature and rewhisk to combine all of the ingredients before using.

2. Put the flank steak on the baking sheet and sprinkle both sides evenly with 1 tsp of the salt and ½ tsp of the pepper. Let sit at room temperature for 1 hour. About 20 minutes before you are ready to cook, preheat the oven to 400°F/200°C, and place a rack in the center of the oven.

CONTINUED

3. Roast the steak for 7 to 9 minutes, or until the thermometer inserted into the thickest part of the steak registers 130° to 135°F/54° to 57°C for medium-rare. Transfer the steak to a cutting board and let rest for at least 15 minutes to allow the juices to redistribute. Leave the oven on.

4. Meanwhile, in a small bowl, toss the potatoes with 1 tbsp of the olive oil, ½ tsp salt, and ¼ tsp pepper. Transfer the potatoes to the same baking sheet that was used for the steak. In the same small bowl, whisk together the remaining 2 tbsp olive oil, the balsamic vinegar, brown sugar, remaining ½ tsp salt, and remaining ¼ tsp pepper. Add the onions to the bowl, breaking up the rings and mixing well until evenly coated. Place the onion rings on the baking sheet next to the potatoes. Roast the vegetables for 18 to 20 minutes, or until the potatoes can be easily pierced with a fork. Remove from the oven and let cool to room temperature.

5. Divide the romaine equally among individual bowls. Slice the steak against the grain into thin strips. Top each salad with equal amounts of the steak, potatoes, onions, tomatoes, and avocado. Drizzle each serving evenly with the vinaigrette and finish with the blue cheese before serving.

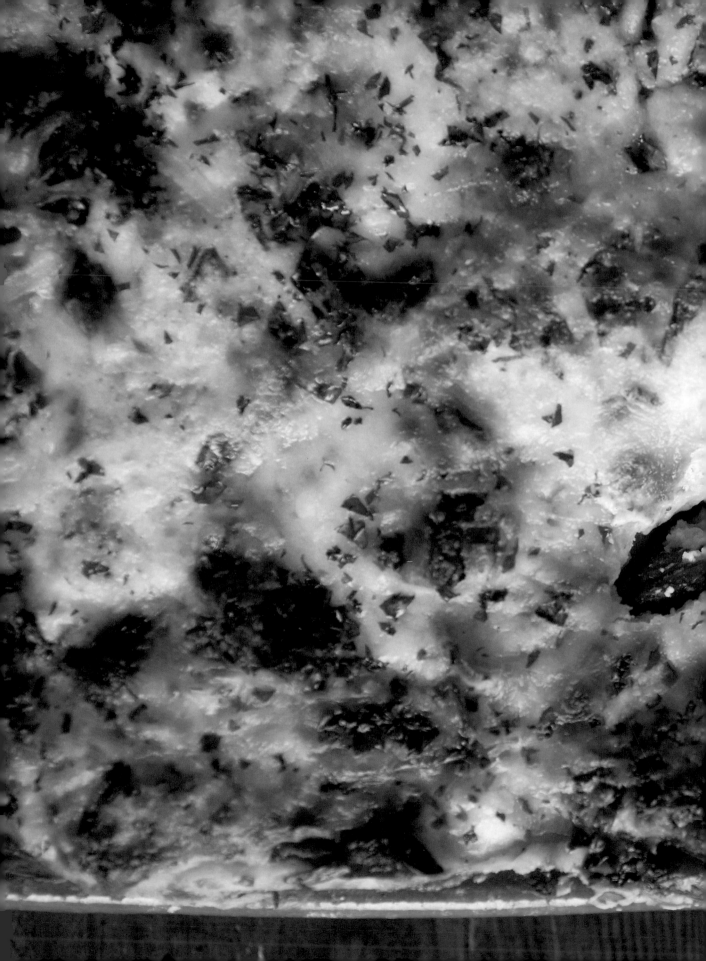

mains

BRAISED CHICKPEAS AND VEGETABLES
with Couscous, Harissa Yogurt, and Soft Eggs

Harissa is a North African condiment that my chefs introduced me to, and now I put it on pretty much everything. It's a thick, oily, chunky paste made with red chiles, chile oil, and garlic, and just a dab makes everything taste better. At Flour we use a *harissa* that includes rose petals (see page 43) that make it wonderfully complex.

We braise vegetables and chickpeas with cumin and turmeric and steam handfuls of couscous to go alongside. Spicy, pungent *harissa* yogurt gets mixed in at the end, and soft poached eggs top it all off. This dish is exotic, healthful, and filling and makes a lovely light dinner or brunch dish.

SERVES 6

⅔ cup/120 g dried chickpeas, or one 15-oz/430-g can chickpeas

4 tbsp/60 ml vegetable oil

8 oz/225 g spinach, tough stems removed

Kosher salt

Freshly ground black pepper

1 medium onion, cut into ½-in/12-mm pieces

3 garlic cloves, smashed and minced

1 medium carrot, peeled and cut into ½-in/12-mm pieces

1 medium zucchini, trimmed, quartered lengthwise, and cut crosswise into ½-in/12-mm pieces

1 medium yellow squash, trimmed, quartered lengthwise, and cut crosswise into ½-in/12-mm pieces

1 medium red bell pepper, cut into 1-in/2.5-cm pieces

1 tsp ground cumin

1½ tsp ground turmeric

1½ cups/340 ml Vegetable Stock (page 279)

1 cup/180 g couscous

¾ cup/180 g plain full-fat Greek yogurt

¼ cup/60 g *harissa* paste

½ cup/30 g chopped fresh cilantro

½ cup/30 g chopped fresh mint

6 large eggs

1 lime, cut into 6 wedges

SPECIAL EQUIPMENT: large stockpot with lid

1. If using dried chickpeas, place them in a bowl or other container, add 5 to 6 cups/1.2 to 1.4 L water, cover, and refrigerate overnight. The next day, drain and rinse the chickpeas. In a medium saucepan, bring the chickpeas and about 6 cups/1.4 L fresh water to a boil over high heat. Reduce the heat to medium-low and simmer for 1 to 1½ hours, or until the chickpeas are tender. Remove from the heat, drain, and set aside. If using canned chickpeas, drain, rinse under cold running water, and set aside.

CONTINUED

2. In the stockpot, heat 1 tbsp of the vegetable oil over high heat until hot. Add the spinach, reduce the heat to medium-high, and cook, stirring frequently, for 2 to 3 minutes, or until the spinach wilts. Season with ¼ tsp each salt and pepper, transfer to a small bowl, and set aside.

3. In the same pot, heat 2 tbsp vegetable oil over medium-high heat until hot. Add the onion and garlic and reduce the heat to medium. Cook, stirring frequently, for 3 to 4 minutes, or until the onion is translucent.

4. Add the chickpeas, carrot, zucchini, yellow squash, bell pepper, cumin, and turmeric and cook over medium heat, stirring frequently, for about 5 minutes. Add the stock, raise the heat to high, and bring to a boil. Reduce the heat to low and add 1 ¾ tsp salt and ¼ tsp pepper.

5. Stir in the couscous and turn off the heat. Cover the pot and leave on the stove for 5 minutes. Remove the cover and fluff up the couscous with a fork. Replace the cover and let sit for another 5 minutes. Remove the cover and fluff up the couscous again. Taste the couscous. If too chewy, cover and let stand for another 5 minutes.

6. While the couscous is steaming, chop the reserved spinach and drain off any excess liquid. Set aside.

7. In a small bowl, stir together the yogurt, *harissa*, and ½ tsp salt until well blended. Set aside.

8. When the couscous is done, add the spinach, cilantro, and mint and stir to combine. Divide the couscous equally among six shallow bowls and set aside in a warm spot.

9. In a large skillet, heat the remaining 1 tbsp oil over medium heat. Working in batches if necessary to prevent crowding, carefully crack each egg directly into the pan, keeping the yolk intact. Season each egg with a pinch each of salt and pepper. Pour 1 to 2 tbsp water into the pan, cover, and cook for 3 to 4 minutes, or until the tops of the egg whites are opaque and set and the yolks are still runny. Using a spatula, top each serving of couscous with an egg. Repeat with the remaining eggs if cooking in batches.

10. Garnish each bowl with a generous spoonful of the yogurt and a lime wedge before serving, and pass the remaining yogurt at the table. The lime and the *harissa* yogurt are crucial condiments to the couscous, so make sure everyone uses both!

MUSHROOM AND LEEK LASAGNA
with Creamy Béchamel

About a year before Flour opened, *Food & Wine* magazine contacted me for an article that they were writing about pastry chefs who were delving into savory food. I knew that my dream bakery-to-be would also be part café, with sandwiches and soups and such, and I had big plans for possibly doing take-out dinner specials as well. This lasagna was one of the specials on my original menu. The magazine ran it with a gorgeous picture, and when the article appeared, people were calling me trying to place orders for it. I had to explain over and over that I hadn't actually opened yet and that I was still searching for the right space for Flour. It was months before I would find the perfect location, but boy was it nice to know that people seemed excited about what I wanted to offer. This lasagna is rich and satisfying, with a nutmeg-scented béchamel, sweet mild leeks, and heady garlic-infused mushrooms. Be sure to rinse the leeks thoroughly before chopping; dirt loves to settle in the inner portion of the white parts.

MAKES ONE 9-BY-13-IN/
23-BY-33-CM LASAGNA
(SERVES 8 TO 10)

1 lb/455 g dry lasagna noodles

½ cup/120 ml olive oil, plus more for the noodles

1 cup/225 g soft fresh goat cheese, at room temperature

1 cup/250 g fresh whole-milk ricotta cheese

½ cup/30 g chopped fresh basil

2½ cups/280 g shredded part-skim mozzarella cheese

1½ tsp kosher salt

¾ tsp freshly ground black pepper

1 large egg, beaten

1½ lb/680 g mushrooms, such as oyster, chanterelle, trumpet, hen-of-the-woods (maitake), or portobello, wiped clean and thinly sliced

5 garlic cloves, smashed and minced

3 medium leeks, white and tender green parts, well rinsed and coarsely chopped

1 batch Roasted Tomatoes (page 276), roughly chopped

BÉCHAMEL

6 tbsp/85 g unsalted butter

⅓ cup/45 g all-purpose flour

4 cups/960 ml whole milk, at room temperature

¾ tsp kosher salt

¼ tsp freshly ground black pepper

½ tsp freshly grated nutmeg

SPECIAL EQUIPMENT: large stockpot, colander, 9-by-13-in/23-by-33-cm baking dish

1. Bring the stockpot filled with salted water to a boil over high heat. Add the lasagna noodles, stir well, and cook for 8 to 10 minutes, or until al dente. Drain the noodles in a colander, rinse under cold running water, and drain again. Toss with a little olive oil and set aside in the colander.

2. In a medium bowl, combine the goat cheese, ricotta, basil, 1 cup/110 g of the mozzarella, ¼ tsp of the salt, and ⅛ tsp of the pepper and stir to combine. Add the egg and mix until thoroughly blended. Set aside.

CONTINUED

3. In a large skillet, heat 2 tbsp of the olive oil over medium-high heat. Add about one-third of the mushrooms and cook, stirring and tossing occasionally, for about 2 minutes, or until softened. Stir in one-third of the garlic, add ¼ tsp salt and ⅛ tsp pepper, and cook for 2 minutes longer. Transfer the cooked mushrooms to a plate. Repeat twice with the remaining mushrooms and garlic, using ¼ tsp salt, ⅛ tsp pepper, and 2 tbsp oil for each batch. Set aside.

4. In the same skillet, heat the remaining 2 tbsp olive oil over medium-low heat. Add the leeks and cook for 10 to 12 minutes, or until softened and golden. Add the tomatoes and cook for another 2 to 3 minutes. Add ½ tsp salt and ¼ tsp pepper, mix well, and set aside.

5. **TO MAKE THE BÉCHAMEL:** In the same skillet, melt the butter over medium-high heat. Whisk in the flour and cook, whisking continuously, for about 2 minutes. Slowly add the milk while continuing to whisk and then bring to a simmer over medium-high heat. Reduce the heat to medium and cook, whisking frequently, for about 5 minutes, or until the sauce has lost its floury taste and thickened. Add the salt, pepper, and nutmeg. Set aside.

6. Preheat the oven to 350°F/180°C, and place a rack in the center of the oven.

7. Spread half of the béchamel in the bottom of the baking dish and top with a single layer of the lasagna noodles, overlapping them so that about five noodles fit in the bottom of the pan. Scatter half of the mushrooms over the noodles, and top with dollops of half of the goat cheese mixture. Cover with another layer of overlapping noodles and spread evenly with half of the remaining béchamel. Spread the tomato and leek mixture evenly over the sauce. Cover with a third layer of overlapping lasagna noodles and top with dollops of the remaining goat cheese mixture. Top with the remaining mushrooms and any of the mushroom liquid. Cover with a final layer of lasagna noodles and spread the remaining béchamel evenly over the noodle layer. Top evenly with the remaining 1½ cups/170 g mozzarella.

8. Bake for 50 minutes to 1 hour, or until golden brown on top and bubbling. Let the lasagna stand for 10 to 15 minutes before serving. The lasagna can be cooled, covered, and refrigerated overnight. To serve, bring to room temperature, cover with aluminum foil, and reheat in a 325°F/165°C oven for 20 to 25 minutes.

TRIPLE-CHEESE PIZZA

We make pizza every day at Flour using whatever strikes our chefs' fancy as toppings. Sometimes we go exotic, sometimes simple, but always we start with our delicious, amazingly easy pizza dough. It is soft and a bit sticky and makes for a crispy, chewy, light crust. It's wonderfully forgiving as well: you can use it as soon as two hours after you've made it or up to two days later. As with making great pastries, the key to making great pizza is to start with the best ingredients available. For this classic cheese pizza, don't skimp on the sauce (make this easy one in forty minutes, which is mostly just simmering time, and use high-quality canned tomatoes, such as San Marzano) and get the real stuff for the cheeses. If you like, chop up some fresh basil to sprinkle on top of the sauce before piling on the cheese.

MAKES TWO 12-BY-16-IN/
30.5-BY-40.5-CM PIZZAS
(SERVES 2 OR 3 REALLY HUNGRY PEOPLE
OR 4 TO 6 REGULAR PEOPLE)

SIMPLE TOMATO SAUCE

3 tbsp olive oil

1 garlic clove, smashed

1 small onion, cut into ½-in/12-mm pieces

One 28-oz/800-g can "no salt added" crushed tomatoes, with juice

½ tsp kosher salt

½ tsp freshly ground black pepper

1 tsp granulated sugar, if needed

1 batch Flour Focaccia dough (see page 282), or 2 lb/910 g store-bought pizza dough

All-purpose flour for working with the dough

Small handful of cornmeal for sprinkling on the pan or stone

1 cup/250 g fresh whole-milk ricotta cheese

1 lb/455 g part-skim mozzarella cheese, shredded

1 cup/100 g freshly grated Parmesan cheese

1 tbsp extra-virgin olive oil

½ tsp kosher salt

½ tsp freshly ground black pepper

SPECIAL EQUIPMENT: two large rimmed baking sheets or one large pizza stone, rolling pin, pizza peel or rimless baking sheet if using pizza stone

1. **TO MAKE THE TOMATO SAUCE:** In a large skillet, heat the olive oil over medium-high heat. Add the garlic and onion, reduce the heat to medium, and cook, stirring occasionally, for 6 to 8 minutes, or until the onion is soft and golden. Remove the garlic and discard. Add the tomatoes and mix well with the onion. Season with the salt and pepper, reduce the heat to low, and cook for 25 to 30 minutes, or until the sauce has reduced and thickened. (Taste and adjust the seasoning with salt and pepper.) If the sauce tastes too acidic, add the sugar. Let cool completely before using; you should have about 2 cups/480 ml. The sauce can be stored in an airtight container in the fridge for up to 3 days.

CONTINUED

2. If you will be baking the pizzas the next day or the day after, uncover the risen dough and punch it down in the middle a few times to deflate it. Using the same oiled piece of plastic wrap or lint-free cloth, re-cover the dough and refrigerate overnight or up to 48 hours until ready to use.

3. About 20 minutes before you are ready to bake the pizzas, preheat the oven to 500°F/260°C, and place one rack in the center and one rack in the top third of the oven. If you are using a pizza stone, place the stone in the center rack of the oven and if you have two stones place the second stone on the top rack.

4. Lightly flour a work surface, turn the risen dough out onto it, and divide the dough in half. Flour your hands and gently stretch one piece of the dough into an oblong. Generously flour the dough and the work surface. Using the rolling pin, and working from the center of the dough outward, roll out the dough into a rectangle or oval that fits your baking sheet or pizza stone. Depending on how long the dough has rested, it can be very elastic and hard to roll out, so you may need to be patient and persistent. Keep flipping the dough over and moving it from side to side, and lift it up every now and then and stretch it with your hands. It will slowly start to stretch and eventually, with patient rolling, you will get the dough to fit the sheet. I promise.

5. Liberally sprinkle one baking sheet with about half of the cornmeal and transfer the pizza rectangle to the baking sheet. Repeat with the second piece of dough and the second baking sheet. If you are using a pizza stone, sprinkle the pizza peel or rimless baking sheet with half of the cornmeal and transfer the rolled-out crust to the peel. The stone will likely be a bit smaller than a baking sheet, so stretch the dough so it is about ⅛ in/3 mm thick and make a slight rim around the edge with the excess dough.

6. If using baking sheets, spread each crust with an equal amount of the tomato sauce. Dot both pizzas evenly with the ricotta, then sprinkle evenly with the mozzarella and finally with the Parmesan. If using the pizza peel and stone, top the crust as directed, using just half of the ingredients.

7. If using baking sheets, place one baking sheet on the center oven rack and the second sheet on top rack and bake for 18 to 20 minutes. Start checking the pizzas after 15 minutes, as ovens bake very differently at such high temperatures. To ensure the pizzas bake evenly, about midway through the baking, switch the sheets between the oven racks and rotate each sheet from back to front. The pizzas are ready when both the cheese topping and underside of the crust are golden brown. (Lift a corner of the crust and take a peek.) If using the pizza stone, slide the pizza off of the peel onto the stone and bake for 18 to 20 minutes. You don't need to rotate the stone, but do start checking the pizza after 15 minutes. The doneness cues are the same—golden brown on the top and bottom.

8. Remove the baking sheets from the oven. If using a pizza stone, use the peel to retrieve the pizza, then assemble the second pizza on the peel, slide it onto the stone, and bake it the same way. Drizzle the pizzas evenly with the olive oil and sprinkle with the salt and pepper. Serve immediately.

TARTE FLAMBÉE VARIATION: An Alsatian classic, this pizza is called a *tarte flambée* or *Flammeküche*, and it is typically baked in a wood-fired oven over the highest heat possible. I've adapted this classic for a home oven, and the results are still spectacular. Make this at your own risk—once it comes out you won't be able to stop eating it.

Omit the tomato sauce and the mozzarella, Parmesan, and ricotta cheeses. Cook 12 slices thick-cut applewood-smoked bacon in the oven until barely crisp (for directions on cooking the bacon, see page 150) and cut into ½-in/12-mm pieces. Divide 1 cup/240 ml crème fraîche evenly between the two pizza crusts, spreading it evenly and leaving a ½-in/12-mm border uncovered along the edges. Divide 1 cup/90 g Caramelized Onions (page 278) between the two crusts, distributing the onions evenly over the crusts, then sprinkle each pizza with 2 tsp finely chopped fresh thyme and ½ tsp each kosher salt and freshly ground black pepper. Scatter the bacon evenly over the pizzas, and then scatter 1¼ lb/570 g Gruyère cheese, shredded, evenly over the pizzas. Proceed as directed.

ALOHA VARIATION: Our long-time former manager, Aaron, introduced me to this pizza. Every so often at Flour, we host a pizza party for the staff, and Aaron would always request at least one pizza topped with ham and pineapple. I used to cringe at the idea, but it turns out that this combo is pretty darn popular with everyone, and he usually had to share his special pie with at least a few fellow staff members. We occasionally run this combo as our pizza of the day at Flour, and on those days Aaron would trade in his daily lunch of a banana bread–ham sandwich (I'm not kidding) for this pizza. The Hawaiian-inspired name goes along with his sunny personality.

Omit the Parmesan and ricotta cheeses. Spread the pizza crusts evenly with the tomato sauce as directed. Divide 8 oz/225 g smoked ham or Canadian bacon, chopped, evenly between the crusts, scattering it over the tomato sauce. Top with 1 medium pineapple, peeled, cored, and cut into ½-in/12-mm pieces, distributing the pieces evenly. Finally, sprinkle evenly with the mozzarella. Proceed as directed.

NEW ENGLAND–STYLE BAKED BEANS
with Thick-Cut Bacon

Chef Corey grew up in Maine, and when he joined the Flour family we were introduced to all sorts of New England dishes that weren't part of our repertoire. Among them were these baked beans. He often reminisced about eating these beans while he was growing up and how much he missed the flavors.

When Flour hit its tenth anniversary, we threw a dinner party for the whole staff to celebrate a decade of "making life sweeter." For this occasion, Corey created a multicourse meal called 10 Years, 10 Beers. As the name suggests, we paired courses with beers, and it was a huge success. The most popular course by far was these baked beans, full of smoky flavor and not at all too sweet. For a traditional dinner, serve the beans with more bacon crumbled on top and accompany them with thick slices of grilled country bread and a green salad.

SERVES 3 OR 4

1 lb/455 g dried white beans, like navy or flageolet, rinsed

5 slices thick-cut applewood-smoked bacon, chopped into 1-in/2.5-cm pieces

1 medium onion, cut into ½-in/12-mm pieces

⅓ cup/80 ml molasses

¼ cup/55 g packed brown sugar

⅓ cup/80 ml cider vinegar

1 tbsp Dijon or whole-grain mustard

1½ tsp kosher salt

2 tbsp tomato paste

SPECIAL EQUIPMENT: large stockpot

1. In the stockpot, combine the beans and water to cover by about 2 in/5 cm and bring to a boil over high heat. Reduce the heat to medium-low, cover, and cook, adding more water as needed to keep the beans covered, for about 1 hour, or until the beans are tender. Remove from the heat and drain. Set aside.

2. Return the stockpot to the stove. Add the bacon and cook over medium-high heat, stirring often, for 3 to 4 minutes, or until the fat has rendered and the bacon starts to crisp. Add the onion and cook, stirring frequently, for 3 to 4 minutes longer, or until translucent. Reduce the heat to low and add the molasses, brown sugar, vinegar, mustard, and salt. Mix well and cook for 2 to 3 minutes. Add the drained beans and stir until well mixed. Cook over low heat for 20 to 30 minutes, or until the liquid has been absorbed.

3. Stir in the tomato paste and 2 cups/480 ml water and continue to cook for 1 hour longer. The beans should be thick but not stiff, soft but not soupy. (Taste and adjust the seasoning with more salt or mustard if needed, and add more water as needed to achieve a good consistency.) Serve immediately.

SLOW-BAKED ATLANTIC SALMON
with Tabouli

This is the absolute best way to cook salmon. It's a technique that Chef Aniceto taught me after his years at a four-star French restaurant. Grilling or searing tends to coagulate the proteins in a harsh way that can make the salmon, which is already a strongly flavored fish, taste unpleasantly fishy. This slow, even baking method cooks much more gently, leaving the salmon with a delicate, buttery texture and flavor.

Chef Aniceto pairs the salmon with a simple lemony tabouli, a Middle Eastern bulgur wheat salad full of fresh herbs and summer vegetables. This one is a bit heavier on the bulgur than is traditional, making it more of a side salad than a condiment, which is how it is often used. Persian cucumbers are small, slender, crispy seedless cucumbers typically sold in small plastic packages. They are really crunchy and ideal for this salad, but if you can't find them, an English cucumber is a good substitute. This is an easy recipe that you'll appreciate having at your fingertips to make again and again with this salmon or on its own.

SERVES 4

TABOULI

1 cup/200 g bulgur wheat, fine grind or no. 1 grind

1 to 1½ cups/240 to 360 ml boiling water

6 radishes, trimmed and quartered lengthwise

2 Persian cucumbers or ½ English cucumber, thinly sliced crosswise

1 cup/170 g halved cherry tomatoes

3 tbsp minced red onion

¼ oz/15 g julienned fresh mint leaves

¼ cup/15 g julienned fresh flat-leaf parsley

3 tbsp extra-virgin olive oil

1 tbsp plus 2 tsp freshly squeezed lemon juice

½ tsp grated lemon zest

½ tsp kosher salt

¼ tsp freshly ground black pepper

4 tbsp/60 ml extra-virgin olive oil

1½ lb/680 g salmon fillet with skin intact, cut into 4 equal pieces

1 tsp kosher salt

½ tsp freshly ground black pepper

½ lemon

SPECIAL EQUIPMENT: Microplane or other fine-rasp grater, rimmed baking sheet

1. **TO MAKE THE TABOULI:** Put the bulgur wheat in a small heatproof bowl and pour 1 cup/ 240 ml of the boiling water over it. Cover tightly with plastic wrap and place in a warm area for about 20 minutes. After 20 minutes, uncover and fluff up the bulgur wheat with a fork. If it is still hard or chewy, add ¼ cup/60 ml boiling water, re-cover, and steam for another 5 minutes. Repeat once more if necessary. You want the bulgur wheat to be fluffy and tender. Set aside.

CONTINUED

2. In a large bowl, combine the radishes, cucumbers, tomatoes, red onion, mint, and parsley. Drizzle with the olive oil and lemon juice and toss until evenly coated. Add the lemon zest, salt, and pepper and toss again. Add the bulgur wheat and mix until well combined. (Taste and adjust the seasoning with salt and/or lemon juice if needed.) The salad can be stored in a covered container in the fridge for up to 3 days. For the best flavor and texture, bring to room temperature before serving.

3. Preheat the oven to 300°F/150°C, and place a rack in the middle of the oven.

4. Smear the baking sheet with 1 to 2 tsp of the olive oil and place the salmon, skin-side down, on the baking sheet. Drizzle about half of the remaining oil over the salmon and sprinkle evenly with the salt and pepper. Bake for 12 to 15 minutes, or until the fish turns opaque and feels firm when you press the thickest part. The baking time will depend on the thickness of the fillet. Keep in mind that even after the fish comes out of the oven, it will continue to cook because of carryover cooking (retained heat).

5. Remove the salmon from the oven and baste it with the remaining oil. Squeeze the lemon half over the salmon pieces and let the fish rest on the baking sheet for 5 to 8 minutes. To serve, divide the tabouli evenly among four dinner plates, and top each with a salmon fillet.

PAN-SEARED MAINE CRAB CAKES
with Spicy Celery Root Rémoulade

Corey, our chef at Flour in the South End, spent a number of years cooking at the famed Fore Street restaurant in Portland, Maine. His time there has greatly influenced his cooking: his food is classic, deeply flavorful, and honest. These crab cakes showcase his skills superbly. Lump crabmeat is barely held together with a minimum of mayonnaise, bread crumbs, and an egg, so what you taste first and foremost is the fresh, pure flavor of Maine crab. Cook these cakes long and low in the skillet so they slowly form a deep golden brown crust, and you'll be rewarded with the best crab cakes you've ever eaten.

Rémoulade is a popular seafood condiment that resembles tartar sauce. In France, it is combined with celery root to make *celeri rémoulade*. I love the crisp bite that finely shredded celery root brings to the rémoulade here, which we use as a spicy, creamy, crunchy bed for the crab cakes.

SERVES 3 AS MAIN OR
6 AS AN APPETIZER

SPICY CELERY ROOT RÉMOULADE

2 tbsp good-quality mayonnaise

1 tbsp Dijon mustard

1¼ tsp hot pepper sauce

2 scallions, white and green parts, minced

½ large celery stalk, minced

½ tsp celery seeds

½ tsp kosher salt

½ tsp freshly ground black pepper

1 tbsp freshly squeezed lemon juice

½ tsp Worcestershire sauce

1 small celery root

CRAB CAKES

5 tbsp/75 ml vegetable oil

¼ red bell pepper, finely diced

2 tbsp finely diced white onion

1 scallion, white and green parts, minced

1 lb/455 g fresh-cooked Maine lump crabmeat, picked over for shell fragments and cartilage

6 tbsp/25 g fresh bread crumbs

¼ cup/60 ml good-quality mayonnaise

1 tbsp Dijon mustard

½ tsp celery seeds

1 large egg, beaten

½ tsp kosher salt

¼ tsp freshly ground black pepper

2 tbsp chopped fresh flat-leaf parsley for garnish

SPECIAL EQUIPMENT: mandoline, box grater, or food processor with large-hole shredding attachment

1. **TO MAKE THE RÉMOULADE:** In a medium bowl, combine the mayonnaise, mustard, hot pepper sauce, scallions, celery, celery seeds, salt, pepper, lemon juice, and Worcestershire sauce and stir until well mixed. Using a sharp chef's knife, carefully peel off the rough, knobby exterior from the celery root. Using the mandoline, cut the celery root into paper-thin slices, then stack the slices and cut into fine julienne, or shred the celery root on the large holes of the box grater or with the food processor fitted with the shredding attachment. Immediately fold the celery root into the mayonnaise mixture. The mixture will resemble a slaw. Cover and refrigerate until serving or for up to 1 day.

2. **TO MAKE THE CRAB CAKES:** In a medium skillet, heat 1 tbsp of the vegetable oil over medium-high heat. Add the bell pepper, white onion, and scallion and sauté for 3 to 5 minutes, or until the onion is translucent. Using a rubber spatula, scrape the vegetables into a small bowl and let cool.

3. In a medium bowl, combine the crab, bread crumbs, mayonnaise, mustard, celery seeds, egg, salt, and pepper and mix very gently until well combined, keeping the crab in large pieces if possible. Mix in the cooled onion mixture, cover, and refrigerate for about 30 minutes.

4. Remove the crab mixture from the fridge and gently shape it into six cakes, each about 2½ in/ 6 cm wide and 1½ in/4 cm thick. They will be fairly tall and compact, like hockey pucks. Chill again for 15 to 20 minutes.

5. In a large skillet, heat 2 tbsp of the vegetable oil over medium heat. Add three cakes, reduce the heat to low, and cook, without agitating the pan or turning the cakes, for 6 to 8 minutes, or until the bottoms turn brown. The cakes are very delicate and may look like they are falling apart because so few bread crumbs are binding them, so be patient. Using the spatula, very gently turn the cakes over and cook the other side for another 5 to 6 minutes, or until golden brown and crispy on the second side. Transfer the cakes to a platter and tent loosely with foil. Repeat with the remaining 2 tbsp oil and three cakes.

6. Divide the rémoulade equally among three plates for a main course or six plates for an appetizer and top each with two crab cakes for a main or one crab cake for an appetizer. Sprinkle with the parsley and serve immediately.

COREY'S HOMEMADE CHICKEN POTPIE

Homemade chicken potpie made entirely from scratch is a revelation. Maybe you've had one frozen from a box, you remember the one in your school cafeteria, or you've ordered one in a home-style restaurant. I guarantee you those won't compare to this one. Chef Corey made this potpie as a dinner special one cold, blustery December week, and it sold so quickly that it became a staple on our dinner menu that entire winter. Customers started asking for it even in the summertime, and we decided to offer it year-round. We start with homemade stock, chicken breasts, peas, carrots, and potatoes, all thickened with a little flour. The potpie filling goes into a flaky, buttery pie shell and is topped with a crust that bakes to a gorgeous golden brown. If you don't already have one, buy or borrow a deep-dish pie pan. You want a baking vessel that is deep and large enough to accommodate all of the hearty fresh vegetables and chicken.

A homemade potpie is perfect for busy families, because it can be made in advance, frozen, and then baked straight from the freezer for an unbeatable wholesome, hearty dinner. A terrific variation of this recipe is to skip the bottom crust and top the filling with cheddar-scallion biscuits (see page 197). Try both to see which one is your favorite.

SERVES 6 TO 8

PÂTE BRISÉE

1¾ cups/245 g all-purpose flour

1 tbsp granulated sugar

1 tsp kosher salt

1 cup/225 g cold unsalted butter, cut into 12 pieces

2 egg yolks

3 tbsp cold milk

FILLING

2 tbsp unsalted butter

1 medium onion, cut into ½-in/12-mm pieces

1 large carrot, peeled and thinly sliced crosswise

1 celery stalk, thinly sliced

1 small russet potato, unpeeled and cut into ½-in/12-mm pieces

1 lb/455 g boneless, skinless chicken breasts, cut into 1- to 2-in/2.5- to 5-cm pieces

5 tbsp/45 g all-purpose flour

1½ cups/360 ml Chicken Stock (page 280)

1 cup/140 g fresh or frozen English peas

2 tsp chopped fresh thyme

1½ tsp kosher salt

½ tsp freshly ground black pepper

2 tbsp heavy cream

1 large egg, beaten

SPECIAL EQUIPMENT: stand mixer with paddle attachment or handheld mixer, rolling pin, 9-by-2-in/23-by-5-cm deep-dish aluminum pie pan or glass or ceramic pie dish (at least 6-cup/1.4-L capacity), parchment paper, pie weights, pastry brush, rimmed baking sheet

1. **TO MAKE THE PÂTE BRISÉE:** Using the stand mixer or the handheld mixer and a medium bowl, beat together the flour, sugar, and salt on low speed for 10 to 15 seconds. Scatter the butter over the flour mixture and beat on low speed for 1 to 1½ minutes, or until the flour is no longer bright white and holds together when you clump it and lumps of butter the size of pecans are visible throughout. In a small bowl, whisk together the egg yolks and milk. Add the yolk-milk mixture all at once to the flour-butter mixture and beat on low speed for 20 to 30 seconds, or *just* until the mixture barely comes together. It will look really shaggy and more like a mess than a dough.

CONTINUED

2. Dump the dough out onto a clean, dry work surface and gather it into a tight mound. Using the palm of your hand, smear the dough, starting at the top of the mound and sliding your palm down the sides of the mound along the work surface, until most of the butter chunks are smeared into the dough and the whole thing comes together. Wrap the dough tightly in plastic wrap and press down to make a flattened disk. Refrigerate for at least 1 hour before using. The dough can be stored in the refrigerator for up to 4 days or in the freezer for up to 4 weeks (wrap it in a second layer of plastic wrap if storing for more than 1 day or freezing it). If frozen, transfer the dough to the refrigerator and allow it to thaw for 1 day before using it.

3. Divide the dough into two pieces, one twice as large as the other. The smaller portion will be used for the top crust. On a well-floured work surface, roll out the larger dough portion into a circle about 12 in/30.5 cm in diameter and 1/8 in/3 mm thick. Roll the dough circle around the rolling pin and then unfurl it on top of the pie pan or dish. Gently press the dough into the bottom and sides of the pan, leaving a 1/4-in/6-mm lip extending beyond the pan rim (to allow for shrinkage in the oven). Refrigerate the pie shell for at least 30 minutes. The pie shell can be tightly wrapped in plastic wrap and refrigerated for up to 1 day or frozen for up to 2 weeks. The frozen pie shell can be baked directly from the freezer.

4. Preheat the oven to 350°F/180°C, and place a rack in the center of the oven.

5. Line the chilled pie shell with parchment paper, fill it with pie weights, and blind bake (see page 36) for 30 to 35 minutes, or until the entire shell is light brown. Transfer the pie shell to a wire rack and leave the oven on. Remove the weights and the parchment and let the shell cool completely.

6. MEANWHILE, MAKE THE FILLING: In a large saucepan, heat the butter over medium-high heat until it foams. Add the onion and cook for 2 to 3 minutes, or until it softens a bit. Add the carrot, celery, and potato and sauté, stirring, for 4 to 5 minutes, or until the vegetables start to soften. Add the chicken and continue to cook over medium-high heat, stirring with a wooden spoon, for another 2 to 3 minutes, or until the chicken pieces start to turn opaque. Stir in the flour, mixing to coat all of the meat and vegetables, and cook, stirring occasionally, for 2 to 3 minutes longer. By this time the filling will start to look a bit sludgy and a brown film should be forming on the bottom of the pan. Add the stock and bring to a simmer. Add the peas, thyme, salt, pepper, and cream and stir well. Simmer, scraping up the browned bits clinging to the bottom of the pan, for about 5 minutes, or until the filling thickens. Remove from the heat and spoon the filling into the prebaked pie shell.

7. Roll out the remaining dough portion into a circle about 10 in/25 cm in diameter and 1/8 in/3 mm thick. Roll the dough circle around the rolling pin and then unfurl it over the filled pie shell, letting the edge of the round overhang the rim of the pan by 1/4 to 1/2 in/6 to 12 mm (you will trim off this excess once the pie is baked). Using the pastry brush, brush the top crust evenly with the egg and poke a hole in the center of the crust to allow steam to escape. (At this point, the potpie can be well wrapped in plastic wrap and frozen. When you want to eat it, discard the plastic wrap, place the pie on the baking sheet, and put the frozen pie in the preheated oven. Add 20 to 25 minutes additional baking time, and tent a piece of aluminum foil over the crust if it starts to overbrown before the pie is ready.)

8. Place the pie on the baking sheet to catch any overflow. Bake for about 30 minutes, or until the entire top crust is golden brown. Transfer to a wire rack and let cool for about 15 minutes. Using a small paring knife, trim away any excess crust along the edge before serving.

CHEDDAR-SCALLION BISCUIT TOPPING VARIATION:
If you prefer a bottomless potpie with a buttery biscuit topping, omit the pâte brisée. Prepare the filling as directed and spoon it into the unlined deep-dish pie pan. To make the biscuit topping, in the stand mixer fitted with the paddle attachment, combine 1¾ cups/245 g all-purpose flour; ½ cup/100 g medium-coarse cornmeal; 1½ tsp baking powder; ½ tsp baking soda; 1 tsp kosher salt; 3 oz/85 g Cheddar cheese, cut into ¼-in/6-mm pieces; and 4 scallions, white and green parts, minced. Beat on low speed for 10 to 15 seconds, or until combined. Cut ½ cup/115 g cold unsalted butter into 8 to 10 pieces, scatter the pieces over the flour mixture, and beat on low speed for about 30 seconds, or until the butter is broken down into pieces the size of a pecan.

In a small bowl, whisk together ½ cup/120 ml cold nonfat buttermilk, ½ cup/120 ml cold crème fraîche, and 1 cold whole egg until thoroughly mixed. On low speed, pour the buttermilk mixture into the flour-butter mixture and beat for 20 to 30 seconds, or just until the dough comes together. There will still be a little loose flour mixture at the bottom of the bowl. (Alternatively, if you don't have a stand mixer, use a pastry cutter, two knives, or a fork to cut the butter into the dry ingredients until the butter chunks are about the size of lima beans; use a wooden spoon to mix the wet ingredients into the dry ingredients.)

Remove the bowl from the mixer stand. Gather and lift the dough with your hands and turn it over in the bowl so that it starts to pick up the loose flour at the bottom. Turn the dough over several times until all of the loose flour is mixed in. Using a ½-cup/120-ml measure, an ice-cream scoop, or a large spoon, drop mounds of the biscuit dough on top of the potpie filling until the whole top is covered. Brush the biscuit tops with 1 egg yolk, beaten, and bake in the preheated 350°F/180°C oven for 45 to 55 minutes, or until the biscuits are golden brown. Transfer to a wire rack and let cool for about 30 minutes before serving.

BUTTERMILK-FRIED CHICKEN

Within Flour, Chef Aniceto is known among the other chefs for having the most adventurous and diverse specials. His time at two four-star French restaurants, a Middle Eastern bakery-café, and a nose-to-tail farm-driven bistro, along with his own perpetual food curiosity, have led him to introduce all of us to ingredients and techniques that we'd never have known about without him. So imagine my surprise when he came up with a dinner special that was as American as apple pie. Fried chicken, done right, is a rare treat. He bemoans the fact that because all of our dinner specials are made in advance to be reheated at home, customers don't get to enjoy chicken straight out of the fryer. It's a testament to how delicious this chicken is that it's just as good (some would say better) cold as it is hot. Now you can try it yourself. Note that the chicken has to marinate for a day in the buttermilk, so you need to start this recipe a day in advance.

SERVES 4

One 4- to 4½-lb/1.8- to 2-kg whole chicken

1 tsp paprika

1 tsp freshly ground black pepper

1 tsp garlic powder

1 tsp onion powder

1 tsp dry mustard

2 cups/480 ml nonfat buttermilk

3 fresh tarragon sprigs, roughly chopped

1 medium onion, peeled and cut into ½-in/12-mm pieces

1 tbsp kosher salt

2 cups/280 g all-purpose flour

4 cups/960 ml vegetable oil, for frying

SPECIAL EQUIPMENT: sharp boning knife, 9-by-13-in/ 23-by-33-cm baking dish or other shallow container; large, deep, heavy skillet; deep-fry thermometer; rimmed baking sheet

1. The day before you plan to serve the chicken, cut the chicken into ten pieces. First, take a drumstick and pull it away from the body. Feel for the thigh joint where the thigh meets the body and cut at the joint—if you stick a boning knife along the joint you'll feel the joint where it's soft (versus the bone where it's hard) and you'll be able to cut through. Repeat on the other side. Separate the thighs from the drumsticks again by cutting at the joint. Set aside. Press the body of the chicken (breast-side up) flat against your cutting board. You'll hear the back bones crack a bit. Lift up the body and slice down the middle of the chicken to separate the bony back from the breast. (Reserve the back bones to make stock.) Cut the breast in half right down the middle of the bone; you may have to switch to a larger chef's knife to cut through the bone. Cut the wings off the breast, including some of the breast meat so that the wings have some good meat to them. Set the wings aside. Cut the remaining breast halves crosswise in half again. You will now have ten pieces of chicken all approximately the same size. Arrange the chicken pieces in a single layer in the baking dish.

CONTINUED

2. In a small container, mix together the paprika, pepper, garlic powder, onion powder, and dry mustard until blended.

3. Pour the buttermilk into a small bowl. Add about half of the spice mixture and whisk it into the buttermilk. Stir in the tarragon, onion, and salt. Pour the marinade over the chicken pieces, cover with plastic wrap, and refrigerate overnight.

4. The next day, in a medium bowl, whisk together the remaining spice mixture and the flour, then transfer the mixture to a pie pan or other flat, shallow pan with a rim. Remove the chicken pieces from the buttermilk, shaking them to remove any excess liquid. Dredge each piece on both sides in the flour mixture and shake off any excess. Set aside on a large platter or plate.

5. Pour the vegetable oil into the skillet and heat to 375°F/190°C on the deep-fry thermometer. While the oil heats, line the baking sheet with paper towels and set aside. Using kitchen tongs or a slotted spoon, carefully place all of the dark meat (these pieces will need to cook a bit longer) into the skillet. The temperature will drop to between 350° and 325°F/180° and 165°C. Cook on both sides, turning once or twice, for 12 to 15 minutes, or until the chicken is browned and cooked through. Transfer to the prepared baking sheet to drain. Repeat with the white meat, which will take 8 to 10 minutes. The chicken can be cooked in advance, covered and stored in the fridge, and reheated in a 350°F/180°C oven for about 10 minutes to restore crunch before serving.

JEFF'S SPICY TURKEY BURGERS
with Tomato-Onion Jam

I had never eaten ground turkey until Chef Jeff made these burgers for a lunch special. Before he even had a chance to bring them out to the front to sell, the kitchen staff (including me) had devoured pretty much all of them. Most chefs would go crazy if that happened to them. Chef Jeff has such a heartfelt love of feeding people that he was thrilled that the burgers were so well received, even if we didn't have any to sell that day. (At least that's what he told me!)

These burgers are full of spice and herbs, with a kick of chipotle to bring it all up a notch. We serve them with a sweet, tangy tomato jam on our homemade focaccia rolls. These are a healthful alternative to a fatty beef burger with just as much flavor, if not more.

MAKES 4 BURGERS

Small handful of cornmeal for sprinkling on the baking sheet

½ batch Flour Focaccia dough (see page 282), or 1 lb/455 g store-bought pizza dough

Small handful of all-purpose flour for sprinkling on the rolls

TOMATO-ONION JAM

3 tbsp extra-virgin olive oil

½ medium onion, cut into ½-in/12-mm pieces

1 lb/455 g plum tomatoes, halved, pulp and seeds removed, and roughly chopped

½ tsp kosher salt

¼ tsp freshly ground black pepper

¼ tsp hot red pepper flakes

TURKEY BURGERS

3 slices day-old white bread

3 tbsp olive oil

½ medium onion, minced

2 garlic cloves, smashed and minced

1 lb/455 g ground turkey

2 tbsp Dijon mustard

1 tbsp seeded and minced canned chipotle chile

1 large egg

3 tbsp chopped fresh basil

2 tbsp chopped fresh flat-leaf parsley

4 oz/115 g feta cheese, crumbled

½ tsp kosher salt

¼ tsp freshly ground black pepper

4 lettuce leaves for serving

SPECIAL EQUIPMENT: baking sheet, food processor, meat thermometer

CONTINUED

1. Sprinkle the baking sheet evenly with the cornmeal and set aside.

2. Shape the dough into a rough 4-in/10-cm square and divide the square into four equal pieces. Shape each piece of dough into a ball by stretching it flat on a work surface and bringing the edges up to meet in the center. Turn the dough piece over and keep tucking the edges underneath until you have a small ball with a taut surface. Place the dough ball on the prepared baking sheet and repeat with the remaining three dough pieces. Sprinkle the dough balls with some of the flour, lightly cover them with plastic wrap or a lint-free cloth, and place them in a warm area (78° to 82°F/25° to 27°C is ideal) for about 2 hours, or until the dough has doubled in size and is soft and wobbly.

3. About 30 minutes before you are ready to bake the rolls, preheat the oven to 400°F/200°C, and place a rack in the center of the oven.

4. Uncover the dough balls. Sprinkle them with the remaining flour, and slap them flat with the palm of your hand to deflate them. Bake the rolls for 15 to 20 minutes, or until golden brown. Transfer the rolls to a wire rack to cool.

5. Brush the cornmeal off the baking sheet and set the pan aside for cooking the burgers. Reduce the oven temperature to 350°F/180°C.

6. **WHILE THE ROLLS ARE RISING, MAKE THE TOMATO-ONION JAM:** In a medium saucepan, heat the extra-virgin olive oil over medium heat. Add the onion and tomatoes and cook, stirring occasionally, for 30 to 40 minutes, or until the mixture has thickened. Add the salt, pepper, and red pepper flakes and stir until well mixed. Remove from the heat and let cool. The jam can be made up to 4 days in advance and stored in an airtight container in the refrigerator. Bring to room temperature before serving.

7. **TO MAKE THE TURKEY BURGERS:** In the food processor, process the day-old bread until it turns to crumbs. You should have about 1 cup/85 g. Set aside.

8. In a large skillet, heat 1 tbsp of the olive oil over medium heat. Add the onion and cook, stirring occasionally, for 4 to 6 minutes, or until softened. Add the garlic and cook for another 2 minutes. Remove from the heat.

9. In a large bowl, combine the turkey, cooked onion and garlic, mustard, chile, reserved bread crumbs, egg, basil, parsley, feta, salt, and pepper. Using your hands, mix until well blended. Form the turkey mixture into four large, flat, thin patties 4 to 5 in/10 to 12 cm in diameter. The patties will shrink up and get thick as you cook them, so pat them very flat at this point to compensate.

10. In the same skillet used for the onion, heat 1 tbsp of the oil over medium heat. Add two burgers and cook, turning once, for about 2 minutes per side, or until nicely seared. Transfer the seared burgers to the baking sheet. Add the remaining 1 tbsp oil to the pan and sear the remaining two burgers.

11. Bake the burgers for 14 to 16 minutes, or until they are cooked through. Check the doneness by inserting the meat thermometer into the thickest part of a burger; it should register an internal temperature of 165°F/74°C.

12. Split the rolls and spread one cut side of each roll evenly with the tomato-onion jam. Top the bottom of each roll with a lettuce leaf and then a burger. Close each burger with a roll top and serve.

ROASTED PORK LOIN

with Chive Spaetzle, Slow-Roasted Balsamic Onions, and Oregano Mojo

When Chris, our opening chef at Flour1, decided to leave to open his own restaurant, I knew I couldn't hire just anyone to replace him. In three short years, his immense culinary skills, which he translated into wildly popular soups and inventive sandwiches, had put Flour on the Boston map. We found the perfect replacement in our next chef, Aniceto, who hailed from a four-star French restaurant and blew me away during his interview by making a creamy sweet corn soup with Thai basil. Aniceto spent the next five years pushing the menu in every way possible, introducing our customers (and me) to new ingredients and flavors and techniques. He eventually left Flour to get back into restaurant work, but I didn't have to miss his food for long. When we launched our third location in Cambridge, he rejoined Flour as part of the opening team.

This pork loin combines four great recipes, two from Chris and two from Aniceto, into one swoon-worthy main course. The pork and spaetzle recipes come from Aniceto, who offered the pork loin one year for our holiday menu. It filled our normally sweet-smelling kitchen with the most mouthwatering garlicky, oregano aroma. The kitchen stood by patiently for tastes as Aniceto carved it up. The onions and oregano *mojo* recipes are courtesy of Chris, who combined them with roasted pork in a sandwich special that customers still ask about today.

SERVES 4 TO 6

BRINE

About ½ cup/105 g kosher salt

About ½ cup/110 g packed brown sugar

3 cinnamon sticks

1 orange, halved

About 10 fresh thyme sprigs

3 garlic cloves, smashed

1 tbsp fennel seeds

1 tsp coriander seeds

3 bay leaves

One 2½- to 3-lb/1.2- to 1.4-kg boneless pork loin

OREGANO MOJO

1 cup/55 g finely chopped fresh oregano

½ cup/120 ml extra-virgin olive oil

⅓ cup/80 ml freshly squeezed lime juice

3 large garlic cloves, smashed and minced

1 tsp kosher salt

1 tsp freshly ground white pepper

SLOW-ROASTED BALSAMIC ONIONS

1 tsp kosher salt

½ tsp freshly ground black pepper

1 cup/240 ml balsamic vinegar

3 tbsp extra-virgin olive oil

3 medium onions

CHIVE SPAETZLE

2 cups/280 g all-purpose flour

3 large eggs

¾ cup/180 ml whole milk

3 tbsp minced fresh chives

3 tbsp minced fresh flat-leaf parsley

1½ tsp kosher salt

3 tbsp extra-virgin olive oil

TO ROAST THE PORK

2 tbsp kosher salt

2 tbsp freshly ground black pepper

3 tbsp vegetable oil

3 garlic cloves, smashed

5 to 6 fresh oregano sprigs

SPECIAL EQUIPMENT: large stockpot, one or two rimmed baking sheets, pastry brush, large saucepan and colander or perforated pan, roasting rack, meat thermometer

1. **THE DAY BEFORE SERVING, MAKE THE BRINE:** Pour 2 1/2 qt/2.5 L water into the stock-pot, add the salt, brown sugar, cinnamon, orange, thyme, garlic, fennel seeds, coriander seeds, and bay leaves and bring to a boil over high heat, stir-ring to dissolve the salt and sugar. Remove the pot from the heat and let the brine cool completely.

2. Add the pork to the brine, making sure it is totally submerged. Cover and refrigerate overnight.

3. **ONCE THE PORK IS IN THE BRINE, MAKE THE OREGANO *MOJO*:** In a small bowl, combine the oregano, olive oil, lime juice, garlic, salt, and pepper and mix thoroughly. Cover and refrigerate for at least 24 hours before using. The *mojo* can be made up to 1 week in advance and stored in an air-tight container in the refrigerator.

4. **TO MAKE THE ROASTED ONIONS:** Preheat the oven to 325°F/165°C and place a rack in the center of the oven. Sprinkle the baking sheet with the salt and pepper, add the vinegar and olive oil, and stir carefully to combine.

5. Peel the onions, cut a thin slice off both ends, and then cut crosswise (horizontally) into rounds 1/2 in/12 mm thick. Arrange the onion rounds in a single flat layer in the liquid on the baking sheet. Turn the rounds over a few times to coat them evenly with the vinegar-oil mixture, being careful to keep them intact.

6. Cover the baking sheet with aluminum foil or top with the second baking sheet and roast for 20 minutes. Remove the pan from the oven, then, using the pastry brush, baste each round with the vinegar-oil mixture. Re-cover the pan and return it to the oven, rotating it back to front for even roasting. Roast for another 20 minutes. Repeat basting and rotating every 20 minutes for 1 1/2 to 2 hours, or until the inner ring of each onion round is fork-tender. Remove from the oven and set aside until the onions are cool enough to handle, then toss them into a bowl (and adjust the season-ing with more salt if needed). The onions can be made up to 1 week in advance and stored in an air-tight container in the fridge. Serve cool or at room temperature.

7. **TO MAKE THE SPAETZLE:** Scoop the flour into a large bowl, make a well in the middle of the flour, and add the eggs to the well. Using a wooden spoon, slowly stir together the eggs and flour until blended. Add the milk and beat with the spoon until incorporated. The batter will be some-what lumpy. Stir in the chives, parsley, and salt. Cover and refrigerate for 1 hour.

8. Fill the large saucepan with salted water and bring to a boil over high heat. While the water is heating, fill a large bowl with ice cubes, add cold water just to cover the ice, and set aside. Rest the colander in the rim of the pan of boiling water, making sure the bottom is not touching the water. (If it does touch the water, recruit a second pair of hands to hold the colander above the water.)

9. Using a bowl scraper or rubber spatula and working in batches, scrape a large scoop of the chilled batter into the pan or colander. Then, using a back-and-forth motion, scrape the batter through the holes into the boiling water, where it will set into little noodles. In about 45 seconds, the noodles will bob to the top. Using a slotted spoon, remove the noodles and plunge them into the ice bath. Repeat until all of the batter is cooked and the noodles are cooled, then drain the noodles and transfer them to a medium bowl. Add 1½ tbsp of the oil and toss until evenly coated. Store in an airtight container in the fridge until ready to serve. Reserve the remaining 1½ tbsp oil for heating the spaetzle just before serving.

10. **TO ROAST THE PORK:** Remove the pork from the brine and pat dry with paper towels until completely dry. Let the pork come to room temperature for about 30 minutes, and then pat dry again. Preheat the oven to 325°F/165°C, and place a rack in the center of the oven.

11. Place the roasting rack on the baking sheet (you can rinse the baking sheet you used for the onions) and set aside. Sprinkle the pork evenly all over with the salt and pepper. Heat a large skillet over high heat, then add the vegetable oil. When the oil is hot, carefully add the pork loin, fat-side down, then throw in the garlic and oregano. Reduce the heat to medium-high and sear the pork on the first side for 2 to 3 minutes, or until the bottom caramelizes and develops color. Turn the pork over and cook for another minute until it browns.

12. Transfer the pork to the roasting rack on the baking sheet. Pour the drippings and anything left in the skillet over the pork. Roast the pork for 60 to 70 minutes, or until the meat thermometer inserted into the thickest part registers an internal temperature of 135°F/55°C. Remove from the oven and let rest for 10 to 15 minutes before serving.

13. Rinse the skillet used for the pork roast, place it over medium-high heat, and add the remaining 1½ tbsp oil. Add the spaetzle and cook, stirring occasionally, for 7 to 8 minutes, or until crispy and golden brown. Transfer to a serving bowl.

14. Cut the pork loin into slices ½ in/12 mm thick and arrange on a platter to serve. Pass the spaetzle, slow-roasted onions, and oregano *mojo* at the table.

BONELESS BEEF SHORT RIBS
with Parmesan Polenta

One of the responsibilities of every Flour manager is to taste the food and pastry as much as possible, every single day. That might sound obvious and easy, but sometimes we get so caught up in running the bakeries that we forget to eat. I often have to remind everyone, including myself, to take things home if they're too busy to try things at work. Chef Corey offered these short ribs on his dinner menu one crazy cold winter week, and I brought them home to my husband for dinner. Our former long-time general manager, Aaron, brought them home to his wife the same night. That night we both texted Corey with different variations of the message: "Best. Dinner. Ever."

Chef Corey serves the ribs with his ridiculously easy and amazingly delicious polenta. Once you have made this polenta, I guarantee that you will declare it one of the mainstays of your recipe collection. I made it for my parents recently, and what should have served four people served one mom and one dad quite happily.

SERVES 4

2 lb/910 g boneless beef short ribs

1 tbsp kosher salt

1 tsp freshly ground black pepper

1 tbsp vegetable oil

1 medium onion, cut into ½-in/12-mm pieces

1 celery stalk, thinly sliced

1 large carrot, peeled and thinly sliced crosswise

3 garlic cloves, smashed and minced

2 tbsp tomato paste

About 4 cups/960 ml Vegetable Stock (page 279)

1 tbsp Worcestershire sauce

2 fresh thyme sprigs

1 fresh rosemary sprig

PARMESAN POLENTA

3 cups/720 ml Vegetable Stock (page 279) or water

2 cups/480 ml whole milk

1½ tsp kosher salt

1 cup/160 to 200 g (depending on coarseness) coarsely ground polenta

1 cup/100 g freshly grated Parmesan cheese

½ tsp freshly ground white pepper

¼ cup/15 g chopped fresh flat-leaf parsley for garnish

SPECIAL EQUIPMENT: Dutch oven

1. The night before serving, cut the short ribs into four equal pieces, and rub liberally all over with salt and pepper. Refrigerate in a covered container overnight.

2. The next day, remove the short ribs from the fridge and let sit at room temperature for about 1 hour.

3. About 20 minutes before you are ready to cook the ribs, preheat the oven to 350°F/180°C, and place a rack in the center of the oven.

4. In the Dutch oven, heat the vegetable oil over high heat until it is shimmering. Carefully add the short ribs, fat-side down, and sear for 2 minutes. Do not disturb or move the pot or ribs for the entire 2 minutes to allow the ribs to sear and caramelize. After 2 minutes, turn the ribs and sear the second side for about 1 minute. Sear the remaining two sides for 30 seconds to 1 minute each. When the ribs are seared on all sides, remove them from the pot and set aside.

5. Reduce the heat to medium-high and add the onion, celery, carrot, garlic, and tomato paste to the Dutch oven. Using a wooden spoon, immediately stir and scrape up all of the caramelized bits from the bottom (these browned bits, called the *fond*, add lots of flavor to your ribs) and cook for 6 to 8 minutes, or until the vegetables have softened and are browned and covered with *fond*.

6. Place the ribs on top of the vegetables. Pour in enough stock to reach three-fourths of the way up the sides of the ribs. (If you have run out of stock, use water.) Add the Worcestershire sauce, thyme, and rosemary and bring to a boil. Cover the pot, transfer to the oven, and braise for about 3 hours, or until the meat is completely tender when stabbed with a fork.

7. **JUST BEFORE THE SHORT RIBS ARE READY TO COME OUT OF THE OVEN, BEGIN MAKING THE POLENTA:** In a large saucepan, bring the stock, milk, and salt to a boil over high heat. Whisking continuously, add the polenta in a slow, steady stream. Reduce the heat to very low and simmer, stirring often with a wooden spoon, for 15 to 18 minutes, or until the polenta is thick and creamy. Remove from the heat and stir in the Parmesan and pepper. (Taste and adjust with more salt if needed.) Keep warm until serving.

8. Remove the pot from the oven and let the ribs rest in the sauce for 10 to 15 minutes.

9. Divide the polenta equally among four plates and top with the short ribs. Spoon some of the braised vegetables with the meat juices over the ribs. Sprinkle with the parsley and serve immediately.

paRty time

Great food makes a great party. More than almost any factor, the food you serve at a party shapes the mood, the theme, the degree of formality, and, let's be honest, your guests' memories of your fete. At Flour, we adore being a part of special occasions. It's an honor when customers ask us to prepare the food for a once-in-a-lifetime celebration, a casual gathering of friends, and everything in between. These favorite recipes will become your go-to dishes the next time you want to serve something memorable.

snacks

FLOUR PICKLES

At Flour2, Chef Jeff often makes a big batch of pickles for snacking. He loves to add them to sandwich specials and to chop them up and mix them into potato and egg salads. One day he decided to put a few pickles into a little take-out container and sell them up front along with the panoply of pastries that fill the counter. They were gone within a few minutes. These pickles have since gained quite a loyal following, and when customers don't see them on the counter, they often request them.

MAKES 1½ QT/930 G

4 English cucumbers, cut crosswise into rounds ¼ in/6 mm thick

1½ cups/300 g granulated sugar

1½ cups/360 ml Champagne vinegar

2 tbsp kosher salt

4 tsp pickling spice

1 tsp mustard seeds

1 tsp celery seeds

1 tsp fennel seeds

1 tsp ground turmeric

1 tsp freshly ground black pepper

½ tsp ground cloves

½ tsp chili powder

1. Put the cucumber rounds in a large container with a lid. In a medium saucepan, combine the sugar and vinegar, bring to a boil over high heat, and boil until the sugar dissolves. Remove the pan from the heat, add the salt, pickling spice, mustard seeds, celery seeds, fennel seeds, turmeric, pepper, cloves, and chili powder and stir to combine. Pour the brine over the cucumbers and set aside at warm room temperature for 2 to 3 hours, or until cool.

2. When the pickles have cooled to room temperature, cover and refrigerate them. The pickles are ready to serve after they have chilled for at least 8 hours. They may be stored in an airtight container in the fridge for up to 3 weeks.

SPECTACULAR SPICED PECANS

One of my must-haves for any recipe is that I have to want to eat it all the time. When I'm testing a recipe, I take a tester piece of whatever I am making—pie, cake, cookie—and if I find myself reaching for it again long after the official tasting is over, I know I have a winner. Aniceto, who was the chef at Flour1 for four years and is now back with us as the chef at Flour3, shared with us a spicy, nutty treat that he learned to make during his time at Radius restaurant in Boston. He had used it there as a salad garnish, and he regaled us with tales of having to make double or triple batches to avoid running out, because so many cooks would grab the nuts right off the cooling tray. As soon as Aniceto told me that, I knew I wanted to replicate this addictive snack. It's a simple treat with just a few ingredients, but I'll bet that once you eat one, you won't be able to stop.

MAKES ABOUT 2½ CUPS/300 G

2 cups/200 g pecan halves

½ cup/100 g granulated sugar

1½ to 2 tsp cayenne pepper (use a smaller amount for milder spice)

¼ tsp kosher salt

SPECIAL EQUIPMENT: rimmed baking sheet, parchment paper

1. Preheat the oven to 350°F/180°C, and place a rack in the center of the oven. Line the baking sheet with parchment paper.

2. In a saucepan, combine the pecans, sugar, cayenne, salt, and ¼ cup/60 ml water over medium heat, stirring constantly with a wooden spoon. Continue stirring for 8 to 10 minutes (the timing will vary depending on your stove), or until the sugar crystallizes, coats the pecans, and turns a sandy white. It may seem like there is no way the sugar will become sandy, so be patient and keep stirring, and soon you'll be rewarded with sandy-coated nuts.

3. Remove the pan from the heat and pour the mixture onto the prepared baking sheet, spreading the nuts in a single layer. Bake for 12 to 15 minutes, or until the pecans are toasted inside. To test if they are ready, break a nut open; the interior should be a light golden brown. Let the pecans cool on the baking sheet for 20 to 30 minutes, or until they are cool enough to handle, then transfer them to an airtight container. They will keep at room temperature for up to 2 weeks.

GOUGÈRES

I had been making *pâte à choux*, the light pastry dough used to fashion cream puffs, for years as a professional pastry chef before I learned about this savory version. Once I heard about it, it was like a light bulb had gone off in my head: *of course* you can make a tremendous predinner nibble if you whip up some *pâte à choux* and mix a ridiculous amount of cheese into it. These cheesy, gooey pastry puffs go together quickly and store well in the freezer, and you are guaranteed to look like a pro when you serve a warm batch of them to your friends and family.

MAKES ABOUT 18

½ cup/115 g unsalted butter

1 tbsp granulated sugar

¼ tsp kosher salt

1 cup plus 1 tbsp/150 g unbleached all-purpose flour

4 large eggs

1½ cups/170 g shredded Gruyère cheese

SPECIAL EQUIPMENT: two rimmed baking sheets, parchment paper, stand mixer with paddle attachment (optional), pastry bag and 1-in/2.5-cm round pastry tip (optional)

1. Preheat the oven to 400°F/200°C, and place one rack in the center and one rack in the top third of the oven. Line the baking sheets with parchment paper.

2. In a medium saucepan, combine the butter, sugar, salt, and 1 cup/240 ml water and heat over medium heat until the butter has melted. Do not let the mixture come to a boil or some of the water will evaporate. Add the flour all at once, then stir the flour into the liquid with a wooden spoon until it is fully incorporated. The mixture will look like a really stiff pancake batter. Keep stirring vigorously over medium heat until the mixture slowly starts to look more like loose dough and less like stiff batter. It will also lose its shine and look more matte. Stir continuously for 3 to 5 minutes, or until the dough starts to leave a film at the bottom of the pan.

3. Remove the pan from the heat and transfer the dough to the stand mixer. Beat the dough on medium-low speed for 1 minute. This will allow some of the steam to escape and the dough to cool slightly. (Or, in a medium bowl, vigorously beat the mixture by hand with a wooden spoon for 2 to 3 minutes.) Crack the eggs into a small pitcher and whisk to break up the yolks. On medium-low speed (or beating vigorously by hand), gradually add the eggs to the dough. When the eggs have been added, increase the speed to medium and beat for about 20 seconds, or until the dough is glossy and shiny. Remove the bowl from the mixer and add the Gruyère. Using the wooden spoon or a rubber spatula, mix well to incorporate the cheese completely.

4. Fit the pastry bag with the pastry tip and fill the bag with the dough. If you don't have a pastry bag and tip, cut 1 in/2.5 cm from one corner of a plastic storage bag and fill the plastic bag with the dough. Pipe out balls about 1½ in/4 cm in diameter onto the prepared baking sheets, spacing the balls about 2 in/5 cm apart. If the balls form a peak on top, moisten your fingertip with water and tap down the peaks.

5. Place the baking sheets in the oven. The heat of the oven will immediately start turning the liquid in the batter into steam, which will cause the pastries to inflate. After about 10 minutes, when the pastries have puffed up and are starting to turn golden brown, reduce the oven temperature to 325°F/165°C, then switch the baking sheets between the oven racks and rotate the sheets back to front. Continue to bake for another 25 to 28 minutes, or until the pastries are evenly golden brown without any pale spots. Let the pastries cool on the baking sheets on wire racks until they are cool enough to handle, then serve immediately.

Note: The pastries can be cooled completely and stored in an airtight container at room temperature for up to 1 day. Refresh them in a 300°F/150°C oven for about 5 minutes before serving. They can also be stored in an airtight container in the freezer for up to 3 weeks and then refreshed in a 300°F/150°C oven for 10 to 12 minutes, or until warm and crisp.

FLAKY PARMESAN CHEESE STRAWS

When I opened Flour, I quickly learned how to apply my pastry skills to the savory side of the kitchen. Buttery biscuits became toppings for potpies, flaky pie dough became the base for wonderfully tender quiches, cream-puff pastry turned into cheesy *gougères*. These Parmesan straws are among my favorite of the sweet-pastry-turned-savory-treat persuasion. Puff pastry is typically used in the dessert kitchen to create sweet treats like napoleons (*mille-feuille*) and *palmiers*. Here, the magic of puff with its thousands of layers of butter and dough make these cheese straws shatteringly crisp. You can make them ahead of time and store them in your freezer, so that you always have an impressive predinner snack ready to bake and serve to guests.

MAKES 24 STRAWS

½ batch Puff Pastry dough (page 286)

1 large egg

1½ cups/150 g freshly grated Parmesan cheese

SPECIAL EQUIPMENT: rimmed baking sheet, parchment paper, rolling pin, pastry brush, pizza cutter (optional)

1. Line the baking sheet with parchment paper and set aside.

2. Place the puff pastry on a generously floured work surface and roll into a rectangle about 20 in/50 cm wide and 8 in/20 cm from top to bottom. Break the egg into a small bowl and whisk with a fork. Using the pastry brush, brush the dough with about half of the egg. Sprinkle the dough evenly with about half of the cheese, and then press down with your hands so the cheese adheres to the dough. Flip the dough over and repeat on the second side with the remaining egg wash and cheese.

3. Using the pizza cutter or a sharp knife, cut the rectangle vertically into strips about ¾ in/2 cm wide and 8 in/20 cm long. One at a time, pick up each strip in the center and gently twist it in opposite directions as you move your fingers to the ends of the strip, working until you have a tightly twisted cheese straw. As the twisted straws are shaped, place them about 1 in/2.5 cm apart on the prepared baking sheet. When the pan is full, place it in the fridge and allow the dough to rest for at least 20 minutes or overnight. (The straws can be stored in an airtight container in the freezer for up to 3 months, then baked straight from the freezer as directed.)

4. Meanwhile, preheat the oven to 350°F/180°C, and place a rack in the center of the oven.

5. Remove the cheese straws from the refrigerator and bake for 30 to 40 minutes, or until golden brown. Let cool on the pan and serve. Straws are best eaten the day they are baked but you can store them in an airtight container for up to 2 days and re-crisp in a 300°F/150°C oven for 6 to 8 minutes.

SCALLION PANCAKES

I grew up eating scallion pancakes in every shape and form. They were an easy snack that my mom bought frozen in the Asian grocery store, we made them carefully from scratch with my aunt when she visited from Taiwan, and we ordered them every time we went out for dinner at a Chinese restaurant. I learned quickly that there are huge variations in what you get, from a flaky, salty delicacy to a greasy, chewy, flavorless forgery.

When I opened Flour, it hit me that our popular focaccia dough would make an awesome fried dough, that guilty pleasure sold at outdoor fairs. And then I had a eureka moment and realized that the focaccia would make an even more awesome scallion pancake. The yeasted dough would fry up lighter and airier than the traditional dough, and I could combine the best of both worlds. At Myers+Chang, we use the focaccia dough from Flour, spread it with a mixture of sesame oil and scallions, shape it into rounds, and then fry the rounds to make the ultimate scallion pancake. They are a staff and customer favorite.

MAKES 3 LARGE PANCAKES

8 or 9 scallions, white and green parts, minced

¼ cup/60 ml sesame oil

1¼ tsp kosher salt

½ batch Flour Focaccia dough (see page 282), or 1 lb/455 g store-bought pizza dough

About 1½ cups/360 ml vegetable oil, for frying

SOY DIPPING SAUCE

3 tbsp soy sauce

½ tsp Sriracha sauce

½ tsp sesame oil

1 tbsp peeled and finely minced fresh ginger

1 tsp rice vinegar

1 tbsp granulated sugar

1 scallion, white and green parts, minced

SPECIAL EQUIPMENT: rimmed baking sheet, rolling pin

1. In a small bowl, mix together the scallions, sesame oil, and salt.

2. Cut the dough into thirds. On a well-floured work surface, roll out one portion of the dough into a thin 5-by-10-in/12-by-25-cm rectangle. Repeat with the remaining two dough portions. Spread the scallion mixture evenly over the dough rectangles, leaving a ½-in/12-mm border uncovered on all sides. Starting at a long side, roll up each rectangle jelly-roll style and pinch the seam with your fingers to seal. Spiral each cylinder into a tight coil and tuck the ends under the coil. Place in a warm area, cover loosely with plastic wrap, and let rest for about 2 hours to allow the dough to proof and relax. (At this point, the dough can be stored in an airtight container in the fridge overnight or in the freezer for up to 1 week; thaw in the fridge overnight before using.)

3. Line the baking sheet with a double layer of paper towels. Set aside.

CONTINUED

4. On a generously floured work surface, press each coil into a flat circle, deflating any air pockets and squishing the scallions gently into the dough. With the rolling pin, slowly and carefully roll out each flattened circle into a 10-in/25-cm round. Flour the dough and work surface as needed to prevent the dough from sticking. (It's okay if some of the scallion mixture comes out.) As you finish rolling each round, set it aside.

5. In a large skillet, heat the vegetable oil over medium-high heat until it is shimmering.

6. **WHILE THE OIL IS HEATING, MAKE THE DIPPING SAUCE:** In a small bowl, whisk together the soy sauce, Sriracha sauce, sesame oil, ginger, vinegar, sugar, and scallion until the sugar has dissolved. Set aside. (The sauce can be made up to 1 week in advance and stored in the fridge in an airtight container.)

7. To check if the oil is ready, sprinkle a bit of flour into the skillet. If it sizzles on contact, the oil is ready. Carefully add one pancake to the hot oil and fry, turning once, for 1 to 2 minutes per side, or until golden. Transfer the pancake to the prepared baking sheet. Repeat with the remaining pancakes, always allowing the oil to return to temperature before adding the next one.

8. Cut the pancakes into quarters, arrange on a platter, and serve hot with the dipping sauce.

GOAT CHEESE, PORTOBELLO, AND CUMIN EMPANADITAS

When I was the pastry chef at Mistral, I would stuff myself with the empanadas, little turn-overs filled with meat and cheese, that the prep staff would bring to work daily for lunch. Gloria, Tommy, Luiz, and Vanel introduced me to their world of Latin American foods that I'd never tried before. I promised them I would create a dish in their honor when I left Mistral to open Flour. These *empanaditas*, or mini empanadas, were my farewell gift. I flavored goat cheese with roasted portobello mushrooms and a pinch of earthy cumin and used the mixture to fill puff pastry pockets. My meat-loving friends were skeptical of this vegetarian version, but once they tried these pastries, they went crazy for them. They were also among the first items I put on our opening catering menu. Make a bunch, store them in your freezer, and have a flaky, tasty treat ready to bake off whenever you want something quick and wonderful for guests.

MAKES ABOUT 24 EMPANADITAS

2 or 3 large/225 g portobello mushrooms
2 tbsp vegetable oil
½ tsp kosher salt
¼ tsp freshly ground black pepper
8 oz/225 g soft fresh goat cheese, at room temperature
½ tsp ground cumin
1 batch Puff Pastry dough (page 286)
1 large egg

SPECIAL EQUIPMENT: rimmed baking sheet, parchment paper, rolling pin, pastry brush

1. Remove and discard the stems from the mushrooms and wipe the caps clean. Using a spoon, scrape out the dark gills on the underside of each cap. Roughly chop the mushrooms into about 1-in/2.5-cm pieces.

2. In a medium skillet, heat the vegetable oil over high heat. Add the mushrooms, reduce the heat to medium, and cook, stirring with a wooden spoon, for 4 to 5 minutes, or until the mushrooms soften. Add the salt and pepper and remove from the heat.

3. When the mushrooms are cool enough to handle, chop them finely and transfer them to a medium bowl. Add the goat cheese and cumin and mix thoroughly with a wooden spoon. Set aside.

4. Line the baking sheet with parchment paper. On a well-floured work surface, roll the puff pastry into a rectangle about 28 in/65 cm wide and 12 in/30.5 cm from top to bottom. The dough may seem pretty tough and difficult to roll out at first. Don't be afraid to be firm with the dough as you roll it into the rectangle, flip it upside down, turn it side to side, and pound it with the rolling pin to flatten it. Using a 3½- to 4-in/9- to 10-cm round cutter, cut out as many circles as possible. Gather up and reroll the scraps and cut out as many additional circles as possible. You should have about twenty-four circles.

5. Break the egg into a small bowl and whisk with a fork. Using the pastry brush, brush the entire top surface of each pastry circle with some of the egg wash. Place a rounded 1 tsp of filling on one half of each circle, leaving a narrow border uncovered to allow for sealing the circle. Working carefully, stretch the dough circle and fold it in half to make a half-moon. With your fingers, pinch the edges together. Then, using the tines of the fork, firmly press the edges to seal well. Repeat with the remaining dough circles. As the half-moons are formed, transfer them to the prepared baking sheet, spacing them about 1 in/2.5 cm apart. When the pan is full, place it in the fridge and allow the dough to rest for about 15 minutes. (At this point, the pastries can be well wrapped in plastic wrap and stored in an airtight container in the freezer for up to 3 months, then baked straight from the freezer as directed. Add on 4 to 5 minutes to baking time.)

6. Meanwhile, preheat the oven to 350°F/180°C, and place a rack in the center of the oven.

7. Using the pastry brush, brush the tops of the pastries with the remaining egg wash. Use a paring knife to cut a small slit in the top of each empanadita to allow steam to escape. Bake for 40 to 50 minutes, or until evenly golden brown and baked through. Look at the sides of the empanaditas where the pastry has puffed up to make sure they are golden brown. Transfer the empanaditas to a wire rack and let cool for at least 30 minutes before serving to allow the filling to cool. They taste best on the day they are baked, but you can hold them in an airtight container for up to 2 days and then refresh them in a 300°F/150°C oven for 5 to 8 minutes, or until warmed through.

dESSeRts

PAVLOVA
with Plums, Figs, and Plum Wine

Named after Russian ballerina Anna Pavlova and created in her honor during a tour of Australia and New Zealand, a Pavlova is a delicate, crisp-yet-soft meringue shell filled with fruit and cream. Not only is it fun and easy to make, it's also gorgeous and delicious. I created this Pavlova to serve at Myers+Chang, where we are always looking for desserts to complement our addictive menu. At the restaurant, we make individual meringues and top them with fresh plums and figs marinated in plum wine that meld marvelously with the simple vanilla whipped cream. This large version is impressive and dramatic and makes for a great dinner-party dessert.

SERVES 8 TO 10

PAVLOVA

6 egg whites

1¼ cups/250 g granulated sugar

2 tbsp cornstarch, sifted

⅛ tsp kosher salt

1 tsp vanilla extract

PLUM COMPOTE

3 ripe black or red plums

10 or 12 ripe figs

1 cup/240 ml plum wine

½ cup/100 g granulated sugar

Pinch of kosher salt

WHIPPED CREAM

2 cups/480 ml heavy cream

¼ cup/35 g confectioners' sugar

1 tsp vanilla extract

A few fresh mint leaves for garnish

SPECIAL EQUIPMENT: rimmed baking sheet, parchment paper, stand mixer with whisk attachment or handheld mixer

1. **TO MAKE THE PAVLOVA:** Preheat the oven to 200°F/95°C, and place a rack in the center of the oven. Line a baking sheet with parchment paper, and trace a 9-in/23-cm circle in the center of the paper. Flip the parchment over (so your pencil or pen won't mark your Pavlova) and coat the parchment liberally with nonstick cooking spray. Then coat it again.

CONTINUED

2. Using the stand mixer or handheld mixer and a large bowl, beat the egg whites on medium speed for about 1 minute. The whites will start to froth and turn into bubbles and eventually the yellowy viscous part will disappear. Keep beating until you can see the tines of the whisk or beaters leaving a slight trail in the whites. With the mixer still on medium speed, slowly add the granulated sugar in six to eight equal additions, beating for about 30 seconds after each addition. It should take 4 to 5 minutes to add all of the sugar. When all of the granulated sugar has been incorporated into the egg whites, increase the mixer speed to medium-high and beat for about 1 minute longer. Using a rubber spatula, fold in the cornstarch, salt, and vanilla. The meringue batter will be gloppy and sticky looking.

3. Scrape the meringue batter into a tall mountain in the middle of the circle on the prepared baking sheet. With the back of a spoon, create a well in the middle of the meringue and spread it out to fill the 9-in/23-cm circle. You want to shape the meringue into a bowl with sides 2 to 3 in/5 to 7.5 cm high.

4. Bake the meringue for 3 to 4 hours, or until it is firm to the touch and if you press it with your fingertips they do not poke through the surface. It should be crispy on the outside and somewhat soft on the inside. Turn off the heat and let the meringue sit in the closed oven for another 2 hours.

5. Remove the meringue from the oven and carefully peel it off the parchment paper. (The meringue can be made up to 2 days in advance and stored in an airtight container at room temperature.)

6. **TO MAKE THE PLUM COMPOTE:** Halve and pit the plums and cut them into slices ¼ in/6 mm thick. Trim the stem off each fig and then quarter the figs lengthwise. Put the fruit in a heatproof medium bowl. In a small saucepan, combine the wine, granulated sugar, and salt and heat over high heat just to a boil, stirring to dissolve the sugar. Reduce the heat to medium and simmer for 1 to 2 minutes, or until the syrup thickens slightly. Pour the syrup over the plums and figs and set aside for at least 3 hours, or until cool. (The compote can be made up to 2 days in advance and stored in an airtight container in the refrigerator. Bring back to room temperature before using.)

7. **WHEN READY TO SERVE THE PAVLOVA, MAKE THE WHIPPED CREAM:** Using the mixer or a whisk and a bowl, whip together the cream, confectioners' sugar, and vanilla until soft peaks form. Don't overwhip! You want your cream to be soft and billowy.

8. Spread the cream over the meringue, leaving 2 to 3 in/5 to 7.5 cm around the edge of the meringue exposed. Using a slotted spoon, remove the plums and figs from the syrup, reserving the syrup, and arrange the fruit on the cream. Drizzle the entire dessert with a few spoonfuls of the syrup and garnish with the mint. Serve immediately.

LEMON-GINGER MOUSSE

People often ask me if I recommend cooking school as a good way to get started in the culinary field. Although I didn't go to culinary school myself, I do know many chefs who did, and I always say it depends on both the person and the school.

But if I could have that person work for pastry chef Rick Katz, as I did for my first pastry job, I would tell them that working under Rick would be more valuable than going to the ten best schools rolled into one. Among the many lessons that Rick taught me was that you don't need to depend on fillers such as gelatin and cornstarch to make delectable desserts. With mousses, for example, he preferred to stabilize them instead with more chocolate or more butter or more anything-that-helped-enhance-flavor. I took that lesson with me, and when I was creating a light lemony mousse to serve at Myers+Chang, I recalled how Rick made a luscious mousse by simply folding firmly whipped cream into lemon curd. So I infused whipped cream with fresh and ground ginger, made a bright lemon curd, and gently folded the two together. It is Christopher's all-time favorite item on our menu. The mousse is delicious as is, or try layering it with fruit and cake cubes for a fun quick trifle.

SERVES 6 TO 8

2½ cups/600 ml heavy cream

3-in/7.5-cm piece fresh ginger, unpeeled and roughly chopped

½ tsp ground ginger

2½ cups/735 g Lemon Curd (page 291)

½ cup/80 g chopped crystallized ginger for garnish

SPECIAL EQUIPMENT: sieve, stand mixer with whisk attachment or handheld mixer

1. In a medium saucepan, combine the cream and fresh and ground ginger and bring to just under a boil over high heat. Remove from the heat and let the cream sit for about 1 hour to infuse with the ginger. Transfer to an airtight container and refrigerate for at least overnight or up to 4 days.

2. When you are ready to serve the mousse, strain the chilled cream into the bowl of the stand mixer or into a large bowl if using a handheld mixer. Whip the cream on medium speed until it holds a stiff peak. Then, using a rubber spatula, fold the lemon curd into the whipped cream just until fully incorporated.

3. Divide the mousse equally among serving bowls and top with the candied ginger. Serve immediately.

SUGARED CRÊPES
with Rum-Butterscotch Bananas

Most people don't make crêpes at home any-more, and that's a shame, because they are not only easy but also really fun to make. And you can make them in advance, which makes them ideal for a dinner party, when the last thing you want to be doing is fretting over the stove or oven trying to pull together your impressive dessert course.

A few tips before you start: First, make sure your butter and milk are at room temperature so they will combine easily to make the batter. If your milk is cold, it will cause the melted butter to harden, and you'll have lumps of butter in your batter. Second, a nonstick skillet or crêpe pan will make easy work of cooking the crêpes. The first few crêpes you make are likely to stick or burn or come out lopsided, because you're not yet sure how quickly to spread the batter or what the exact heat level should be. Once you get the hang of it, though, crêpes are fun to cook. Finally, when you are flipping a crêpe, use a spatula or your fingers to first lift up the edges all around to release it from the pan. That way, when you finally turn the crêpe over it won't stick on one side and tear. The amount of batter this recipe makes assumes that you'll mess up a few, so don't fret if the first ones come out wrong.

MAKES ABOUT 12 CRÊPES
(SERVES 4 TO 6)

CRÊPES

1 cup/140 g all-purpose flour
2 tsp granulated sugar
½ tsp kosher salt
4 large eggs, at room temperature
5 tbsp/70 g unsalted butter, melted and cooled, plus 1 to 2 tbsp, at room temperature
1¾ cups/420 ml milk, at room temperature

RUM-BUTTERSCOTCH BANANAS

½ cup/110 g packed brown sugar
⅓ cup/80 ml heavy cream
2 tbsp unsalted butter
1 tsp vanilla extract
2 tbsp dark rum
⅛ tsp kosher salt
4 bananas, perfectly ripe, cut on the diagonal into slices ½ in/12 mm thick

1 to 2 tbsp unsalted butter, melted, for crisping the crêpes

2 to 3 tbsp confectioners' sugar, for sugaring the crêpes

Vanilla ice cream or crème fraîche for serving (optional)

SPECIAL EQUIPMENT: 10-in/25-cm nonstick pan, baking sheet, sieve, candy thermometer

1. **TO MAKE THE CRÊPES:** The night before, in a large bowl, stir together the flour, granulated sugar, and salt. In a medium bowl, whisk together the eggs, melted butter, and milk. Make a well in the center of the dry ingredients and pour the wet ingredients into the well. Whisk the wet and dry ingredients together until well combined and no lumps remain. Transfer the batter to an airtight container and refrigerate overnight.

2. The next day, remove the crêpe batter from the fridge and give it a good whisk to recombine everything. Heat the skillet over medium heat. Add 2 to 3 tsp of the room-temperature butter and then tilt the skillet from side to side to cover the bottom evenly with melting butter. Using your right hand (if you are right-handed) and position-ing it at one side of the skillet, pour in a scant ¼ cup/60 ml of the batter and then immediately lift up and tilt the skillet with your left hand, mov-ing it back and forth to distribute the batter evenly

over the bottom of the pan. Cook for 1 to 2 minutes, or until the edges of the crêpe start to curl up and look dry. The bottom of the crêpe should start to look golden brown. When you can pull up the crêpe from the edge, carefully flip it over with a spatula and cook it for another 25 to 30 seconds, or until the bottom is lightly browned. Transfer the crêpe to a plate and repeat with the remaining batter. If the crêpes start to stick to the skillet, add a little more butter to reseason the pan. As the crêpes are ready, stack them one on top of another—no parchment or wax paper is needed between them. (The crêpes can be made up to 2 days in advance, well wrapped in plastic wrap, and stored in the fridge.)

3. About 20 minutes before serving, preheat the oven to 350°F/180°C, and place a rack in the center of the oven.

4. **TO PREPARE THE BANANAS:** In a small, heavy saucepan, combine the brown sugar with about ¼ cup/60 ml water, or enough to dissolve the sugar, and stir until the sugar has dissolved. Bring to a boil over high heat and continue to boil, swirling the pan continuously as it starts to boil to ensure even caramelization, until the syrup reaches 280°F/138°C on the candy thermometer. Immediately remove from the heat and slowly whisk in the cream. Work carefully, as the steam coming off the caramel is very hot and the cream may cause the caramel to splatter.

5. Return the pan to medium-high heat and boil for 2 to 3 minutes. Slowly whisk in the butter and vanilla, and then mix in the rum and salt. Add the bananas and toss to coat evenly. Reduce the heat to low and cook for about 1 minute, or until the bananas have softened a bit and are completely covered in butterscotch. Keep warm.

6. Fold each crêpe into quarters and arrange them, touching and overlapping a bit, on the baking sheet. Brush the crêpes with the melted butter for crisping, then, using the sieve, dust them evenly with the confectioners' sugar. Heat the crêpes in the oven for 3 to 4 minutes, or until they are warmed through and the sugar has started to melt.

7. Remove the crêpes from the oven and transfer them to dessert plates, putting two or three crêpes on each plate. Spoon an equal amount of the bananas over each serving and top with ice cream, if desired.

APPLE PITHIVIER

When I started working at Payard Pâtisserie in New York City, I had already been a pastry chef in Boston for a few years. I couldn't wait to see what this French guy could teach me. On my first day, I was handed a stack of recipes—all in French—and immediately realized it would be a challenging year. I spoke and read basic French, but I was pretty hazy on much of the baking vocabulary, and there were many words I'd never even seen before. *Pithivier* was one of them. I didn't even know how to pronounce it. (It's pee-tee-vee-YAY.) "Watch and learn," Chef Payard told me. He sandwiched a mound of rum-scented almond cream between two large squares of homemade puff pastry and then quickly scalloped the edges of the pastry to look like a sunflower. Slash-slash-slash went his paring knife over the top pastry as he etched sun rays into the surface. The whole thing went into the oven and emerged golden brown with a glorious starburst pattern on top. It put every other pastry I had ever made previously to shame.

At Flour, we give our own spin to the *pithivier* by omitting the rum and adding a thick layer of caramelized apple butter atop the almond cream. It's a spectacular dessert.

SERVES 8 TO 10

VANILLA APPLE BUTTER

6 apples, such as Granny Smith, peeled, halved, cored, and roughly chopped

4 tbsp/55 g unsalted butter

1 cup/200 g granulated sugar

¼ tsp kosher salt

½ vanilla bean

1 batch Puff Pastry dough (page 286)

1 cup/240 ml Frangipane (page 292)

1 large egg

SPECIAL EQUIPMENT: rimmed baking sheet, parchment paper, rolling pin, bench scraper (optional), offset spatula (optional), pastry brush

1. **TO MAKE THE APPLE BUTTER:** In a large saucepan, combine the apples, butter, sugar, and salt. Split the vanilla bean in half lengthwise and scrape the seeds directly into the pan (save the pods for adding to a canister of granulated sugar for vanilla sugar). Place over low heat and cook, stirring occasionally, for 30 to 40 minutes, or until the apples break down and the mixture thickens and turns golden brown. The mixture will release a lot of water at first and bubble a lot and then it will slowly start to caramelize and get a bit darker; there may still be some pieces of whole apple, which is fine. Remove from the heat and let cool. (The apple butter can be stored in an airtight container in the fridge for up to 4 days or in the freezer for up to 2 weeks.)

2. Line the baking sheet with parchment paper and set aside. On a well-floured work surface, roll the puff pastry into a rectangle about 24 in/61 cm wide and 12 in/30.5 cm from top to bottom. The dough may seem pretty tough and difficult to roll out at first. Don't be afraid to be firm with the dough as you roll it into the rectangle, flip it upside down, turn it side to side, pound it with the rolling pin to flatten it. Use a chef's knife to trim away any rough edges. Then, using the knife or a bench scraper, cut the dough in half vertically. You should have two 12-in/30.5-cm squares.

CONTINUED

3. Set one square aside and place the other square on the prepared baking sheet. In the center of the square, draw an 8-in/20-cm circle with your finger or lightly with a paring knife (without cutting all the way through). Using the offset spatula or the back of a spoon, spread the frangipane evenly on the pastry, filling just the circle. Top the frangipane with an even layer of the apple butter.

4. Crack the egg into a small bowl and whisk with a fork. Using the pastry brush, brush some of the egg over the pastry around the circle.

5. Again on a well-floured surface, roll the second puff pastry square so that it is slightly larger than 12-in/30.5-cm square. Drape the second square directly over the top of the first square. Using your fingers, press firmly all around the edges of the pastry to seal the two squares together. There will be a big mound in the center where the frangipane and apple butter are. Again, using your fingers, press firmly all around the circle; you want to enclose the frangipane and apple butter as much as you can within the circle.

6. With a small paring knife, cut a scalloped petal pattern around the edge of the puff pastry to create a circle with a total of six or seven petals. Discard the puff pastry scraps (or save them for a quick treat: sprinkle with cinnamon-sugar and bake until golden). Refrigerate the pastry for at least 30 minutes or up to 2 days to allow the puff to chill and relax. (If chilling for longer than 30 minutes, cover the pastry with plastic wrap to prevent it from drying out. At this point, you can also wrap the unbaked pastry well with plastic wrap and freeze it for up to 2 weeks.)

7. Preheat the oven to 350°F/180°C, and place a rack in the center of the oven.

8. Using the pastry brush, brush the entire top of the pastry, including the petals, with the remaining egg wash. Poke a hole in the middle of the circular mound at the center of the *pithivier* and then, starting from the center of this hole, use the tip of the paring knife to trace a curved sun-ray pattern into the mound, spacing the rays 1/2 to 1 in/12 mm

to 2.5 cm apart and covering the entire mound with the curved rays. You should have eighteen to twenty-four rays. Don't cut all the way through the puff; just lightly score the dough with the tip of the knife. Trace a crosshatch pattern on the petals.

9. Bake for 1 hour to 1 hour and 10 minutes, or until the dough is entirely golden brown and baked through. Look at the sides of the *pithivier* where the puff pastry has puffed up to make sure the sides are also golden brown. Remove from the oven and let cool on the pan on a wire rack for at least 1 hour before serving to allow the filling to cool. This pastry is best served the same day, but you can hold it in an airtight container at room temperature for up to 2 days and then refresh it in a 300°F/150°C oven for 5 to 8 minutes before serving.

FRENCH MACARONS

When I was a pastry cook at Payard, I was introduced to these classic French cookies. Until then, I had known only the American-style macaroons with two o's, usually made with coconut and usually not a sandwich cookie. *Macarons*—with one o—were more like little art pieces that happened to taste amazing.

A great *macaron* has four key attributes: an eggshell-gossamer exterior that shatters when you bite into it to reveal a soft, moist almondy interior; a little foot at the base of each cookie that shows off a tiny ruffle of the cookie's interior; a filling that extends to the edge of the cookie so that every bite includes filling; and a cookie soft enough and a filling firm enough so that when you bite down nothing squishes out. The basic cookie recipe lends itself to many variations, four of which follow. You can also try different fillings.

Here are some helpful hints that will produce a great batch of cookies:

- Because confectioners' sugar and almond flour are particularly tricky to measure in a volume measure, you will get the best results if you weigh them for this recipe.

- Use perfectly flat baking sheets and brand-new parchment paper (or silicone baking mats) to ensure a nice round cookie (otherwise they may spread into amoebas).

- Make sure the bowl in which you whip the egg whites is spotlessly clean or the whites will not reach their optimal loft.

- I've had the most success preheating the oven to 325°F/165°C, lowering it to 300°F/150°C immediately after placing the cookies in it, and then rotating the pan back to front at least once during baking to ensure the cookies bake evenly.

- Wait until the cookies are completely cool before you remove them from the baking sheet.

- Remember that even misshapen, bowlegged cookies are delicious.

MAKES ABOUT 24 COOKIES

CONTINUED

1¼ cups/125 g almond flour

1½ cups/210 g confectioners' sugar

4 egg whites, at room temperature and at least a day old (see note)

¼ cup/50 g granulated sugar

1½ cups/400 g Buttercream (page 293)

SPECIAL EQUIPMENT: two perfectly flat baking sheets, parchment paper or two silicone baking mats, sifter or sieve, stand mixer with whisk attachment or handheld mixer, pastry bag and ½-in/12-mm round piping tip

1. Preheat the oven to 325°F/165°C, and place a rack in the middle of the oven. Line the baking sheets with parchment or baking mats and set aside.

2. In a medium bowl, sift together the almond flour and confectioners' sugar. Set side.

3. Using the stand mixer or a handheld mixer and a large bowl, beat the egg whites on medium speed for 1 to 2 minutes, or until soft peaks form. The whites will start to froth and turn into bubbles, and eventually the yellowy viscous part will disappear. Keep beating until you can see the tines of the whisk or beaters leaving a slight trail in the whites. To test for the soft-peak stage, stop the mixer and lift the whisk or beaters out of the whites; the whites should peak and then droop. With the mixer still on medium speed, add 1 tbsp of the granulated sugar and continue to beat for 30 to 45 seconds. Add the remaining granulated sugar, 1 tbsp at a time and beating after each addition for 30 to 45 seconds. When all of the sugar has been incorporated into the egg whites, beat the whites for 1 to 2 minutes, or until they become glossy and shiny.

4. Using a rubber spatula, fold in about half of the almond flour–confectioners' sugar mixture just until most of it is incorporated. Then add the remainder and fold for about 45 seconds, or until the mixture is smooth and a little stiff. It should drop smoothly off the spatula.

5. Fit the pastry bag with the piping tip and fill the bag with the batter. Pipe rounds about 1 in/ 2.5 cm in diameter onto the prepared baking sheets, spacing them 1 in/2.5 cm apart. Try to pipe straight down and flick the tip of the bag when you are done so that a peak doesn't form on the top of the round. The batter should be stiff enough to hold a mound shape but loose enough so that it relaxes into a little circle once it has been piped. When you have finished piping, rap the baking sheets on the countertop a few times to flatten out the mounds and to pop any bubbles that may be in the batter. Let the cookies rest for 20 to 30 minutes, or until they are no longer tacky to the touch.

6. Put one baking sheet in the oven and immediately reduce the heat to 300°F/150°C. After 8 minutes, rotate the baking sheet back to front. These cookies take a total of 15 to 20 minutes, depending on your oven, and are done when they are pale golden brown on top. Remove from the oven and let the cookies cool completely on the pan on a wire rack. Increase the oven temperature to 325°F/165°C, and when the oven is fully preheated, bake the second pan of cookies the same way.

7. Remove the cookies from the pans and line them up by size in pairs. Rinse and dry the pastry bag and piping tip, fit the bag with the tip, and fill the bag with the buttercream. Pipe a large, rounded 1 tbsp buttercream onto the flat side of one cookie in a pair. Top with the second cookie, flat-side down, and press to make a sandwich. The cookies can be stored in an airtight container at room temperature for up to 5 days or in the freezer for up to 2 weeks.

Note: Separate the eggs the night before you plan to make the cookies and store the egg whites in a covered container in the fridge. About 4 hours before you are ready to start the cookies, remove the egg whites from the fridge and let them come to room temperature.

VANILLA MACARONS VARIATION: Split ¼ vanilla bean in half lengthwise and scrape the seeds into the glossy, stiffly beaten egg whites or add 2 tsp vanilla extract, then proceed as directed. If using the seeds, make sure they are evenly distributed in the batter by using the spatula to press the clumps of seeds against the side of the bowl a few times to smear them out.

HAZELNUT MACARONS VARIATION: Substitute ¼ cup/ 25 g hazelnut flour for ¼ cup/25 g of the almond flour and proceed as directed.

LEMON CURD–FILLED MACARONS VARIATION: Omit the buttercream and substitute 1¼ cups/365 g chilled Lemon Curd (page 291).

CHOCOLATE GANACHE–FILLED MACARONS VARIATION: Omit the buttercream and substitute 1 cup/240 g Ganache (page 294).

KOUIGN-AMANN

A specialty of Brittany, the small, rich *kouign-amann*, literally "butter cake," is possibly the most extraordinary pastry of all time. Imagine a flaky croissant–type pastry filled with layers of butter and sugar, and then more butter and sugar, and baked until the sugar caramelizes into a marvelously sticky, crispy coating. The first time I had one—in Paris, of course—I knew I had to make it at Flour. It remains for me the most delicious pastry I've ever eaten.

Nicole, our executive pastry chef, spent hours perfecting the recipe to make sure it has the right balance of sugar to butter to dough, and then tweaked it so that it could be baked in a muffin tin rather than ring molds. Read through the recipe a few times to make sure you understand the directions. If you've made laminated doughs of any kind before (puff pastry, croissant), you'll have no problem with this one. If you haven't, it is not difficult to make, but you'll need to familiarize yourself with the simple technique of folding and turning the dough, explained in the recipe. These small cakes are more of an after-party treat or decadent breakfast than an opulent plated dessert, although if you were to serve them with some ice cream and berries, I guarantee that you would be showered with compliments.

MAKES 12 SMALL CAKES

1⅛ tsp active dry yeast, or 0.35 oz/10 g fresh cake yeast

2¾ cups/385 g all-purpose flour

1¼ tsp kosher salt

1 cup/225 g unsalted butter, at warm room temperature, plus 1 tbsp melted

1½ cups/300 g granulated sugar, plus more for rolling and coating

SPECIAL EQUIPMENT: stand mixer with dough hook (optional), baking sheet, rolling pin, bench scraper (optional), 12-cup standard muffin tin

1. In the stand mixer, mix together the yeast and 1 cup/240 ml tepid water until the yeast dissolves. Add the flour, salt, and 1 tbsp melted butter and mix on low speed for 3 to 4 minutes, or until the dough comes together and is smooth. (If the dough is too wet, add 2 to 3 tbsp flour; if it is too dry, add 2 to 3 tsp of water.) The dough should be soft and supple and should come away from the sides of the bowl when the mixer is on. To make the dough by hand, in a medium bowl, dissolve the yeast in 1 cup/240 ml water as directed and stir in the flour, salt, and melted butter with a wooden spoon until incorporated. Then turn the dough out onto a floured work surface and knead by hand for 8 to 10 minutes, or until the dough is soft, smooth, and supple.

2. Transfer the dough to the baking sheet and cover with plastic wrap. Leave in a warm place for 1 hour to allow the dough to proof. Then transfer the dough to the fridge and leave it for another hour.

3. Transfer the dough from the fridge to a generously floured work surface. Roll it into a rectangle about 16 in/40.5 cm wide and 10 in/25 cm from top to bottom. With your fingers, press or smear the room-temperature butter directly over the right half of the dough, spreading it in a thin, even layer to cover the entire right half. Fold the left half of the dough over the butter, and press down to seal the butter between the dough layers. Turn the dough 90 degrees clockwise so that the rectangle is about 10 in/25 cm wide and 8 in/20 cm top to bottom, and generously flour the underside and top of the dough.

CONTINUED

4. Press the dough down evenly with the palms of your hands, flattening it out before you start to roll it out. Slowly begin rolling the dough from side to side into a rectangle about 24 in/61 cm wide and 12 in/30.5 cm from top to bottom. The dough might be a little sticky, so, again, be sure to flour the dough and the work surface as needed to prevent the rolling pin from sticking. Using the bench scraper or a knife, lightly score the rectangle vertically into thirds. Each third will be about 8 in/20 cm wide and 12 in/30.5 cm from top to bottom. Brush any loose flour off the dough. Lift the right third of the dough and flip it over onto the middle third. Then lift the left third of the dough and flip it on top of the middle and right thirds (like folding a business letter). Your dough should now be about 8 in/20 cm wide, 12 in/30.5 cm from top to bottom, and about 1½ in/4 cm thick. Rotate the dough clockwise 90 degrees; it will now be 12 in/30.5 cm wide and 8 in/20 cm from top to bottom, with the folded seam on top. The process of folding in thirds and rotating is called turning the dough.

5. Repeat the process once more, patiently and slowly roll the dough into a long rectangle, flipping it upside down as needed as you roll it back and forth, and then fold the dough into thirds. The dough will be a bit tougher to roll out and a bit more elastic.

6. Return the dough to the baking sheet and cover it completely with plastic wrap, tucking the plastic wrap under the dough as if you are tucking it into bed. Refrigerate the dough for about 30 minutes. This will relax the dough so that you'll be able to roll it out again and give it more turns. Don't leave the dough in the fridge much longer than 30 minutes, or the butter will harden too much and it won't roll out properly.

7. Remove the dough from the refrigerator and place it on a well-floured work surface with a long side of the rectangle facing you and the seam on top. Again, roll the dough into a rectangle about 24 in/61 cm wide and 12 in/30.5 cm from top to bottom. Sprinkle ¾ cup/150 g of the sugar over the dough and use the rolling pin to gently press it in. Give the dough another fold into thirds and turn as directed previously. The sugar may spill out a bit. That's okay, just scoop it back in.

8. Once again roll the dough into a rectangle 24 in/61 cm wide and 12 in/30.5 cm from top to bottom. Sprinkle the remaining ¾ cup/150 g sugar over the dough and use the rolling pin to press the sugar gently into the dough. Give the dough one last fold into thirds and turn. Return the dough to the baking sheet, cover again with plastic wrap, and refrigerate for another 30 minutes.

9. Meanwhile, liberally butter the cups of the muffin tin and set aside.

10. Remove the dough from the refrigerator. Sprinkle your work surface generously with sugar, place the dough on the sugar, and sprinkle the top with more sugar. Roll the dough into a long rectangle 24 in/61 cm wide and 8 in/20 cm from top to bottom. The sugar will make the dough gritty and sticky, but it will also make the dough easier to roll out. Using a chef's knife, cut the dough in half lengthwise. You should have two strips of dough, each 24 in/61 cm wide and 4 in/10 cm from top to bottom. Cut each strip into six 4-in/10-cm squares.

11. Working with one square at a time, fold the corners of the square into the center and press down so they stick in place. Shape and cup the dough into a little circle, and press the bottom and the top into more sugar so that the entire pastry is evenly coated with sugar. Place the dough circle, folded-side up, into a cup of the prepared muffin tin. It will just barely fit. Repeat with the remaining squares. Cover the tin with plastic wrap and let the cakes proof in a warm place (78° to 82°F/25° to 27°C is ideal) for 1 hour to 1 hour and 20 minutes, or until the dough has pouffed up.

12. About 20 minutes before you are ready to bake, preheat the oven to 400°F/200°C, and place a rack in the center of the oven.

13. When the dough is ready, place the muffin tin in the oven, reduce the heat to 325°F/165°C, and bake for 30 to 40 minutes, or until the cakes are golden brown. Remove the cakes from the oven and let them cool just until you can handle them, then gently pry them out of the muffin tin onto a wire rack and leave them to cool upside down. They are extremely sticky and will stick to the muffin tin if you don't pop them out while they are still warm. Let cool completely before serving.

MAPLE-APPLE UPSIDE-DOWN BUTTERMILK CAKE

This is the best upside-down cake ever: the maple syrup infuses the apples and the cake and makes the whole thing taste like a stack of appley pancakes. Be careful when reducing the maple syrup; it tends to come to a boil quickly and then it will boil hard unless you keep an eye on it and adjust the heat as needed to make sure it is reducing slowly.

SERVES 8 TO 10

1½ cups/355 ml maple syrup

1 cup/225 g plus 2 tbsp unsalted butter, at room temperature

4 Granny Smith or other firm tart apples, halved, peeled, cored, and each half cut into 8 slices

2 cups/280 g all-purpose flour

1 tsp baking powder

½ tsp baking soda

1 tsp kosher salt

2 large eggs, at room temperature

2 egg yolks, at room temperature

¾ cup/180 ml nonfat buttermilk, at room temperature

1 tbsp vanilla extract

1⅓ cups/270 g granulated sugar

Crème fraîche, unsweetened whipped cream, or vanilla ice cream for serving

SPECIAL EQUIPMENT: 10-by-3-in/25-by-7.5-cm round cake pan, stand mixer with paddle attachment or handheld mixer

1. Preheat the oven to 350°F/180°C, and place a rack in the center of the oven. Butter and flour the cake pan.

2. In a medium saucepan, carefully bring the maple syrup to a boil over medium-high heat. Reduce the heat to medium-low and simmer for 40 to 45 minutes, or until thickened, dark, and reduced to about 1 cup/235 ml. (It foams up in the pan, so be sure to use a pan that is large enough so that it doesn't boil over. Once it foams, reduce the heat to maintain a low simmer; if it keeps foaming it will start to burn.)

3. Remove the pan from the heat and whisk in the 2 tbsp butter. Pour the maple syrup into the prepared cake pan. Arrange the apple slices in concentric circles in the bottom of the pan, making a second layer on top of the first if they don't all fit in a single layer.

CONTINUED

4. In a small bowl, whisk together the flour, baking powder, baking soda, and salt. In a separate bowl, whisk together the whole eggs, egg yolks, buttermilk, and vanilla. Set aside both bowls.

5. Using the stand mixer or a handheld mixer and a large bowl, beat the remaining 1 cup/225 g butter and the sugar on medium speed, stopping to scrape down the sides of the bowl and paddle several times, for 6 to 7 minutes, or until light, pale, and fluffy. On low speed, add about one-third of the flour mixture and beat for about 15 seconds, or until almost fully incorporated. Add about one-half of the egg-buttermilk mixture and beat until almost thoroughly incorporated. Stop the mixer and scrape down the sides of the bowl and the paddle. Add half of the remaining flour mixture and beat until almost fully incorporated. Add the remaining egg-buttermilk mixture and beat until almost fully incorporated. Remove the bowl from the mixer and fold in the remaining flour mixture with a rubber spatula just until fully incorporated. Top the apples and maple syrup with dollops of the batter and then spread evenly with the spatula.

6. Bake the cake for 60 to 70 minutes, or until golden brown and the middle springs back when you poke it gently with your finger. Let cool in the pan on the wire rack for about 1 hour.

7. Carefully invert the cake onto a serving plate while it is still warm, so that the apples will release from the pan. Slip any dislodged apple slices back into place. Serve warm with crème fraîche.

TRIPLE-CHOCOLATE MOUSSE CAKE

I learned how to make this cake at my first baking job, which was with Rick Katz, pastry chef extraordinaire, at his Bentonwood Bakery. When I eventually opened Flour, this was one of the cakes I knew I had to feature. It's my personal favorite, and I'm not even a true chocolate nut. Don't let the ingredients list or lengthy instructions deter you from making this dreamy creamy cake. It's quite sensational, with three beautiful chocolate mousses peeking out from between thin layers of flourless chocolate cake and the whole thing draped in a dark chocolate glaze. Read the recipe all the way through before you begin and you'll see that many of the steps are really quite simple.

A few words to help you along:

- The mousses are not technically mousses but chocolate-flavored whipped creams. You combine melted chocolate and heavy cream in three different chocolate variations, and after a night in the refrigerator, the cream chills enough for the mousses to be whipped to a light, fluffy filling.

- The baked cake layers are easy to manipulate after they come out of the oven and are still on the parchment paper on which they are baked. You bake off two sheets of cake, let them cool, and then cut each sheet in half, so you end up with four cake layers.

- To ensure that the final result is as pretty as it can be, you need to freeze the assembled cake overnight so that it is solid enough to trim the sides cleanly and neatly. The glaze doesn't cover the sides of the cake completely, which means the three different mousses can show their stuff.

- You can make the cake up to a month in advance, store it in the freezer, and then finish it off the day you want to serve it.

- Along the same lines, this recipe makes a cake that is fairly large—about 8 by 12 in/ 20 by 30.5 cm or so. When it is fully frozen, you can cut it into two smaller cakes and store them, well wrapped, in the freezer for up to 1 month. Given the number of steps that go into making this cake, it is nice to have two options for this cake: either one larger impressive cake or two smaller ones for two different occasions.

SERVES 10 TO 12

CONTINUED

WHITE CHOCOLATE MOUSSE

1½ cups/360 ml heavy cream

½ vanilla bean

3 oz/85 g white chocolate

⅛ tsp kosher salt

MILK CHOCOLATE MOUSSE

1½ cups/360 ml heavy cream

1 tsp dark-roast coffee or espresso grinds

3 oz/85 g milk chocolate

⅛ tsp kosher salt

DARK CHOCOLATE MOUSSE

1½ cups/360 ml heavy cream

3 oz/85 g bittersweet chocolate

⅛ tsp kosher salt

FLOURLESS CHOCOLATE CAKE

10 large eggs, separated

¼ cup/60 ml brewed coffee, at room temperature

10 oz/280 g semisweet or bittersweet chocolate, melted and cooled

¼ tsp kosher salt

1¼ cups/250 g granulated sugar

CAKE-SOAKING SYRUP

½ cup/120 ml hot brewed coffee

6 tbsp/75 g granulated sugar

TO FINISH

1 cup/240 g Ganache (page 294), warmed

Berries or other fresh fruit and chocolate curls for garnish

SPECIAL EQUIPMENT: sieve, two 13-by-18-in/33-by-46-cm rimmed baking sheets, parchment, stand mixer with whisk attachment or handheld mixer, offset spatula, clean cardboard, pastry brush

1. **TO MAKE THE THREE MOUSSES (AT LEAST 2 DAYS IN ADVANCE):** Start with the white chocolate mousse. Pour the cream into a medium saucepan. Split the vanilla bean in half lengthwise, scrape the seeds directly into the cream, and then toss in the pod halves. Heat the cream over medium-high heat until scalded, that is, just until small bubbles form along the sides of the pan. While the cream is heating, chop the white chocolate into small pieces and place in a small heatproof bowl. Pour the scalded cream over the white chocolate, let it stand for a minute or so,

and whisk together until the chocolate is completely melted. Pour the mixture through the sieve into a small storage container, add the salt, and refrigerate overnight. Repeat to make the milk chocolate mousse, except scald the heavy cream with the coffee grinds instead of the vanilla bean. Then repeat to make the dark chocolate mousse.

2. **TO MAKE THE CAKE (AT LEAST 1 DAY IN ADVANCE):** Preheat the oven to 350°F/180°C, and place one rack in the center and one rack in the top third of the oven. Line the baking sheets with parchment paper, and coat the parchment liberally with nonstick cooking spray.

3. In a medium bowl, whisk together the egg yolks, brewed coffee, melted chocolate, and salt; set aside. Using the stand mixer or a large bowl and the handheld mixer, beat the egg whites on medium speed for 2 to 3 minutes if using the stand mixer or 4 to 6 minutes if using the handheld mixer, or until soft peaks form. The whites will start to froth and turn into bubbles, and eventually the yellowy viscous part will disappear. Keep beating until you can see the tines of the whisk or beaters leaving a slight trail in the whites. To test for the soft-peak stage, stop the mixer and lift the whisk or beaters out of the whites; the whites should peak and then droop. With the mixer still on medium, slowly add the sugar a spoonful or two at a time. It should take at least 2 minutes to add all of the sugar—go slowly! When all of the sugar has been added, increase the speed to medium-high and beat for 1 or 2 minutes longer, or until the whites are glossy and smooth and the peaks hold their shape without drooping. Using a rubber spatula, fold one-third of the whites into the yolk-chocolate mixture to lighten it, and then gently fold in the remaining whites just until no light streaks are visible.

4. Divide the batter evenly between the two prepared baking sheets. The batter will be pretty thin and delicate (that's because of the egg whites, which are easy to deflate). Using the offset spatula, carefully spread the batter to cover each baking sheet fully. Concentrate on spreading the batter

toward the corners and the edges of the baking sheets; the centers will be easier to fill once the edges are filled with batter. The batter should be about ½ in/12 mm deep. Don't worry about the tops being perfectly smooth.

5. Bake the cakes, switching the sheets between the oven racks and rotating the sheets back to front about halfway during baking, for 16 to 18 minutes, or until the top of each cake is "crispy" when you touch it (that is, the cakes will be dry on top, but if you poke your finger through the crispy top, you will feel the soft cake underneath). Let the cakes cool in the pans on wire racks for 10 minutes. At this point, you can proceed to the next step, or you can wrap the cakes, still in their pans, with plastic wrap and leave them out at room temperature for 1 day.

6. **TO MAKE THE SOAKING SYRUP (1 DAY IN ADVANCE):** In a small bowl, stir together the coffee and sugar until the sugar has dissolved. Set aside.

7. Run a paring knife around the edge of a cake to release it from the sides of the baking sheet. Using the tip of the knife, cut each cake in half vertically, pressing firmly to cut through the parchment. (You'll need a very sharp knife for this, or you can even use kitchen shears.) You should now have four cake layers, each about 8 by 12 in/20 by 30.5 cm. Cut the cardboard so that it is just slightly larger than a cake layer.

8. Remove one cake layer with the parchment attached from a baking sheet and flip it over onto the cardboard base. Carefully peel off the parchment. In a medium bowl, using the handheld mixer or a whisk, whip the white chocolate mousse until it holds stiff peaks. Using the offset spatula, spread it evenly across the cake layer all the way to the edges. Remove a second cake layer and flip it over onto the white chocolate mousse. Carefully peel off the parchment. If at any point the cake tears or breaks, just patch it together and keep the cake layer as even as possible on top of the mousse. Brush this layer with about one-third of the cake-soaking syrup. In a medium bowl, whip the milk chocolate mousse until it holds stiff peaks and spread it evenly across the second cake

layer. Remove a third cake layer and flip it over onto the milk chocolate mousse. Carefully peel off the parchment. Brush this layer with about half of the remaining soaking syrup. In a medium bowl, whip the dark chocolate mousse until it holds stiff peaks and spread it evenly across the third cake layer. Remove the final cake layer from its pan and flip it over onto the dark chocolate mousse. Carefully peel off the parchment. Brush this last layer with the remaining cake-soaking syrup. Lightly wrap the cake in plastic wrap, place in the freezer, and freeze for about 8 hours or up to overnight, or until it is frozen solid. (At this point, the cake can instead be put into the freezer just until it has firmed up and then it can be well wrapped and frozen for up to 2 weeks.)

9. **TO FINISH THE CAKE (4 TO 5 HOURS IN ADVANCE OF SERVING):** Remove the cake from the freezer and place it on a cutting board. Using a chef's knife dipped in very hot water, trim about ½ in/12 mm off of each side of the cake, so that the exposed layers of mousse and cake are even. (These trimmings make for great snacking.) Dip and wipe the knife clean several times as you trim to make sure you get a neat, sharp edge on the cake. Trim the cardboard underneath so it is flush with the cake.

10. Place the cake on its cardboard base on a cooling rack set on a baking sheet. Pour the warm ganache over the top of the cake. Using the off-set spatula, spread the ganache in an even layer. It will begin to firm up right away when it hits the cold cake, so work quickly to even the surface. Let the excess ganache drip down the sides, leaving some parts of the cake exposed. Let the ganache set for several seconds, then transfer the cake to a serving plate. Let the cake thaw in the fridge before serving.

11. Decorate the cake with fruit and chocolate curls, then slice and serve. Dip your serving knife in hot water before each cut to ensure neat slices.

BEST BOSTON CREAM PIE

It's a little risky to try making your own version of Boston cream pie, an iconic dessert that's been around longer than any of us, in a city so steeped in tradition. Boston cream pie isn't really a pie, either. First served in 1856 in the Parker House hotel in Boston, now known as the Omni Parker House, it's actually a vanilla sponge cake filled with pastry cream and topped with chocolate glaze. I learned how to make this version of the classic from Rick Katz, the first pastry chef I ever worked for. His Boston cream pie was lighter and less cloyingly sweet than the original, which meant lightening up the cake, the filling, and the glaze. The cake is a simple sponge cake that lends itself to being soaked with a flavored syrup (hence, the name "sponge" cake). The filling is not just straight pastry cream, as in the original version, but a creamier, fluffier combination of pastry cream and whipped cream. And the glaze is pure chocolate ganache—bittersweet chocolate and heavy cream—which makes for the most decadent finish ever.

SERVES 4 TO 6

SPONGE CAKE

4 large eggs, separated, plus 3 egg whites

1 cup/200 g granulated sugar

2 tbsp freshly squeezed lemon juice

¾ cup/90 g all-purpose flour

Pinch of kosher salt

CAKE-SOAKING SYRUP

⅓ cup/80 ml hot brewed coffee

⅓ cup/70 g granulated sugar

1 cup/240 ml heavy cream

1¾ cups/420 ml Pastry Cream (page 290)

1 cup/240 g Ganache (page 294), warmed

SPECIAL EQUIPMENT: 13-by-18-in/33-by-46-cm rimmed baking sheet, parchment paper, stand mixer with whisk attachment or handheld mixer, sifter or sieve, offset spatula, clean cardboard

1. **TO MAKE THE SPONGE CAKE:** Preheat the oven to 350°F/180°C, and place a rack in the middle of the oven. Line the baking sheet with parchment paper.

2. Using the stand mixer or the handheld mixer and a medium bowl, beat together the egg yolks, ¼ cup/50 g of the sugar, and the lemon juice on high speed for at least 6 to 8 minutes if using the stand mixer or 10 to 12 minutes if using the handheld mixer, or until thick and doubled in volume. Stop the mixer once or twice and scrape down the sides of the bowl and the whisk to ensure the sugar and yolks are evenly mixed. Transfer to a large bowl and set aside.

CONTINUED

3. Clean the bowl and the whisk attachment or beaters (they must be spotlessly clean) and beat the egg whites on medium speed for 2 to 3 minutes with the stand mixer or 4 to 6 minutes with the handheld mixer, or until soft peaks form. The whites will start to froth and turn into bubbles, and eventually the yellowy viscous part will disappear. Keep beating until you can see the tines of the whisk or beaters leaving a slight trail in the whites. To test for the soft-peak stage, stop the mixer and lift the whisk or beaters out of the whites; the whites should peak and then droop. With the mixer on medium speed, add the remaining ¾ cup/150 g sugar very slowly, a spoonful or so at a time, taking about 1 minute to add all of the sugar. Continue beating on medium speed for 2 to 3 minutes longer, or until the whites are glossy and shiny and hold a stiff peak when you slowly lift the whisk or beaters straight up and out of the whites.

4. Using a rubber spatula, gently fold about one-third of the whipped whites into the yolk mixture to lighten it. Then gently fold in the remaining egg whites. Sift the flour and salt together over the top of the mixture and fold in gently until the flour is completely incorporated. Pour the batter into the prepared baking sheet.

5. Using the offset spatula, carefully spread the batter evenly to cover the entire baking sheet. Concentrate on spreading the batter toward the corners and edges of the pan. The center will be easier to fill once the edges are filled with batter. Don't worry about the top being perfectly smooth; it is more important that the batter be spread evenly so that the cake is the same thickness throughout. Bake the cake, rotating the baking sheet back to front about halfway through the baking, for 18 to 24 minutes, or until the top is pale golden brown and springs back when pressed in the center with your fingertips and the cake doesn't stick to your fingers. Let the cake cool in the pan on the wire rack for about 5 minutes.

6. Line a large cutting board with parchment. Run a paring knife around the edge of the still-warm cake to release it from the sides of the baking sheet, and invert the cake onto the parchment. Carefully peel off the parchment and allow the cake to cool completely. Using a chef's knife, cut the cake in half crosswise and then in half lengthwise. You should now have four cake layers each about 5½ by 8 in/14 by 20 cm. Cut the cardboard so that its dimensions are just slightly larger than the cake layer dimensions.

7. **TO MAKE THE SOAKING SYRUP:** In a small bowl, stir together the coffee and sugar until the sugar has dissolved.

8. Using the pastry brush, brush the top of all four cake rectangles evenly with the soaking syrup, using up all of the syrup.

9. Place one cake layer, syrup-side up, on the prepared cardboard rectangle. In a medium bowl, using a mixer or a whisk, whip the heavy cream until it holds very firm, stiff peaks. Fold in the pastry cream until well combined. Using the offset spatula, spread about one-third of the cream mixture over the cake layer. There is a tendency for the cream to mound in the center, so be sure to spread the cream out to the edges of the cake. In fact, to make the best-looking cake possible, it is better if the cream layer is slightly thicker along the edge than in the center.

10. Place a second cake layer, syrup-side up, on top of the cream layer and press down gently so the cake layer is level. Using the offset spatula, spread about half of the remaining cream mixture over the cake layer. Again, you want to spread the cream a bit thicker along the edge of the rectangle to prevent the final cake from doming.

11. Place a third cake layer, syrup-side up, on top of the cream and press down slightly to level the cake. Using the offset spatula, spread the remaining cream mixture over the cake, again making it a bit thicker along the edges than in the center. Top the cake with the final cake layer, syrup-side up, and press down gently so that the top layer is flat. Lightly wrap the cake with plastic wrap, place in the freezer, and freeze for about 8 hours or up to overnight, or until it is frozen solid. (At this point, the cake can instead be put into the freezer just until it has firmed up and then it can be well wrapped and frozen for up to 2 weeks.)

12. At least 3 hours in advance of serving, remove the cake from the freezer and place it on a cutting board. Using a chef's knife dipped in very hot water, trim the edges of the cake so that they are neat and even. (These trimmings make for great snacking.) Dip and wipe the knife clean several times as you trim to make sure you get a neat, sharp edge on the cake. Trim the cardboard underneath so it is flush with the cake.

13. Place the cake on its cardboard base on a cooling rack set on a baking sheet. Pour the warm ganache over the top of the cake. Using the offset spatula, spread the ganache in an even layer. It will begin to firm up right away when it hits the cold cake, so work quickly to even the surface. Let the excess ganache drip down the sides of the cake, leaving some parts of the cake exposed. Let the ganache set for several seconds, then transfer the cake to a serving plate. Let the cake thaw at room temperature before serving.

BITTERSWEET CHOCOLATE-ESPRESSO TERRINE

When I was the pastry chef at Rialto in Cambridge, there were a few recipes that we would always pull out for special occasions and large parties. *Torta*—a dense, fudgy flourless cake—was one of the desserts from those days that I was most excited to add to my repertoire. It was a crowd-pleaser because of its incredibly deep chocolate flavor, and it was also a pastry kitchen favorite because it could be easily made in big batches to feed hundreds. You'll be pleasantly surprised at how straightforward it is to put together and how impressive the results are. I now make this cake daily at Myers+Chang. It has become our most popular dessert.

SERVES 8 TO 10

¾ cup plus 1 tbsp/135 g unsalted butter, cut into small pieces

2½ oz/70 g unsweetened chocolate, chopped

6 oz/170 g bittersweet chocolate (68 percent cacao), chopped

½ cup/120 ml brewed espresso

3 large eggs

3 egg yolks

½ cup plus 2 tbsp/125 g granulated sugar

½ tsp kosher salt

½ cup/70 g confectioners' sugar for finishing

Lightly sweetened whipped cream for serving

SPECIAL EQUIPMENT: parchment paper, 8-in/20-cm cake pan, roasting pan or 10-in/25-cm cake pan, sieve

1. Preheat the oven to 350°F/180°C, and place a rack in the center of the oven. Cut a parchment paper circle to fit the cake pan. Coat the pan bottom with nonstick cooking spray or butter the bottom, then line pan with the parchment circle.

2. Put the butter, unsweetened chocolate, and bittersweet chocolate in a medium metal or heatproof glass bowl and place the bowl over (not touching) barely simmering water in a medium saucepan. Heat, stirring occasionally, until the chocolate is completely melted and smooth. Remove the bowl from the heat and whisk in the espresso. Let cool for about 20 minutes.

3. In a separate medium bowl, whisk together the whole eggs, egg yolks, granulated sugar, and salt until combined. Pour the chocolate mixture into the egg mixture and fold together until thoroughly combined. Pour the batter into the prepared pan.

4. Place the cake pan in the roasting pan and pour hot water into the roasting pan to reach about halfway up the sides of the cake pan. (The water bath helps the cake to bake slowly and gently, which leads to a smoother textured cake.) Carefully transfer both pans to the oven and bake for 40 to 50 minutes, or until the cake is mostly set when you jiggle it. Remove both pans from the oven and leave the cake pan in the water bath for about 1 hour, or until the cake has cooled. Remove the cake pan from the water, cover the pan with plastic wrap, and refrigerate for 2 to 3 hours to firm up.

5. Remove the cake from the fridge. Invert a flat serving plate on top of the pan and flip the pan and plate together. Rap the pan on the counter to pop out the cake and carefully peel off the parchment. Using the sieve, dust the top of the cake with the confectioners' sugar. Use a thin knife dipped in hot water and wiped dry to slice the cake and serve cold with the whipped cream. The cake can be stored in an airtight container in the refrigerator for up to 1 week.

CROQUEMBOUCHE

Croquembouche (crow-kem-BOOSH) translated from French means "crunch-in-mouth," and its elaborate name only hints at the full glory that is a *croquembouche*. Cream puffs filled with vanilla cream and dipped in caramel, piled high into a pyramid, and then swathed in sparkly, glittery strands of golden spun sugar—this is the dessert of fairy tales. Or, if you're French, the pièce de résistance of weddings and christenings.

Break down the recipe into parts so you don't get overwhelmed. You can make the *pâte à choux* puffs one day, the pastry cream filling another. You need to fill the puffs and assemble the pyramid no more than about five hours before serving, so give yourself ample time for these finishing steps.

Making spun sugar is like riding a bike or tying a shoe: it's not hard to do once you know how to do it, but describing it to someone who has never done it before can be tricky. First, don't frustrate yourself unnecessarily by attempting this dessert on a humid day. Spun sugar melts rapidly in humidity, and the dessert will be an exercise in futility. Practice shaking your wrist back and forth briskly while holding a fork so that you have the general movement down. Wait patiently for the caramel to thicken, so that it will turn to spun sugar when you flick it around; it should have the consistency of thin honey. Dip your fork into the caramel, hold the fork high above the tower of puffs, and then flick firmly and decisively back and forth over the tower. Keep dipping your fork in the caramel and spinning sugar over the tower until the entire *croquembouche* is covered. Then, to make a spun-sugar topper, you will use the same motion, but you will be dropping the strands onto parchment paper. When you have enough strands, you will gather them up and set them on top of your masterpiece. When the *croquembouche* is finished, take the time to admire your breathtaking pastry before your guests dig in. Once they start eating it, it's really hard to stop.

SERVES 8 TO 10

CONTINUED

¾ cup/170 g unsalted butter

4 tsp granulated sugar

¼ tsp kosher salt

1⅔ cups/230 g all-purpose flour

6 large eggs

VANILLA CREAM

¾ cup/180 ml heavy cream

1¾ cups/420 ml Pastry Cream (page 290)

SPUN SUGAR

2 cups/400 g granulated sugar

SPECIAL EQUIPMENT: two rimmed baking sheets, parchment paper, stand mixer with paddle attachment and whisk attachment (optional), pastry bag and one 1-in/2.5-cm round piping tip and one ⅛- to ¼-in/3- to 6-mm round piping tip, cardboard cake circle or flat plate 8 to 10 in/20 to 25 cm in diameter

1. **TO MAKE THE *PÂTE À CHOUX*:** Preheat the oven to 400°F/200°C, and place one rack in the center and one rack in the top third of the oven. Line two baking sheets with parchment paper.

2. In a medium saucepan, combine the butter, sugar, salt, and 1½ cups/360 ml water over medium heat until the butter has melted. Do not let the mixture come to a boil or some of the water will evaporate. Add the flour all at once, then stir the flour into the liquid with a wooden spoon until it is fully incorporated. The mixture will look like a really stiff pancake batter. Keep stirring vigorously over medium heat until the mixture slowly starts to toughen and looks more like loose dough and less like stiff batter. It will also lose its shine and look more matte. Stir continuously for 3 to 5 minutes, or until the dough starts to leave a film at the bottom of the pan.

3. Remove the pan from the heat and transfer the dough to the bowl of the stand mixer fitted with the paddle attachment. Beat the dough on medium-low speed for 1 minute. This will allow some of the steam to escape and the dough to cool slightly. (Or, in a medium bowl, vigorously beat the mixture by hand with a wooden spoon for 2 to 3 minutes.) Crack the eggs into a small pitcher and whisk to break up the yolks. On medium-low speed (or beating vigorously by hand), gradually add the eggs to the dough. When the eggs have been added, increase the speed to medium and beat for about 20 seconds, or until the dough is glossy and shiny.

4. Fit the pastry bag with the 1-in/2.5-cm round tip and fill the bag with the dough. (If you don't have a pastry bag and tip, cut 1 in/2.5 cm from one corner of a plastic storage bag and fill the plastic bag with the dough.) Pipe out balls about 1½ in/4 cm in diameter onto the prepared baking sheets, spacing them about 2 in/5 cm apart. If the balls form a peak on top, moisten your fingertip with water and tap down the peaks. You should have enough dough to pipe out eighteen to twenty-two balls per sheet.

5. Place the baking sheets in the oven. The heat of the oven will immediately start turning the liquid in the batter into steam, which will cause the pastries to inflate. After about 10 minutes, when the pastries have puffed up and are starting to turn golden brown, reduce the oven temperature to 325°F/165°C, then switch the baking sheets between the oven racks and rotate the sheets back to front. Continue to bake for another 25 to 28 minutes, or until the pastries are evenly golden brown. Let the pastries cool completely on the baking sheets on wire racks. (The cooled pastries can be stored unfilled in an airtight container in the freezer for up to 2 weeks. Remove from the freezer and refresh in a 325°F/165°C oven for 6 to 8 minutes, or until thawed. Let cool completely before filling. You can also store them unfilled in an airtight container at room temperature for up to 2 days. Refresh them in a 325°F/165°C oven for 2 to 3 minutes, then let cool before filling.)

6. **TO MAKE THE VANILLA CREAM:** In the stand mixer fitted with the whisk attachment on medium speed or in a medium bowl with a whisk, whip the heavy cream until it holds stiff peaks. Add the pastry cream to the whipped cream and fold together until thoroughly combined. (You should have about 3½ cups/840 ml vanilla cream. Vanilla cream may be made up to a day in advance and stored in the fridge in an airtight container.)

7.   Rinse and dry the pastry bag, fit it with the ⅛- to ¼-in/3- to 6-mm tip, and fill the bag with the vanilla cream. Using the tip of a small, sharp knife, poke a hole in the bottom of each puff, and then pipe the cream into the puffs. Make sure to fill each puff fully with the cream. Set the filled puffs aside.

8.   TO MAKE THE SPUN SUGAR: Put the sugar in the small saucepan and carefully add about ½ cup/120 ml water, or just enough to moisten all of the sugar. Bring the mixture to a boil over high heat, making sure that the sugar is evenly moistened and that you don't splash any sugar crystals on the sides of the pan. When the sugar syrup boils, it will go from bubbling furiously like water to bubbling more languidly as it thickens, which will take 3 to 4 minutes. Once the syrup starts to thicken, watch it carefully, and as soon as you see the syrup begin to turn light golden brown, immediately remove the pan from the heat and gently swirl it to even out the caramelization.

9.   Immediately and carefully dip the bottoms of the filled puffs, one by one, into the caramel and quickly arrange them in a circle about 8 in/20 cm in diameter on the cake circle. If you see cream leaking out of the bottom of a puff, wipe it off before dipping the puff into the caramel. You want to keep the caramel as clean as possible; that is, free of any cream filling. Once you have arranged the first circle, continue dipping puffs and arranging them in concentric circles inside the first circle. The caramel will harden pretty quickly and act as glue as you are building your *croquembouche*. I find that once I dip and put the puff where I want it, I have to hold it in place for only 2 to 3 seconds before it hardens and I can move on to the next puff. Keep building circles on top of the circles, making them smaller as the pyramid gets taller, until you have one last puff for the top of the tower. You'll use thirty-four to thirty-eight puffs total.

10.   At this point, the caramel should be a thick viscous mass similar in consistency to honey. While the caramel is at this temperature, you have only 5 to 8 minutes to make your spun sugar garnish. If it is too thick, like rubber cement, you will want to rewarm the caramel carefully over medium-low heat for a few minutes until it melts a little and thins out.

11.   Holding a fork by the edge of the handle, dip the tines into the caramel and lift the fork straight up so that the dripping caramel starts to fall back into the pan. Before it all drips in, position the fork about 3 ft/1 m above the pastry pyramid and, using a quick, sharp, flinging wrist motion, flick the fork back and forth over the pyramid so that the dripping caramel strands spin into spun sugar, covering the *croquembouche*. Continue dipping the fork in the caramel and covering the puffs with sugar strands, spinning the *croquembouche* as you work so that you get all sides, until the pyramid is covered with caramel strands.

12.   Place a sheet of parchment on a clean, dry work surface (for easy cleanup) and make more spun sugar the same way, dipping the fork into the pan, lifting it straight up, allowing most of the caramel to drip back into the pan, and then flicking your wrist back and forth about 3 feet/1 m above the parchment so that the strands fall onto the paper. After five or six dips and flicks, you should have enough spun sugar on the parchment to gather together into a ball and place on top of the pyramid.

13.   To serve, pluck puffs off one by one with your hands and put them on individual plates. Or, for neater serving, use a set of tongs to pluck the puffs off and transfer them to the plates. The *croquembouche* should be served the day it is made, because the spun sugar will start to melt after 5 to 8 hours. Do not refrigerate the *croquembouche*, as the sugar will melt in the fridge.

BÛCHE DE NOËL

If you are looking for a glorious, showstopping holiday dessert, look no further. The *bûche de Noël*, or Yule log, is a classic Christmas centerpiece, especially within the French pastry tradition. When I was a baker at Payard Pâtisserie in New York City, we made these by the dozen for the entire month of December. Our pastry case was filled with *bûches* of all kinds—chocolate, lemon, raspberry, chestnut—and it was one pastry cook's full-time job to make and decorate these small masterpieces.

This chocolate *bûche* is made with a moist, thin, chocolaty cake that gets soaked liberally with coffee syrup, spread with a white chocolate–whipped cream, and rolled tightly into a log. After a day in the freezer, the roll has firmed up and you can cut it up to resemble a log. Ganache covers the whole thing (except for the exposed spirals on both ends of the log, which are meant to look like tree rings). The best part is decorating the *bûche* with small meringue "mushrooms" and cranberry-rosemary "holly." It's a truly magnificent dessert.

SERVES 10 TO 12

WHITE CHOCOLATE FILLING

1½ cups/360 ml heavy cream

½ vanilla bean

3 oz/85 g white chocolate

⅛ tsp kosher salt

CHOCOLATE CAKE

5 large eggs, separated

3 tbsp brewed coffee, at room temperature

4 oz/115 g semisweet or bittersweet chocolate, melted and cooled

¼ tsp kosher salt

⅔ cup/140 g granulated sugar

½ cup/70 g all-purpose flour

About ¼ cup/20 g cocoa powder for dusting

CAKE-SOAKING SYRUP

¼ cup/60 ml hot brewed coffee

¼ cup/50 g granulated sugar

MERINGUE MUSHROOMS

2 egg whites

¼ cup/50 g granulated sugar

¼ cup/35 g confectioners' sugar

Pinch of kosher salt

About ¼ cup/40 g semisweet or bittersweet chocolate chips or shaved chocolate, melted

TO FINISH

1 cup/240 g Ganache (page 294), at warm room temperature

3 to 4 tbsp cocoa powder for dusting

A few fresh cranberries for making holly

A few fresh rosemary sprigs for making holly

SPECIAL EQUIPMENT: sieve, 13-by-18-in/33-by-46-cm rimmed baking sheet, parchment paper, stand mixer with whisk attachment or handheld mixer, offset spatula, pastry brush, pastry bag and small round piping tip, clean comb or fork

1. **TO MAKE THE FILLING (2 DAYS IN ADVANCE):** Pour the cream into a medium saucepan. Split the vanilla bean in half lengthwise, scrape the seeds directly into the cream, and then toss in the pod halves. Heat the cream over medium-high heat until scalded; that is, just until little bubbles form along the sides of the pan. While the cream is heating, chop the white chocolate into small pieces and place in a small heatproof bowl. Pour the scalded cream over the white chocolate, let it stand for a minute or so, and whisk together until the chocolate is completely melted. Pour the mixture through the sieve into a small storage container, add the salt, and refrigerate overnight.

2. **TO MAKE THE CAKE (1 DAY IN ADVANCE):** Preheat the oven to 350°F/180°C, and place a rack in the center of the oven. Line the baking sheet with parchment paper, and coat the parchment liberally with nonstick cooking spray.

3. In a medium bowl, whisk together the egg yolks, coffee, chocolate, and salt; set aside. Using the stand mixer or a large bowl and the handheld mixer, beat the egg whites on medium speed for 2 to 3 minutes if using the stand mixer or 4 to 6 minutes if using the handheld mixer, or until soft peaks form. The whites will start to froth and turn into bubbles, and eventually the yellowy viscous part will disappear. Keep beating until you can see the tines of the whisk or beaters leaving a slight trail in the whites. To test for the soft-peak stage, stop the mixer and lift the whisk or beaters out of the whites; the whites should peak and then droop. With the mixer still on medium speed, slowly add the sugar a spoonful or two at a time. It should take at least 2 minutes to add all of the sugar— go slowly! When all of the sugar has been added, increase the speed to medium-high and beat for 1 to 2 minutes longer, or until the whites are glossy and smooth and the peaks hold their shape without drooping. Using a rubber spatula, fold one-third of the whites into the yolk-chocolate mixture to lighten it, then gently fold in the remaining whites just until no light streaks are visible. Finally, gently fold in the flour just until fully incorporated. Pour the batter into the prepared baking sheet.

4. Using the offset spatula, carefully spread the batter evenly to cover the entire baking sheet. Concentrate on spreading the batter toward the corners and the edges of the pan; the center will be easier to fill once the edges are filled with batter. Don't worry about the top being perfectly smooth; it is more important that the batter be spread evenly so that the cake is the same thickness throughout. Bake the cake, rotating the baking sheet back to front about halfway through baking, for 14 to 16 minutes, or until the top is firm and dry when you touch it. Let the cake cool in the pan on the wire rack for 10 minutes. Run a paring knife around the edge of the cake to release it from the sides of the baking sheet. Using the sieve, dust the entire top surface of the cake with the cocoa powder. (The cocoa powder will prevent the cake from sticking when you unmold it.) Place a sheet of parchment slightly larger than the baking sheet on a work surface, and invert the cake directly onto the parchment. Let cool for another 10 to 15 minutes, or until cool to the touch. Carefully peel off the parchment from the cake bottom.

5. **TO MAKE THE SOAKING SYRUP (1 DAY IN ADVANCE):** In a small bowl, mix together the coffee and sugar until the sugar has dissolved.

6. Using the pastry brush, brush the top surface of the cake evenly with the syrup.

7. Using the stand mixer, the handheld mixer, or a medium bowl and a whisk, whip the white chocolate filling until it holds stiff peaks. Spread it evenly over the cake, leaving a 1-in/2.5-cm border uncovered on all four edges. Starting at a narrow end, carefully roll the cake jelly-roll style, gently nudging the cake along until you have a neatly coiled roll. At this point, wrap the roll tightly and entirely in plastic wrap and place in the freezer until fully frozen, at least 4 hours or up to overnight.

CONTINUED

8. **TO MAKE THE MERINGUE MUSHROOMS (1 DAY IN ADVANCE):** Preheat the oven to 200°F/95°C, and place a rack in the center of the oven. Line a baking sheet with parchment paper and set aside.

9. Using the stand mixer or the handheld mixer and a medium bowl, beat the egg whites on medium speed for 1 to 2 minutes with the stand mixer or 3 to 4 minutes with the handheld mixer, or until soft peaks form. The whites will start to froth and turn into bubbles, and eventually the yellow viscous part will disappear. Keep beating until you can see the tines of the whisk leaving a slight trail in the whites. To test for the soft-peak stage, stop the mixer and lift the whisk out of the whites; the whites should peak and then droop. With the mixer on medium speed, slowly add the granulated sugar 1 tbsp at a time, mixing for 30 seconds after each addition. When all of the granulated sugar has been incorporated into the egg whites, increase the speed to medium-high and beat for about 10 seconds longer.

10. In a small bowl, using the sieve, sift together the confectioners' sugar and salt. Using a rubber spatula, fold the confectioners' sugar mixture into the beaten egg whites.

11. Fit the pastry bag with the piping tip and fill the bag with the beaten egg whites. Pipe out eight to ten circles about 1½ in/4 cm in diameter onto the prepared baking sheet, spacing them about 1 in/2.5 cm apart. These will be the tops of the mushrooms. Then pipe eight to ten small posts that look like elongated Hershey's kisses onto the baking sheet. To do this, pipe a small mound, then lift the bag straight up as you ease off pressure on the meringue. These will be the stems of the mushrooms.

12. Bake the meringues for about 2 hours, or until they are firm to the touch. Turn off the oven and let them cool in the closed oven overnight.

13. The next day, remove the meringues from the oven. (At this point, the meringue mushroom tops and stems can be stored in an airtight container at room temperature for up to 1 week.) Place a sheet of parchment on a work surface. Remove a mushroom top from the baking sheet and, using the pastry brush, brush the underside with the melted chocolate. Using a paring knife, poke a hole in the middle of the underside of the top. Dip the top of a meringue stem into the chocolate and immediately poke the chocolate-coated tip into the hole to create a mushroom. Place the mushroom on the parchment. Repeat with the remaining mushroom tops and bottoms, adding them to the parchment.

14. **TO FINISH THE CAKE (2 TO 3 HOURS BEFORE SERVING):** Remove the cake from the freezer and place it on a cutting board. Dip a chef's knife in very hot water and trim about ½ in/12 mm off each end of the log. You should have a log about 10 in/25 cm long. With the knife at a 45-degree slant and at about 2 in/5 cm from the right end of the log, cut off a slanted piece of the cake. Your log will now be in two pieces, one stubby piece and one larger piece, each with one diagonal end. Trim off a thin, angled piece at the opposite end of the larger piece, so that both ends of the larger log are trimmed and slanted. This second short piece is extra, and you can eat it. Carefully transfer the larger piece of cake to a serving plate or platter.

15. Using some of the softened ganache, dab a bit on the flat end of the stubby piece of cake and place the stubby piece, flat-end down, on top of the larger piece of cake, positioning it about one-third of the way (2 to 3 in/5 to 7.5 cm) from the right end. The pointed slanted part of the stubby piece will be facing upward. Let the cake sit for about 1 hour, or until it has thawed.

16. When the cake is fully thawed, warm up the remaining ganache (pop it into the microwave for 10 to 15 seconds or place it over hot water for a few minutes) so that it is easily spreadable. Using the offset spatula, completely cover the cake with a layer of ganache, taking care to cover fully the gap between the stubby piece on top of the log and the log. Leave the exposed spiral ends of the log uncovered to show off the inner spiral of the cake. Using the comb, lightly scrape wavy lines along the length of the log and the stub to mimic the natural bark of a log. Using the sieve, dust the meringue mushrooms with the cocoa powder to mimic dirt. Place the mushrooms at various spots along the log, and arrange the rosemary sprigs and cranberries together in a few clusters along the log to mimic branches of holly. Serve immediately or store in the refrigerator for up to 8 hours.

drinks

Okay, not those kinds of drinks—
though many of these drinks could
be given an upgrade with the addition
of a spirit or two. Our drink list is
short and sweet. I never expected
we would have such a following for
our menu of raspberry seltzer and
hot chocolate. And yet every day,
people come through our doors to
treat themselves to these yummy
concoctions. Here are our best and
most popular drink recipes.

CANTALOUPE-MINT SELTZER

You can pretty much take any super-ripe fruit and turn it into a fresh-fruit seltzer. Chef Jeff offers this variation, one of our more popular, at Flour2 all summer long. It's more like a bubbly smoothie. If you prefer a thinner drink, add more soda water. The cantaloupe flavor is incredibly fresh, and the mint tempers the sweetness nicely.

MAKES ABOUT 6 CUPS/1.4 L
CANTALOUPE PURÉE
(ENOUGH FOR ABOUT 6 DRINKS)

15 large sprigs fresh mint , leaves and stems roughly chopped

1 cup/200 g granulated sugar, plus a little more if cantaloupes are not super-sweet

Pinch of kosher salt

2 ripe cantaloupes

2 tbsp freshly squeezed lime juice

1 to 1¼ cups/240 to 300 ml soda water for each drink

SPECIAL EQUIPMENT: sieve, blender or food processor

1. In a small saucepan, combine the mint, sugar, salt, and 1 cup/240 ml water and bring to a boil over high heat, stirring until the sugar has dissolved. Remove from the heat and let steep for at least 1 hour or up to overnight. Strain through the sieve placed over a small bowl and set aside.

2. Halve, seed, peel, and chop the cantaloupes. (You will get 8 to 9 cups/1.4 kg chopped melon.) Try a piece. If it isn't really yummy and sweet, add a little more sugar to the mint syrup and stir to dissolve. In the blender, purée the cantaloupe for about 1 minute, or until smooth. Add the mint syrup and lime juice to the cantaloupe purée and mix well to combine. (The purée can be stored in an airtight container in the fridge for up to 2 days or in the freezer for up to 3 months. Thaw the frozen purée in the refrigerator overnight.)

3. For each drink, spoon about 1 cup/240 ml of the cantaloupe purée into a tall glass, fill the glass with ice, and then pour in 1 cup/240 ml soda water. If you prefer a thinner drink, you can add up to ¼ cup/60 ml more soda water per drink. Using a long spoon, stir until well mixed, then serve.

HOUSE-MADE RASPBERRY SELTZER

1 cup/130 g fresh or frozen raspberries

1 cup/200 g vanilla sugar

2 tbsp freshly squeezed lemon juice

1 tbsp freshly squeezed lime juice

1¼ cups/300 ml soda water for each drink

SPECIAL EQUIPMENT: blender or food processor, sieve

One of the most popular cakes we make at Flour is our Lemon-Raspberry Cake: lemon pound cake, crushed raspberries, lemon curd, buttercream. To give the raspberry layer extra flavor, we soak whole raspberries in a vanilla syrup for several hours and then strain and crush the berries. The happy by-product of this raspberry soaking is vanilla-and-raspberry-infused syrup. When we first opened, I knew I wanted to make some-thing special with the syrup. I'd read about the shrub, a sweetened raspberry-vinegar drink that was popular in colonial times, and thought that it could be a fun drink to offer at Flour. I mixed some of the syrup with raspberry vinegar and then added soda water. Blech! It was awful. I almost gave up on the idea. Then I tried the rasp-berry syrup with lemon and lime juice and a star was born.

This drink has legions of addicts among Flour followers. We sell so many that we can no longer rely on the leftover raspberry syrup to keep us stocked; we now make the syrup from scratch just to keep up with demand. The syrup stores great in the fridge or freezer, so make a batch to keep on hand for when the raspberry seltzer urge hits. Trust me, it will.

MAKES ABOUT 1¾ CUPS/420 ML RASPBERRY SYRUP (ENOUGH FOR ABOUT 9 DRINKS)

1. In a small saucepan, combine the raspberries, vanilla sugar, and 1 cup/240 ml water and bring to a boil over high heat, stirring until the sugar has dissolved. Remove from the heat and let steep for 1 hour.

2. Transfer the raspberry mixture to the blender and purée. Strain through the sieve placed over a small bowl to remove most of the raspberry seeds. Add the lemon and lime juices to the rasp-berry syrup and stir to combine. (The syrup can be stored in an airtight container in the fridge for up to 2 weeks or in the freezer for up to 3 months.)

3. For each drink, put 3 tbsp syrup in the bottom of a tall glass, fill the glass with ice, and then pour in 1¼ cups/300 ml soda water. Using a long spoon, stir until well mixed, then serve.

CRANBERRY-LIME-GINGER SELTZER

1 cup/200 g granulated sugar

3-in/7.5-cm piece fresh ginger, peeled and roughly chopped

2¼ cups/225 g fresh or frozen cranberries

3 tbsp freshly squeezed lime juice

1 cup/240 ml soda water for each drink

SPECIAL EQUIPMENT: sieve, blender or food processor

During the summer, Chef Jeff is making seltzers left and right with every single piece of ripe fruit he can get his hands on. Watermelon, peach, strawberry, honeydew, and cantaloupe are just some of the wonderful fruity drinks he creates.

And then the fall hits, and the fruits we're offered in cold New England dwindle to a paltry selection. But that doesn't stop CJ. One of my favorite fall-winter seltzers is this one. Tart cranberries sweetened with a ginger syrup and brightened with a shot of lime juice make you forget that summer is many, many, long, snowy months away.

MAKES ABOUT 3 CUPS/720 ML PURÉE
(ENOUGH FOR ABOUT 6 DRINKS)

1. In a small saucepan, combine the sugar, ginger, and 1 cup/240 ml water and bring to a boil over high heat, stirring until the sugar has dissolved. Remove from the heat and let steep for 1 hour. Strain through the sieve placed over a small bowl. Reserve the syrup and ginger pieces separately.

2. Add the cranberries to the same saucepan and pour the syrup back into the pan. Place over high heat, bring to a boil, and remove from the heat.

3. In the blender, combine the cranberries and about half of the reserved ginger pieces (discard the other half) and purée for at least 2 minutes, or until very smooth. Transfer the purée to a storage container, stir in the lime juice, and let cool. (The purée can be stored in an airtight container in the fridge for up to 2 days or in the freezer for up to 3 months. Thaw the frozen purée in the refrigerator overnight.)

4. For each drink, spoon about ½ cup/120 ml cranberry purée into a tall glass, fill the glass with ice, and pour in 1 cup/240 ml soda water. Using a long spoon, stir until well mixed, then serve.

MULLED APPLE CIDER

We received a letter from a customer who was incredulous that we'd made something with apples that tasted so good. He was a self-declared apple hater, having never enjoyed anything with apples, not even our apple cake, which is pretty beloved. He was convinced we had mixed our mulled apple cider with some other secret ingredient to make it palatable to his apple-adverse taste buds. The truth is our cider is a perfect example of our Flour food philosophy: take a great product (in this case a high-quality apple cider from a local farm), add a handful of ingredients to highlight its flavor (cinnamon, allspice, clove, ginger, nutmeg, orange), and serve. It's simple and delicious.

MAKES ABOUT 7½ CUPS/1.8 L
(SERVES 4 TO 6)

2 qt/2 L fresh apple cider

2 cinnamon sticks

8 allspice berries

1 orange, unpeeled and thinly sliced

1 tsp whole cloves

1-in/2.5-cm piece fresh ginger, unpeeled and roughly chopped

1 tsp freshly grated nutmeg

SPECIAL EQUIPMENT: sieve

1. In a medium saucepan, combine the cider, cinnamon, allspice, orange slices, cloves, ginger, and nutmeg and bring to a simmer over medium-high heat. Remove from the heat, cover, and let steep for 1 hour.

2. Strain through the sieve into a medium saucepan and reheat until hot. Pour into mugs and serve. The cider can be stored in an airtight container in the fridge for up to 1 week and reheated before serving.

SUPER-RICH HOT CHOCOLATE

This hot chocolate was a no-brainer twelve years ago when we opened. We have ganache all the time in the pastry kitchen, and our customers kept asking for hot chocolate. So we scooped the ganache into the espresso milk pitchers and steamed it on the espresso machine with local organic milk to make our thick, rich, and amazing signature hot chocolate.

We make ganache every morning, and every day, especially during the winter, we go through containers and containers of it to satisfy the hot-chocolate demand. As with any recipe that has very few ingredients, each ingredient must shine, so buy the best chocolate you can afford for the ganache.

SERVES 2

1 cup/240 g Ganache (page 294)

1¾ cups/420 ml whole milk

Big pinch of kosher salt

In a medium saucepan, combine the ganache, milk, and salt and bring to just under a boil over high heat, whisking until blended. Pour into mugs and serve immediately.

KIDS' (OF ALL AGES) CHOCOLATE MILK

At Flour on Farnsworth Street, the mood in the dining room during the weekends (and on any school holiday) is decidedly Romper Room. We're a block away from Boston Children's Museum, a truly terrific museum for kids of all ages, and Flour is the perfect pre- or post-museum stop for hungry families. Chocolate milk wasn't on the original Flour menu, but when we opened up this location, these customers immediately informed us of our omission. Sure we could have easily purchased jugs of chocolate milk from our dairy vendor, or we could have even gone the school-cafeteria route and sold individual cartons. But after looking at the list of ingredients on this kid-friendly staple and stumbling over the third unpronounceable additive, we knew we would make our own. Two simple ingredients plus water and a pinch of salt mixed into milk and you have the best, fastest, easiest chocolate milk ever. You'll never buy it again after making this.

SERVES 3 OR 4

½ cup/60 g cocoa powder

½ cup/100 g granulated sugar

Pinch of kosher salt

3 cups/720 ml whole milk

1. In a small saucepan, combine the cocoa powder, sugar, salt, and 1/2 cup/120 ml water and bring to a boil over high heat, whisking until the solids have dissolved. Transfer the mixture to a heatproof container and let cool for about 1 hour, or until it is cool to the touch and has the consistency of a thick syrup. (The syrup can be stored in an airtight container in the fridge for up to 1 week. It will get thick and fudgy as it sits. Before using, let it come to room temperature or warm it for a few seconds in the microwave or over low heat on the stove just until it regains its thick, syrupy consistency.)

2. When you are ready to serve, in a large bowl, whisk together the chocolate mixture and the milk until thoroughly blended, then ladle into glasses and serve immediately.

Basics

These are our basic recipes, the workhorses that we use daily or several times a day. They are handy for all sorts of cooking and baking, not just for the recipes in this book. Use them often as the foundation for making great food that makes you and those around you happy.

BALSAMIC VINAIGRETTE

This is an easy vinaigrette that we use at Flour to dress almost all of our salads and to drizzle on many of our sandwiches. It's tangy, sweet, and bright and it keeps well in the fridge. If you don't have a blender or food processor, you can most definitely make this by hand. It won't be quite as creamy or thick, but it will still be delicious.

MAKES ABOUT 1½ CUPS/360 ML

⅓ cup/80 ml balsamic vinegar

2 tsp Dijon mustard

1 cup/240 ml vegetable oil

½ tsp kosher salt

¼ tsp freshly ground black pepper

1 tbsp granulated sugar

SPECIAL EQUIPMENT: blender or food processor (optional)

Combine the vinegar and mustard in the bowl of a blender or food processor. With the machine running, very slowly drizzle in the vegetable oil, taking about 1 minute to add all of it. Add the salt, pepper, and sugar and blend until thickened and smooth. Alternatively, combine the vinegar and mustard in a medium bowl and slowly add the oil while whisking continuously, taking about 1 minute to add all of the oil. Add the salt, pepper, and sugar and whisk until thickened and smooth. The vinaigrette can be stored in an airtight container in the fridge for up to 2 weeks. Rewhisk before using to recombine all of the ingredients.

ROASTED TOMATOES

MAKES 16 TOMATO HALVES

8 plum tomatoes

1 tbsp extra-virgin olive oil

½ tsp kosher salt

½ tsp freshly ground black pepper

½ tsp finely minced fresh thyme

SPECIAL EQUIPMENT: rimmed baking sheet

1. Preheat the oven to 300°F/150°C, and place a rack in the center of the oven.

2. Cut the plum tomatoes in half and firmly squeeze each half to remove as many of the seeds and as much of the juice as you can. Place the tomato halves, cut-side up, on the baking sheet. Drizzle evenly with the olive oil and sprinkle with the salt, pepper, and thyme.

3. Roast for 1¼ to 1½ hours, or until the tomatoes are slightly wrinkled and a bit darker. Let cool on the baking sheet. The tomatoes can be stored in an airtight container in the fridge for up to 4 days.

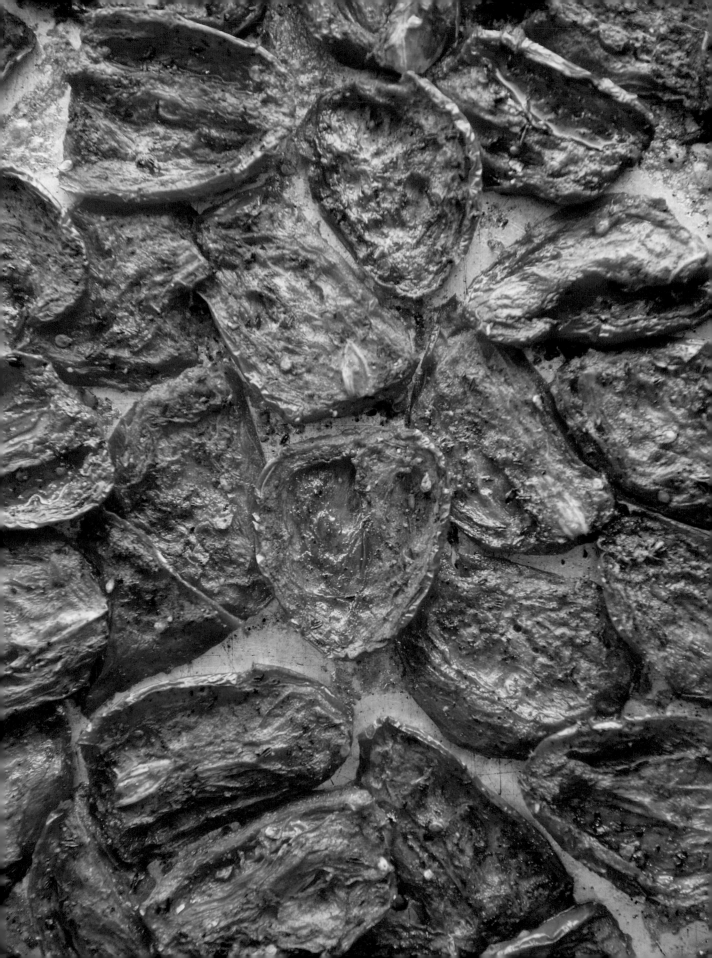

CARAMELIZED ONIONS

MAKES ABOUT 2 CUPS/175 G

2 tbsp vegetable oil

4 medium or 3 large onions, halved and sliced as thinly as possible

1½ tsp kosher salt

1 tsp freshly ground black pepper

2 tsp finely chopped fresh thyme

In a large skillet, heat the vegetable oil over medium heat. Add the onions and cook, tossing and stirring occasionally, for 15 to 20 minutes, or until softened. Reduce the heat to low and continue cooking, stirring occasionally, for another 50 to 60 minutes, or until the onions are completely soft and caramelized. They will look dark brown and mushy. Remove from the heat and add the salt, pepper, and thyme and mix well to combine. The onions will keep in an airtight container in the fridge for up to 1 week.

VEGETABLE STOCK

MAKES ABOUT 2 QT/2 L

1 medium onion	
1 large carrot, peeled	
2 celery stalks	
½ tsp fennel seeds	
½ tsp coriander seeds	
1 bay leaf	

SPECIAL EQUIPMENT: large stockpot, sieve

1. Roughly chop the onion, carrot, and celery into pieces 1 in/2.5 cm thick. In the stockpot, combine the chopped vegetables, the fennel, coriander, bay leaf, and about 2½ qt/2.4 L water and bring to a boil over high heat. Reduce the heat to a simmer and simmer for about 10 minutes. Turn off heat and let the stock sit for 30 minutes.

2. Strain the stock through the sieve into a large container and discard the solids. The stock can be stored in an airtight container in the fridge for 1 week or in the freezer for up to 3 weeks.

CHICKEN STOCK

MAKES ABOUT 2 QT/2 L

3 lb/1.4 kg chicken wings and bones (your mix should be at least half wings for best flavor)

1 medium onion

1 large carrot, peeled

2 celery stalks

2 bay leaves

3 fresh thyme sprigs

SPECIAL EQUIPMENT: large stockpot, sieve

1. Place the chicken wings and bones in the stock-pot. Add about 3 qt/2.8 L water or as needed to cover the wings and bring to a boil over medium-high heat. Skim the foamy impurities off the top and reduce the heat to a gentle simmer. Roughly chop the onion, carrot, and celery into pieces 1 in/2.5 cm thick. Add the chopped vegetables, bay leaves, and thyme to the pot and simmer gently, uncovered, for about 2 hours.

2. Strain the stock through the sieve into a large container and discard the solids. Let stand for a few minutes, then, using a large spoon, skim off the layer of fat that rises to the surface. Don't skim off all of the fat, as it adds a lot of flavor to your stock, just skim off what you can easily spoon off. The stock can be stored in an airtight container in the fridge for up to 1 week or in the freezer for up to 3 weeks.

BEEF STOCK

MAKES ABOUT 2 QT/2 L

5 lb/2.3 kg meaty beef bones, such as shank, short rib, and marrow bones

1 medium onion

1 large carrot, peeled

2 celery stalks

2 bay leaves

3 fresh thyme sprigs

2 tsp tomato paste

1 tsp black peppercorns

SPECIAL EQUIPMENT: rimmed baking sheet, large stockpot, sieve

1. Preheat the oven to 350°F/180°C, and place a rack in the center of the oven.

2. Place the beef bones on the baking sheet and roast for 25 to 30 minutes, or until they are browned. Transfer the bones to the stockpot. Add about 3 qt/2.8 L water or as needed to cover the bones and bring to a boil over medium-high heat. Skim the foamy impurities off the top and reduce the heat to a gentle simmer. Roughly chop the onion, carrot, and celery into pieces 1 in/2.5 cm thick. Add the vegetables, bay leaves, thyme, tomato paste, and peppercorns to the pot and simmer gently, uncovered, for about 2 hours.

3. Strain the stock through the sieve into a large container and discard the solids. Let stand for a few minutes, then, using a large spoon, skim off the layer of fat that rises to the surface. Don't skim off all of the fat, as it adds a lot of flavor to your stock, just skim off what you can easily spoon off. The stock can be stored in an airtight container in the fridge for up to 1 week or in the freezer for up to 3 weeks.

FLOUR FOCACCIA

This is the recipe for our legendary sandwich bread. When I opened Flour, I had originally planned on buying bread from a wholesale bread bakery and using a different bread for each sandwich: *ciabatta* for this, sourdough for that, *pain de mie* for those, and so on. I planned on making one sandwich bread myself—a house-made focaccia—that we would use for only one of our sandwiches. Our opening chef, Chris, loved this focaccia so much he asked if we could make enough of it each day for all of the sandwiches. That wasn't in my game plan at all, but one of the first things you learn when opening a business is how to change your plans fast. We made dozens of loaves that first opening day, and we've never looked back. I honestly think it's a key to the popularity of our sandwiches. It's certainly easier to buy a loaf of bread to make the sandwiches in this book, but I promise you that if you make this bread you'll be rewarded with the best sandwiches you've ever had. We use this versatile dough for our pockets, our egg sandwiches, and our pizzas, as well.

MAKES ABOUT 2¼ LB/1 KG DOUGH, ENOUGH FOR 1 LARGE SANDWICH LOAF (FOR 4 OR 5 SANDWICHES), 10 POCKETS, OR 2 LARGE PIZZAS

1 tsp active dry yeast, or 0.2 oz/5 g fresh cake yeast

3 cups/420 g all-purpose flour

1 cup/150 g bread flour

5 tsp granulated sugar

2 tsp kosher salt

½ cup/120 ml olive oil

Small handful of cornmeal for sprinkling on the baking sheet

SPECIAL EQUIPMENT: stand mixer with dough hook attachment, rimmed baking sheet

1. In the bowl of the stand mixer, combine 1½ cups/360 ml tepid water and the yeast and let sit for 20 to 30 seconds to allow the yeast to dissolve and activate. Dump the all-purpose flour, bread flour, sugar, and salt into the water. Carefully turn the mixer on to low speed and mix for about 10 seconds. (To prevent the flour from flying out of the bowl, turn the mixer on and off several times until the flour is mixed into the liquid, and then keep it on low speed.) When the dough is still shaggy looking, drizzle in the olive oil, aiming it along the side of the bowl to keep it from splashing and making a mess.

2. With the mixer still on low speed, knead the dough for 4 to 5 minutes, or until it is smooth and supple. The dough should be somewhat sticky but still smooth and have an elastic, stretchy texture. (If it is much stiffer than this, mix 1 to 2 tbsp water; if it is much looser than this, mix in 2 to 3 tbsp all-purpose flour.)

3. Lightly oil a large bowl. Transfer the dough to the oiled bowl, cover with an oiled piece of plastic wrap or a damp lint-free cloth, and place in a draft-free, warm (78° to 82°F/25° to 27°C is ideal) area for 2 to 3 hours. An area near the stove or in the oven with only the oven light on is good. The dough should rise until it is about double in bulk. (This is called proofing the dough.)

4. Once the dough has risen, flour your hands and the work surface and turn the dough out onto the work surface. Press the dough into an 8-in/20-cm square and fold the top edge of the square down to the center of the dough. Fold the bottom of the square up to the center of the dough and press the seam firmly with your fingers. Now fold the right side of the square into the center and the left side into the center, and again press the seam firmly. Turn the dough over, seam-side down, and shape the dough with a tucking motion so that it is about 6 in/15 cm square. Transfer the dough to the prepared baking sheet, generously flour the top of the dough, and then cover the dough loosely but completely with a damp lint-free cloth or a piece of plastic wrap. Place in a warm area (78° to 82°F/25° to 27°C) for another hour or so, or until the dough rises a bit and gets puffy and pillowy. (This is proofing, again.) If making hot pockets (see page 89), egg sandwiches (see page 85), or turkey burgers (see page 201): Split the dough in half and reserve half of the dough for another use. Proceed with the desired recipe as directed. These recipes can be easily doubled, in which case use the entire batch of dough and proceed as directed. If making pizza (page 185): Proceed with the pizza recipe as directed.

5. Preheat the oven to 400°F/200°C, and place a rack in the center of the oven. Sprinkle the baking sheet with the cornmeal and set aside.

6. When the dough is ready, remove the cloth or plastic wrap. Using all ten fingers, press and poke and elongate the dough three or four times along its length so that you press and stretch it into an almost-square log that is about 10 in/25cm long, 8 in/20 cm wide, and about 2 in/5 cm tall. Bake for 35 to 45 minutes, or until completely golden brown on the top and bottom. Lift the loaf and make sure the underside is browned before pulling it out of the oven, or you will end up with a soggy loaf. Let cool on the pan on a wire rack for about 30 minutes, or until cool enough to handle, then cut into slices 3/4 in/2 cm thick for sandwiches. The focaccia loaf will keep in a closed paper bag at room temperature for up to 3 days, or tightly wrapped in two layers of plastic wrap in the freezer for up to 2 weeks. If using day-old bread kept at room temperature, I suggest toasting it in a toaster to refresh it. If using bread that has been previously frozen, thaw it at room temperature for 3 to 4 hours and then refresh it in a 300°F/150°C oven for about 5 minutes.

BASIC BRIOCHE

MAKES ABOUT 3¼ LB/1.5 KG,
ENOUGH FOR 2 LOAVES

2¼ cups/315 g all-purpose flour

2¼ cups/340 g bread flour

3¼ tsp active dry yeast, or 1 oz/30 g fresh cake yeast

⅓ cup plus 1 tbsp/80 g granulated sugar

1 tbsp kosher salt

5 large eggs, plus 1 large egg for the egg wash if making loaves

1 cup plus 6 tbsp/310 g unsalted butter, at room temperature, cut into 10 to 12 pieces

SPECIAL EQUIPMENT: stand mixer with dough hook attachment, two 9-by-5-in/23-by-12-cm loaf pans if making loaves, parchment paper if making loaves (optional)

1. Using the stand mixer, combine the all-purpose flour, bread flour, yeast, sugar, salt, 5 eggs, and ½ cup/120 ml water and beat on low speed for 3 to 4 minutes, or until all of the ingredients have come together. Stop the mixer as needed to scrape the sides and bottom of the bowl to make sure all of the flour has been incorporated into the wet ingredients. Once the dough has come together, beat on low speed for 3 to 4 minutes longer. The dough will be stiff and seem quite dry.

2. Still on low speed, add the butter, one piece at a time, mixing after each addition until it disappears into the dough. After all of the butter has been added, continue mixing on low speed, stopping the mixer occasionally to scrape the sides and bottom of the bowl, for about 10 minutes. It is important to mix all of the butter thoroughly into the dough. If necessary, break up the dough with your hands to help incorporate the butter.

3. Once the butter has been completely incorporated, increase the mixer speed to medium and beat for another 15 minutes, or until the dough becomes sticky, soft, and somewhat shiny. It will take some time for it to come together; it will look very shaggy and questionable at the start but in time will turn smooth and silky. When that happens, increase the speed to medium-high and beat for about 1 minute. You should hear the dough make a slap-slap-slap sound as it hits the sides of the bowl. Test the dough by pulling at it; it should stretch a bit and have a little give. (If it seems wet and loose and more like a batter than a dough, add 2 to 3 tbsp flour and mix until it comes together.) If it breaks off into pieces when you pull at it, continue to mix on medium speed for another 2 to 3 minutes, or until it develops more strength and stretches when you grab it. It is ready when you can gather it all together and pick it up in one piece.

4. Transfer the dough to a large bowl or plastic container and cover it with plastic wrap, pressing the wrap directly onto the surface of the dough. Let the dough proof (that is, expand and develop flavor) in the refrigerator for at least 6 hours or up to overnight. (At this point the dough may be frozen in an airtight container for up to 1 week. Thaw overnight in the refrigerator before using.) If you are making a brioche treat (pages 64 to 67), proceed as directed in the individual recipe.

5. Line the bottom and sides of the loaf pans with parchment paper, or butter the pans liberally.

6. Divide the dough in half, and press each half into about a 9-in/23-cm square. (The dough will feel like cold, clammy Play-Doh.) Facing the square, fold down the top one-third toward you, and then fold up the bottom one-third, as if folding a business letter. Press to join the three layers. Turn the folded dough over and place it, seam-side down, into one of the prepared pans. Repeat with the second piece of dough, placing it in the second prepared pan.

7. Cover the loaves lightly with plastic wrap and place in a warm (78° to 82°F/25° to 27°C) area to proof for 4 to 5 hours, or until the loaves have nearly doubled in size. They should have risen to the rim of the pan and have a rounded top. When you poke at the dough, it should feel soft, pillowy, and light, as if it were filled with air—because it is! The loaves have finished proofing and are filled with yeast air pockets. At this point, the texture of the loaves always reminds me a bit of how it feels to touch a water balloon.

8. Preheat the oven to 350°F/180°C, and place a rack in the center of the oven.

9. In a small bowl, whisk the remaining egg until blended. Gently brush the tops of the loaves with the beaten egg. Bake for 35 to 45 minutes, or until the tops and sides of the loaves are completely golden brown. Let cool in the pans on wire racks for 30 minutes, then turn the loaves out of the pans and serve warm or continue to cool on the racks. The bread can be stored tightly wrapped in plastic wrap at room temperature for up to 3 days (if it is older than 3 days, try toasting it) or in the freezer for up to 1 month.

PUFF PASTRY

MAKES ABOUT 1½ LB/680 G

1¾ cups/245 g all-purpose flour

1 tsp kosher salt

6 tbsp/85 g unsalted butter, plus 1 cup/225 g, at room temperature

½ cup/120 ml ice-cold water

SPECIAL EQUIPMENT: stand mixer with paddle attachment, rimmed baking sheet, rolling pin, bench scraper (optional), a lot of patience

1. In the stand mixer, combine the flour, salt, and 6 tbsp/85 g butter and beat on low speed for 6 to 8 minutes, or until the butter is completely mixed into the flour and the mixture resembles damp sand. Add the water and continue to mix on low speed for 20 to 30 seconds, or until the dough comes together. It will be somewhat damp and sticky, with some drier spots. Transfer the dough to a lightly floured work surface and shape it into about a 5-in/12-cm square. Transfer the dough to the baking sheet and cover it loosely with plastic wrap. This dough block is called the *détrempe*. Refrigerate for 20 to 30 minutes.

2. Remove the *détrempe* from the fridge and place it on a generously floured work surface. With your hands, press the dough into a rectangle about 8 in/20 cm wide and 5 in/12 cm from top to bottom. Using the rolling pin or your palms, press, spread, and shape the remaining 1 cup/225 g butter into a rectangle that covers the entire right half of the dough; it should measure about 4 in/10 cm wide and 5 in/12 cm from top to bottom. Fold the left half of the dough over the butter and press down to seal the butter between the dough halves. Turn the dough 90 degrees clockwise so that the rectangle is 5 in/12 cm wide and 4 in/10 cm top to bottom, and generously flour the underside and top of the dough.

3. With your palms, press the dough down, flattening it out to make rolling it a little easier. Slowly begin rolling the dough from side to side into a long rectangle about 15 in/38 cm wide and 10 in/25 cm from top to bottom. The dough may be a little sticky, so be sure to flour the dough and the work surface as needed to prevent the pin from sticking. Using the bench scraper or a knife, lightly score the rectangle vertically into thirds. Each third will be 5 in/12 cm wide and 10 in/25 cm from top to bottom. Brush any loose flour off the dough. Lift the right third of the dough and flip it over onto the middle third. Then lift the left third of the dough and flip it on top of the middle and right thirds (like folding a business letter). Your dough should now be about 5 in/12 cm wide, 10 in/25 cm from top to bottom, and about 1 in/2.5 cm thick. Rotate the dough clockwise 90 degrees; it will now be 10 in/25 cm wide and 5 in/12 cm from top to bottom, with the folded seam on top. (The process of folding and rotating is called turning the dough.)

4. Repeat the process once more, rolling out the dough into a long rectangle, again about 15 in/38 cm wide and 10 in/25 cm from top to bottom, and proceeding as previously directed to give it another turn. This time the dough will be a bit tougher to roll out and a bit more elastic. Try to keep the dough in a nice rectangle, flipping it upside down as needed as you roll it back and forth.

5. Return the dough to the baking sheet and cover it completely with plastic wrap, tucking the plastic under the dough as if you are tucking it into bed. Refrigerate for about 1 hour.

6. Remove the dough from the refrigerator and place it on a well-floured work surface, with one long side of the rectangle facing you and the seam of the dough on top. This time, roll out the dough into a rectangle about 27 in/68 cm wide and 8 in/20 cm from top to bottom. Be firm with the dough. It may be a bit tough to roll out, and you'll need to have patience. Once again score the dough lengthwise into thirds, and then give it another business-letter fold (fold the right third over the middle third, and fold the left third over the middle and right thirds).

7. Repeat to give the dough another turn. Return the dough to the baking sheet and again cover it completely with plastic wrap. Refrigerate for another hour.

8. Remove the dough from the refrigerator and give it two more turns. (Place the dough on a well-floured work surface with a long side facing you, roll it into a rectangle 27 in/68 cm wide and 8 in/20 cm from top to bottom, score it into thirds, give it a business-letter fold, and repeat.)

9. Before using the dough, cover it and return it to the fridge to rest for 1 hour. If you are not using the dough that day, wrap it tightly in plastic and store in the fridge for up to 5 days or in the freezer for up to 3 months.

PASTRY CREAM

MAKES ABOUT 1¾ CUPS/420 ML

1¼ cups/300 g milk

½ cup/100 g granulated sugar

¼ cup/30 g cake flour

½ tsp kosher salt

4 egg yolks

1 tsp vanilla extract

SPECIAL EQUIPMENT: sieve

1. In a medium saucepan, heat the milk over medium-high heat until scalded; that is, until small bubbles form along the sides of the pan. While the milk is heating, in a small bowl, stir together the sugar, flour, and salt. (Mixing the flour with the sugar will prevent the flour from clumping when you add it to the egg yolks.) In a medium bowl, whisk the egg yolks until blended, then slowly whisk in the flour mixture. The mixture will be thick and pasty.

2. Remove the milk from the heat and slowly add it to the egg-flour mixture, a little at a time, while whisking constantly. When all of the milk has been incorporated, return the contents of the bowl to the saucepan and heat over medium heat; whisk continuously and vigorously, for about 3 minutes, or until the mixture thickens and comes to a boil. At first, the mixture will be very frothy and liquid; as it cooks longer, it will slowly start to thicken until the frothy bubbles disappear and it becomes more viscous. Once it thickens, stop whisking every few seconds to see if the mixture has come to a boil. If it has not, keep whisking vigorously. As soon as you see it bubbling, immediately go back to whisking for just 10 seconds, and then remove the pan from the heat. Boiling the mixture will thicken it and cook out the flour taste, but if you let it boil for longer than 10 seconds, the mixture can become grainy.

3. Pour, push, and scrape the mixture through the sieve into a small, heatproof bowl. Stir in the vanilla and then cover with plastic wrap, placing it directly on the surface of the cream to prevent a skin from forming. Refrigerate for at least 4 hours, or until cold, before using. The cream can be stored for up to 3 days in an airtight container in the refrigerator.

LEMON CURD

MAKES ABOUT 2½ CUPS/735 G

1 cup/240 ml freshly squeezed lemon juice

4 tbsp/55 g unsalted butter, cut into small pieces

4 large eggs

2 egg yolks

1 cup/200 g granulated sugar

¼ tsp vanilla extract

⅛ tsp kosher salt

SPECIAL EQUIPMENT: sieve

1. In a medium, nonreactive saucepan, combine the lemon juice and butter, place over medium-high heat, and heat to just under a boil. Meanwhile, in a medium, heatproof bowl, whisk together the eggs and egg yolks until blended, then slowly whisk in the sugar until well combined. Remove the lemon juice mixture from the heat and gradually whisk a little of it into the sugar-egg mixture. Continue whisking the hot liquid into the sugar-egg mixture, a little at a time, until all of it has been incorporated.

2. Return the contents of the bowl to the saucepan and cook over medium heat, stirring continuously with a wooden spoon and making sure to scrape the bottom of the pan frequently to prevent the eggs from scrambling, for 5 to 8 minutes, or until the mixture thickens and coats the spoon thickly. To test, draw your finger along the back of the spoon; the curd should hold the trail for a second or two before it fills.

3. Remove the curd from the heat and strain through the sieve into a medium, heatproof bowl. Whisk in the vanilla and salt. Place a piece of plastic wrap directly on top of the curd to prevent a skin from forming. Cover tightly and refrigerate for 1 to 2 hours, or until cold, before using. The curd can be stored for up to 5 days in an airtight container in the refrigerator.

FRANGIPANE

MAKES ABOUT 1¾ CUPS/390 G

⅔ cup/100 g whole blanched almonds, ¾ cup plus 2 tbsp/100 g sliced blanched almonds, or 1 cup/100 g almond flour

½ cup/115 g unsalted butter, at room temperature

½ cup/100 g granulated sugar

2 large eggs

4 tsp all-purpose flour

⅛ tsp vanilla extract

Pinch of kosher salt

SPECIAL EQUIPMENT: food processor if using whole or sliced nuts, stand mixer with paddle attachment or handheld mixer (optional)

1. If using whole or sliced almonds, grind them in the food processor as finely as possible without turning them into a paste. Set aside.

2. Using the stand mixer or a medium bowl and the handheld mixer, cream together the butter and sugar on medium speed for 1 to 2 minutes if using a stand mixer or 3 to 4 minutes if using a handheld mixer, or until light. Add the ground almonds or the almond flour and beat on medium speed for 1 minute, or until thoroughly incorporated. Stop the mixer and scrape the sides and bottom of the bowl. Or, use a medium bowl and a wooden spoon; creaming the butter and sugar will take 4 to 5 minutes and incorporating the nuts or almond flour will take about 1½ minutes.

3. With the mixer on low speed or with the wooden spoon, beat in the eggs until blended. Add the all-purpose flour, vanilla, and salt and beat just until combined. Use immediately or store in an airtight container in the refrigerator for up to 1 week or in the freezer for up to 3 weeks. If refrigerated, let sit at room temperature for 1 hour before using. If frozen, thaw in the refrigerator overnight, then let sit at room temperature for 1 hour before using.

BUTTERCREAM

¾ cup/150 g granulated sugar

3 egg whites

¾ cup/170 g unsalted butter, at room temperature, cut into 6 to 8 pieces

⅛ tsp kosher salt

SPECIAL EQUIPMENT: stand mixer with whisk attachment or handheld mixer

1. In a small metal or other heatproof bowl, whisk together the sugar and egg whites to make a thick slurry. Place the bowl over (not touching) simmering water in a medium saucepan and heat, whisking occasionally, for 6 to 8 minutes, or until the mixture is hot to the touch. It will thin out a bit as the sugar melts. Remove from the heat and scrape the mixture into the bowl of the stand mixer, or into a medium bowl if using the handheld mixer. Beat on medium-high speed for 6 to 8 minutes if using a stand mixer or 7 to 9 minutes if using a handheld mixer, or until the mixture becomes a light, white meringue and is cool to the touch. Reduce the speed to low and add the chunks of butter, one at a time. The mixture will look curdled at first, but don't worry. Increase the mixer speed to medium and beat for 3 to 4 minutes, or until the buttercream is smooth. Beat in the salt.

2. Use immediately, or store in an airtight container in the refrigerator for up to 4 days. Remove from the fridge 3 to 4 hours before using, and beat with the mixer again until smooth.

ESPRESSO BUTTERCREAM VARIATION: Dissolve 1 tbsp instant espresso powder in 1 tbsp water and add with the salt.

GANACHE

MAKES ABOUT 1 CUP/240 G

4 oz/115 g semisweet or bittersweet chocolate
(56 to 62 percent cacao), chopped, or
¾ cup semisweet or bittersweet chocolate chips

½ cup/120 ml heavy cream

1. Place the chocolate in a small, heatproof bowl. In a small saucepan, heat the cream over high heat until scalded; that is, until small bubbles form along the sides of the pan. Pour the hot cream over the chocolate and let sit for 30 seconds. Slowly whisk the chocolate and cream together until the chocolate is completely melted and the mixture is smooth.

2. Let cool to room temperature. The ganache can be stored in an airtight container in the refrigerator for up to 1 week.

INDEX

ACKNOWLEDGMENTS

Writing a cookbook is sort of like running a marathon. You spend endless hours "training" or testing recipes and at times you question your sanity and want to throw in the towel. Then the book actually comes out—it's a real book!—and instantly you want to do it all over again. I've run sixteen marathons and each time during the race I swore it would be my last . . . until I crossed the finish line. The euphoria of finishing would wash over me and within minutes I was planning for the next race. That's essentially what happened with this book. My editor called me a few weeks after the first Flour book came out and said, "Well?" and I knew I had more to share about all things Flour.

To all of the chefs I worked with in the past I owe sincere thanks for teaching and inspiring me along the way so that I could write this book. Lydia Shire, Susan Regis, Rick Katz, Jody Adams, Francois Payard, and Jamie Mammano shared freely with me their knowledge and passion while I was in their kitchens, shaping how I view my role as chef and mentor.

I am so very fortunate that Flour has always had extraordinary chefs at each location laser-focused on making the best food we can for our customers. Thank you to Chris Parsons, our opening chef, who developed our sandwich and daily specials menu and set the lofty standards for our food for which we have become so well loved; Aniceto Sousa, who took Chris's place (and is now chef at Flour Cambridge) and set the bar even higher by creating a rotating dinner specials menu as well as connecting us to farmers and local purveyors; Corey Johnson, who carried the torch after Aniceto and who is now our executive chef of all Flours and has his hands in everything we make; Jeff Stevens, who opened and remains at Flour Fort Point and helps us daily achieve our goal of making food that you crave and dream about. Thanks to these chefs for allowing me to pick their brains for their recipes and for tolerating me as I followed them around like a shadow, testing and weighing and writing notes as they tried to get work done around me. You guys rock my world.

Thank you to Nicole, our executive pastry chef, whose meticulous nature, keen eye, and gracious spirit allowed me to focus on writing the book, knowing that the pastries and bakeries were being well-watched and cared for. My thanks as well to Aaron, our general manager for the first ten years, and to Peter, Aaron's successor, for ensuring that each location is offering the best in hospitality and service so that I could spend time in the kitchen testing recipes. My pastry chefs also were enormously helpful—Brian Grabowski, Sarah Powers, Liz Hollinger, and Heather Fritz all assisted with testing and prepping and testing some more. The entire Flour team makes me tremendously proud and I thank them for making Flour great every single day.

I didn't test these recipes by myself and I had terrific assistance from volunteers Keith Brooks (who now works at Flour as an opening baker!) and Sacha Madadian, who tested and retested and took copious notes and ate a lot of good and bad versions of all of the recipes. Thanks also to the students at the Cambridge School of Culinary Arts who carefully tested recipes and gave me so much helpful feedback.

An incredible amount of work goes on behind the scenes in producing a book. I can't thank enough my agent, Stacey Glick, whose smart advice and savvy perspective make me so grateful to have her by my side. My editors, Bill LeBlond and Sarah Billingsley, are simply best in class; they help me get out of my own way and push me to create a book that people will actually use and get dirty, which is the highest compliment for any cookbook author. What a joy it was to work with my art director, Alice Chau, who immediately understood the ethos of Flour and designed a book to share that with you. Huge thanks to the marketing duo of Peter Perez and David Hawk for enthusiastically promoting all things Flour to anyone who will listen. My photographer, Michael Harlan Turkell, constantly pushed the limit on the number of pictures one should legally be allowed to take of any one dish, and the result was pictures that capture the mouthwatering deliciousness of our food. Cathy Greve is by far one of my most favorite people to collaborate with ever; her whimsical drawings and distinctive handwriting always make me smile and her generous, kind nature makes me happy every time I see her. Finally, my thanks to Christie Matheson, coauthor of the first Flour book, for teaching me and showing me how it's done; with her guidance from last time I was able to embark on my own with this book.

To our customers! Thanks to the thousands of Flour customers who clamor for our food, allowing us to do what we love every single day, and who fill our days with their awesome kindness and warm support. And to my family at Myers+Chang, thank you for always being so upbeat and encouraging (and keeping me happily well-fed when I needed a break from Flour food), especially when in the throes of writing the book and I wasn't able to be there as much as I wanted to be.

Finally thank you to Mom and Dad. They hardly blinked an eye (or if they did they kept it well hidden from me) when I left my safe business job for the world of cooking, and they have supported me in every way possible throughout the whole journey. And the most thanks of all to Christopher for being my best critic, cheerleader, friend, and partner and for bringing me more joy and happiness than I ever dreamed possible.